FREEDOM FROM MANIPULATION AND CONTROL

A
CURIOUS
ART

NIKKI T. WHITE

ISBN: 978-1-4866-2649-6
eBook ISBN: 978-1-4866-2650-2

Word Alive Press
119 De Baets Street Winnipeg, MB R2J 3R9
www.wordalivepress.ca

WORD ALIVE
—PRESS—

Cataloguing in Publication information can be obtained from Library and Archives Canada.

A Curious Art is a beautiful and timely exploration of leadership, power, and spiritual integrity grounded in Jesus-centred discipleship. Nikki White masterfully contrasts the lives of Saul and David to reveal the dangers of manipulation and control while highlighting the freedom found in humbly surrendering to God's authority. With unflinching honesty and cultural insight, White reminds us that true authority comes not from coercion but from a life aligned with God's character—a message that every Christian leader and follower of Jesus needs to hear.

—Mark Wessner, Ph.D.
President and Associate Professor of Biblical Studies for Leadership,
MB Seminary | National Seminary of the MB Churches of Canada

In *A Curious Art*, White draws on a wide array of theological, devotional, and psychological resources to deepen the reader's discernment for leading in the church today. The author examines power, control, and faith as seen through the lives and leadership of two biblical kings. In Saul's tragic downfall from chosen leader to manipulative ruler, she explores all facets of abuse of power, then highlights our own tendency toward manipulation and control, seen as inevitably leading to a destructive cycle of emptiness and idolatry. The author then shows how sacrificial love, modelled by King David and embodied by Jesus, leads to freedom. *A Curious Art* is an important addition to anyone wanting to lead the church today.

—Rob Rhea, Ph.D.
Vice President of Student Life, Trinity Western University

This work offers a profound exploration of servant leadership, contrasting the corrosive grip of manipulation with the life-giving power of surrender and selflessness. Drawing on the narratives of Saul and David, Nikki weaves biblical insight with practical wisdom to show how true authority is found in serving others, not controlling them. Her engaging storytelling and theological depth will challenge and inspire anyone seeking to lead in a way that reflects Christ's heart for humility and sacrificial love.

—Randy Wollf, Ph.D.
Associate Professor of Leadership, Trinity Western University
Director of MinistryLift
Author of *Maximum Discipleship in the Church: Navigating Church Politics*

Many of us have been victims of abusive power—at home, work, or church—but how aware are we of our own tendencies toward manipulation and control? Do we use people for our own purposes, wield words to hurt or coerce, or try to direct God to do our bidding? Nikki White's *A Curious Art* shines the spotlight on our own control tactics, which are so easy to fall into, then shows that we need not be slaves to those impulses. By contrasting the actions of the abusive, self-absorbed biblical figure of King Saul against the faith-oriented King David (in his better moments), the author shows us how to trust in God's sovereignty and avoid the deadly trap of trying to make life conform to our own demands. *A Curious Art* is full of biblically sound, practical wisdom.

—Joseph Bentz, Ph.D.
Professor of English, Azusa Pacific University
Author of multiple books, including *Nothing Is Wasted*

A Curious Art is a book for our age. At a time when Christian leaders are being exposed for using their influence to manipulate others for personal gain, we are in critical need of someone to challenge us, inspire us, and point us to the sacrificial love of Jesus. Nikki White is deeply immersed in the Scriptures as she draws upon the stories of Saul, Jacob, David, and many others to learn lessons from leaders who have struggled to love and serve the people they lead. Nikki White inspires us to look to the One who embodied his own teachings that *"whoever wants to become great among you must be your servant"* (Matthew 20:26). *A Curious Art* is a must-read for anyone who longs to lead and love like Jesus.

—Matthew Price, M.Th.
Senior Pastor, North Langley Community Church

Nikki's gift for storytelling brings the tale of two kings to life as she convincingly explores manipulation, control, humility, and surrender in this powerful book. We are tempted to believe that power and control are in other people, yet as I learned how insidious and pervasive control is in my own life—in all of us—the path to freedom became clear. Nikki lays the foundation for freedom and highlights the beautiful hope we have through yielding control to the only One who is completely trustworthy, sovereign in his upside-down kingdom.

—Roxanne Koop, MA
Director of Staff Development, Athletes n Action (AIA) Canada

In *A Curious Art*, following the narrative of King Saul, White theologically explores the way we seek to manipulate and control. Echoing prophetic literature, the book challenges and convicts us. I often had to pause to consider ways in which I have been complicit in the "curious arts." However, anchored in the story of David, a man after God's heart, White shows us a path toward freedom through the gospel. I encourage the reader to engage this book with an open heart as well as a curious mind.

—Alex Suderman, Ph.D.
Pastor, Global Mission Worker, Multiply.net

Nikki White uses her sanctified imagination to expose how we followers of Jesus can all fall prey to the need to control our environment and those around us. Her contrast between two kings, Saul and David, serves to highlight antithetical approaches to following our Lord, reminding us that the way of manipulation and control is not much different from the practice of divination and witchcraft, and showing us that the way of humility, submission, and sacrificial love is the only true path to joy, blessing, and freedom.

—Bill Taylor, Ph.D.
Executive Director, Evangelical Free Church of Canada

As director of a clinical counselling practice, I often see the impact of abuse, manipulation, and coercive control on individuals, marriages, and families. The cost is high, the devastation far-reaching. In this book, White clearly and unflinchingly outlines how these tactics are used in relational and systemic spheres, and names it for what it is—the dehumanization of the Imago Dei in others. Through the text, White leads us to a vision of living with disarming vulnerability and true strength, grounded not in a contemporary ethos of increasing power, but in our identity as the beloved of the Father. *A Curious Art* presents a compelling invitation to step outside of the game of vying for control and live fully in the freedom available to us in Christ.

—Andrea Hendy, MA, RCC
Director and Clinical Counsellor

Dedicated again to Dr. John White,
in humble gratitude for his having shared with me
one of his last coherent thoughts.
Dad, this was a game-changer.

CONTENTS

ACKNOWLEDGEMENTS

I AM SO thankful to the men and women who vulnerably and courageously shared their stories of having fallen into, or fallen prey to, the abuse of authority. Your painful life experiences have forever changed me and will, I know, bring hope to all who read the words you have penned.

To Andrea Hendy (MA, RCC) and Roxanne Koop (MA; Canadian Director of Staff Development, Athletes in Action)—whose love has entailed equal parts comfort and challenge—ladies, your friendship means the world to me.

Many thanks also to the editorial team at Word Alive Press, particularly to senior project manager Marina Reis and editor Evan Braun, for their patient encouragement and invaluable insights.

Finally, my grief-tinged thanks to the late Doug Hawes, for noble battles waged with grace.

INTRODUCTION

WHAT HAPPENED? IT all began so innocently, with a charming smile and a few smooth lines. The right words spoken in the right way for, it seemed, the right reasons. He had seemed so believable, but it was all a sham. The bashful bowing of that handsome head hid eyes that might otherwise have betrayed a gleam of stark, selfish desire.

How did such a man manage to evoke such sympathy and compassion? He was convincing, casting himself as the tragic hero of every story, blaming everyone else for everything that went wrong. And he seemed so hurt, so lonely, and so sad; it made you want to comfort him.

Then the lies started: a slight embellishment here, a few essential details omitted there. Bare, cold facts were avoided. Facts illuminate far too harshly; they grate on the nerves when presented without the ambiance of low lighting, soft music, and oh so earnest speech. Facts were exchanged for *story*, far better suited to his purposes.

It worked. He was bewitching.

Then he was just frightening.

What happened to the promises he had made, vows so casually exchanged for a clever sales pitch, slick excuse, and sexy grin? Then came the sharp tongue, veiled threat, and looming presence that flexed itself to tower in rage over the weak and the defenceless. Before a person even knew what was happening, they were cowering.

This was the kind of man he was. This was the kind of father he became.

This was King Saul.

And this is us.

The tale of King Saul is, for some, shocking. How could a man chosen by God, anointed by the prophet Samuel, end up being such a twisted bully?

Yet for those of us who have experienced abuse firsthand, or perhaps even been the perpetrators of abuse in some way, however slight, Saul's story is sadly familiar.

Marriage and family therapists hear this story every day. People groups who have been historically conquered, or else colonized and then marginalized by what seemed like well-intentioned, protective patrons, read Saul's story and nod sagely: this is what people in power do. Ethnic minorities, women, North American Indigenous groups, people on the LGBTQ spectrum, the poor and the disadvantaged and the disabled… they all have tales to tell about being victimized by abusive power, and in today's climate of moral outrage they are telling them loudly.

And the abusers? They stand accused, along with anyone associated with or even genetically descended from them, and have a wide variety of reactions. They may deflect, deny, or angrily dismiss the accusations. Or they may bow their heads in shame, retreating fearfully to a corner where they hope to avoid being noticed. Their fear is well-justified; social media can shred a person's reputation with a single post. Lives are destroyed, and some wonder: is justice thus served? Are human rights championed? Are the victims themselves in danger of becoming corrupted by the heady rush of power that comes with the public shaming of wrongdoers?

Is abuse, along with so many other terms, also being redefined? The reality is that all of us have an overwhelming desire for safety, sustenance, and significance that can easily devolve into an obsessive need for control. We are all capable of abusing power.

Where does this come from?

Christians believe that the lust for power has been in our genetic code since Eden. Like our ancestors, Eve and Adam—whether those are actual persons or an accurate metaphor for all humanity—we are prone to put ourselves in the place of God. When asked to trust in his providence, we are far more likely to take matters into our own hands. The effective use of power is learned almost from the cradle; it is instinctive for self-preservation.

However, even when we become aware of the possibilities of power and the potential for its misuse, we continue using others to serve our own selfish ends. That instinct then becomes a *craft*. We learn to practice the art of skillful manipulation. Intimidation, seduction, deception—these are the tools of the trade. Words become weapons, beauty becomes bait, God is a heavenly slot machine, and souls are trinkets to collect and dangle like cheap jewellery on an aging prostitute's emaciated wrist. We, victims and perpetrators alike, follow in the ways of the evil, doomed ruler of this world.

Why? Because it *works*.

Until it doesn't.

Ironically, the pursuit of control leads ultimately to the loss of human agency. Our one truly free human choice—the choice of masters—is spent and lost when we chose Self over God. In this rebellion, we inevitably also choose Self over Other, and so must always serve, advance, and protect our own interests at the other's expense.

In order to be in control of our own lives, we must absolutely control our own environment, including the people around us. We must control others, bending them to our will so we might always feel safe, significant, and securely provided for. Healthy self-care becomes unhealthy self-service, a daily striving for an endlessly moving target as we are enticed by whatever it is that promises us power to control our lives, like money, sex, knowledge, beauty, fame, and positions of influence. In seizing what we want, rather than turn to God to receive what we need we fall back on cravings that enslave us.

And like King Saul, we slide into obsession, paranoia, isolation, insanity, witchcraft, and death.

It doesn't have to be this way.

In Jesus, God meets us when we are at our worst—our most ugly, selfish, opportunistic moments—and offers us another way. This is the way of true, God-breathed human authority over base, grasping power. It is the way of Jesus.

And yes, it is an uphill battle.

Yet this battle is well worth waging, for Jesus has already won the war to set us free from the dark powers of sin, idolatry, and even death itself.

Our path to freedom lies not in absolute control but in absolute surrender, in yielding ourselves to God and embracing an other-minded vulnerability that refuses to pursue power. In Christ, we eschew the weapons of intimidation, seduction, and deception and, in place of that most unholy of arsenals, pick up the sacred swords of worship, faithfulness, humility, self-disclosure, and sacrificial love. The enemy whispers that we will fail, that God does not care, that the Other warrants neither our forgiveness nor our love. We must grit our teeth and cover one another's ears, for it is our perseverance that defines our victory. To die as those who *"loved not their lives even unto death"* (Revelation 12:11, ESV) is to win.

God is sovereign, and he can be trusted. In the agony of our "nevertheless" moments of suffering, when we feel powerless in the face of injustice and abuse and our own meanness of heart, he leads us to ask a powerful question—not *Why?* but *What?*

We direct our faltering feet to follow his lead, wrestling all the while with fear and rage and trauma and howling grief. God invites us not to repress these emotions but to pour them out to him in weakness and unguarded honesty. He welcomes the rawness of our pain and matches it with his own. Only then can we find that strange cadence, rhyme, and lilting music that lifts the groans and whispers from our parched lips and causes them to soar upward in psalms of bewildering praise.

David knew this as the heart of God. Saul despised it as the weakness of his flesh. Jesus preached it as enemy-love. The Church cherishes it as the way of the cross.

As God's royal priesthood on this earth, we are called to model ourselves not after pathetic power-mongers like King Saul but after the broken, humble, Christlike shepherd-king who reigned in his place, King David. When we can identify and put aside our lust for control, learning to live out of sacrificial love, we become, like David, men and women after God's own heart.

Admittedly, there are some painful and raw moments of self-examination ahead as we look at our motives, practices, and even theology. But a prize awaits: when we refuse to wield the weapons of this world, we will come to know a Teflon-coated freedom and healing from the manipulation and abuse of others. More than that, we will ourselves become the kind of leaders, parents, spouses, pastors, and friends who can turn this world upside down.

ONE
THE MIRROR CRACK'D

But we all, with unveiled face reflecting
as a mirror the glory of the Lord, are
transformed into the same image
from glory to glory, even as from
the Lord the Spirit.
—2 Corinthians 3:18, ERV

Out flew the web and floated wide;
The mirror crack'd from side to side;
"The curse is come upon me," cried
The Lady of Shalott.
—Alfred, Lord Tennyson, *The Lady of
Shalott* (1832)

SCRIPTURE TELLS US that mankind was created in the image of God (Genesis 1:27). While scholars debate what exactly this might mean, we know that, at least in part, the *imago Dei* involves our mirrored reflection of not just God's glory but his authority. To us, as to Adam and Eve, is given the role of exercising some kind of dominion over the earth. What did God intend, and what exactly has mankind done with that authority?

In 1967, American professor of history Lynn White published an article entitled "The Historical Roots of our Ecological Crisis." In this article, White presented Western Christianity as the most anthropocentric religion the world has seen: "Christianity... not only established a dualism of man and nature but also insisted that it is God's will that man exploit nature for his proper ends."[1]

---

[1] Lynn White, "The Historical Roots of Our Ecological Crisis," *Science* 155, 1967, 1203–1207.

Our current environmental predicament certainly argues in favour of White's point: we have indeed abused our authority over nature while, historically, claiming biblical support for doing so. In this regard we have deliberately, and conveniently, misread Genesis. Clearly God did not invest us with authority in order to plunder the planet and turn a profit.

In Genesis 1:26–28, we see mankind being directed to exercise its God-given authority by subduing the earth and having dominion over it (ESV, ASV). Those are fighting words, literally.

The Hebrew word used here for "subdue" is a strong one and evokes an image of military conquest; *kavash* means to place one's foot on the neck of a defeated foe. In the Old Testament, conquered nations are brought into *kavash*.

Likewise, the word used to convey the idea of having dominion (or ruling, in the NIV) is the Hebrew word *radah*, and its twenty-odd occurrences in the Bible also indicate rulership through dominance.

When speaking of the nature of our authority, apparently this is what it *is*. But what is it *for*? The word *radah* is defined in Psalm 72 as a king's mandate to save, serve, and protect. This is how our human authority was first exercised in Eden.

Our best means of determining God's intent in investing mankind with this authority is to look at how he first directed Adam and Eve in its employment. In Genesis 2:15, God takes the man and puts him in the Garden of Eden where subduing and having dominion meant, in this first context, gardening.

Various English translations are given for the Hebrew words *abad* and *shamar*, used here to describe Adam's activities: tending, cultivating, working, taking care of, keeping, and guarding. Significantly, the word *abad* is elsewhere used in the Old Testament to mean "to serve," as a slave. Perhaps a robust conveyance of all these nuances can be found in the old English term "stewardship," wherein one is responsible for the well-being of something (or someone) which belongs to someone else.

In this case, God gives mankind authority over a creation which, ultimately, belongs not to us, but to God.

Why is this important?

Authority has been given to us by God not for our own sake but for the sake of the other—be that another person, or even creation itself—and ultimately it means to be in service to God. As image-bearing royal priests, we know that God has invested us with a degree of genuine authority, but there is a significant difference between having power and having authority. Power is that which is *taken*, whereas authority is that which must be *given.* Power is used *over* others; God-given authority is to be used *for the sake of* others.

The human heart resents authority but craves power, and the only way to grasp power is to exert it over others. When we do so, we break, as it were, the chain of command. Every play for power is a rebellion against God's authority, removing ourselves out from under his command and establishing ourselves as the highest authority in our own lives. Setting ourselves up in the place of God is a good, working definition of idolatry. And idolators make rotten stewards.

Human beings are a part of God's creation. We are meant to steward all of creation, including one another, well. When instead we choose to use others for our own purposes, rather than tend to them for their own sakes and in reverence to the Lord, we cross a significant line. It is no longer God's image which we then reflect. Like Tennyson's tragic Lady of Shallot, our mirror becomes "crack'd from side to side." The distortion, dark and sinister, is a murky shadow of our own idolatrous desires.

In the book *No God but God*, authors Os Guinness and John Seel write that idolatry comes from

> the human need for dominion. Dominion is a God-given human gift of mastery, of the ability to affect our surroundings in stewardship to God. But when we are alienated from God, we search for enough security—from controlling some part of the world—so that God seems unnecessary.[2]

---

[2] Os Guinness and John Steel, *No God but God: Breaking with the Idols of Our Age* (Chicago, IL: Moody Press, 1992), 37.

Adam and Eve lost their dominion, and we, their children, are doing little better. In our futile bid for self-determination, we sacrifice everything. We are on a quest for control. Control over others. Control over God. Control, at any cost—and it costs us everything. We are left untethered, empty, and impotent… with a gnawing, insatiable hunger.

In Adam and Eve's fall in the Garden, we see mankind's cycle of abdicating responsibility, forfeiting authority, and rejecting relationship. Our refusal to serve God and steward his creation and his creatures is rebellion; our choosing to serve and steward ourselves instead is idolatry.

Ironically, this rebellion does not free us, and this idolatry does not enrich us. Rather, we are left bereft, bound, and impotent. Having lost our true authority, all we have left is a pathetic play for power.

It can happen so slowly, so subtly, and be so apparently justifiable, that we may not even be aware of having picked up the tools of the trade. We may not recognize the moment when we go from being the victim to being the victimizer.

TOOLS OF THE TRADE

"I'm not sure how it happened," Cathy told me. "There hasn't been any defining moment; no argument, no therapy. Just a dawning realization. How did I get here? Childhood was part of it, I know. And my first husband, who kept me powerless and voiceless. I was just a teenager, married to a man who responded to my needs with abuse, and to the needs of our children with neglect. When I finally left him, that was my first taste of freedom.

"Then I met Glen.

"He has always been so kind and caring. Being married to a professional man, strangely, has raised my social status, too. It feels empowering. He has always welcomed my voice and given me a sense of agency.

"But when I saw, in times of crisis, how his past traumas could make him an angry, remote stranger, I didn't want to repeat the pattern of my first marriage. I set boundaries on his behaviour, which helped.

"I also started trying to "figure him out," trying to get inside his head, whether he invited me to or not. It made things worse, but I couldn't seem to stop; it was like a compulsion.

"I realize now that I have actually been abusing my own power, my own voice, and using it to judge him. I have been sabotaging his agency, demeaning the image of God in him, and effacing his personhood. Just like my first husband did to me."

***

My friend Cathy came to her senses in time to prevent a relational disaster. Twelve years later, her second marriage has not only survived but thrived. She has found herself consistently gripped by the image of Christ's passion in the gospels and the painful narratives of Isaiah 53.

She is astounded by this portrayal of God—going through injustice, abuse, torture, and murder without fighting back, without trying to survive, without defending himself, without exerting his right to be heard or have personal agency.

To say that this has been a challenge to her paradigm would be a profound understatement. For victims of abusive authority and manipulative control, the thought of such divine passivity can be appalling.

During her first marriage, mute submission to a bully kept Cathy in bondage for years, damaging her daughters. Yet she saw that somehow both the valiant championing of social justice and the utter yieldedness of sacrificial love coexisted in Christ.

What would happen if she tried to embrace that tension herself? Would it work?

Our world rejects such a paradox. To flourish as humans—indeed, to feel intrinsically safe—we seemingly must quickly identify, expose, and eliminate threats. Submissive silence leads only to further injustice.

What happens, though, when our survival instinct becomes so sensitized that it becomes a hair-trigger reactivity? At the time of writing these words, the ubiquitous anxieties and stressors of a global pandemic have exacerbated latent social tensions on a massive scale. The subsequent outraged cries for social justice have become deafening. Suffering refuses to be silenced.

In June 2021, Canada reeled from the discovery of hundreds of unmarked graves, many of them containing the bones of children as young as four, buried on the grounds of former residential schools that were in operation from the 1870s until 1996. First Nations peoples recoiled, forced to relive the trauma of having had their families invaded, their sons and daughters forcibly removed and housed beyond their reach, imprisoned in religious educational institutions where they had their heads shaven, tribal clothing burned, and native words and ways beaten out of them in what amounted to acts of cultural genocide. Those helpless victims were told to submit, in silence, to authority.

Today, Indigenous peoples in Canada are challenging that historic authority and speaking more loudly than ever before.

Women, too, have been recently finding their voice in new and powerful ways. Founders and supporters of the #MeToo movement likewise point to the deadly danger of silence in the face of injustice. The movement originated with Tarana Burke, who called out filmmaker Harvey Weinstein for sexual misconduct. The public exposure of sexual harassment and abuse against women became an unstoppable social force when, in 2017, American actress Alyssa Milano tweeted her encouragement for other survivors to post the words "Me too" on social media. The movement quickly went viral.

A Black-centred political movement called Black Lives Matter, begun around 2012, has also gained international traction. In 2020, the world became privy to the brutal and casual murder of George Floyd at the hands of police officers in Minneapolis, one of whom knelt upon his neck for more than seven minutes until Floyd died. The rage and grief that poured out remain unabated as people rail against the complicity of their silence in the face of systemic racism.

No one is keeping quiet anymore. But is it *working*?

While none can argue that the exposure, opposition, and rectification of injustice are both necessary and right, the current Western climate of social and political polemic has reached new extremes of volatility. Identity politics insists that we view history solely through the lens of white privilege and the oppression of a seemingly infinite number of categories of unique victim groups, suggested by the trajectory of critical race theory. Is this making the world better?

In his book *The Madness of Crowds*, political commentator Douglas Murray points out that, both online and off, "people are behaving in ways that are increasingly irrational, feverish, herd-like" as regards divisive twenty-first-century issues of race, gender, sexuality, and technology.[3]

Rapid online communication and rampant media escalation of both perceived and genuine offences have resulted in a social paralysis on the one hand (fear of being "cancelled") and a hair-trigger social shredding on the other.

And the chasm is widening, as individuals and identifiable groups are forced to choose a side, with accused and abused alike on constant red alert.

What of the Church? The most idealistic among us cling to the hope that there can be forgiveness, grace, reconciliation, enemy love, and restorative justice. But few of us, it seems, want to be the first to extend the olive branch, for fear that our hand might get bitten off. To offer any apology has become tantamount to acceding, implicitly, to the entirety of the other's accusation and all of its associated guilt, with no guarantee of forgiveness, much less a strategy for reconciliation and relationship.

We are quickly running out of cheeks in this us/them, right/wrong scenario where the other must always be kept at arm's length by our accusative, pointing finger.

"Forgiveness flounders," writes Miroslav Volf in *A Spacious Heart,* "because I exclude the enemy from the community of humans even as I exclude myself from the community of sinners."[4]

Here is a world in which there is no middle ground, no compromise, and no degrees of wrongness. It's only *us* and *them*.

Apologies are impossible in such a world. For example, descendants of European colonists may truly grieve the ignorance and cruelty of their forefathers but bristle at being labelled "settlers" by Indigenous peoples and object to being held responsible for sins they personally did not commit.

Even in the Christian Church—despite its core doctrine of the incarnation, anchoring our salvation in a God who becomes man, identifies with sinful humanity in baptism, and willingly dies for sins he himself did not commit—believers rankle against offering a corporate, identificational confession for

---

[3] Douglas Murray, *The Madness of Crowds: Gender, Race, and Identity* (London, UK: Bloomsbury, 2019), 1.

[4] Miroslav Volf and Judith M. Gundry-Volf, *A Spacious Heart: Essays on Identity and Belonging* (Harrisburg, PA: Trinity Press International, 1997), 57.

four hundred years of oppression of Indigenous people. Apologies, where offered, are often couched in "yes, but" disclaimers; where any heartfelt, sincere apologies are offered, they are often met with hostility from Christian peers who feel they do not share the shame and should not be forced to acknowledge it, as well as from Indigenous people who refuse to accept the apology for fear that history will move far too quickly past their pain.

Interestingly, Douglas Murray, himself a self-proclaimed agnostic, argues for the kind of values which the Church has historically upheld. He laments the lack of opportunity for the kind of face-to-face forgiveness that allows us to view one another in ways other than "solely through the prism of power."[5] Murray writes, "Viewing all human interactions in this light distorts, rather than clarifies, presenting a dishonest interpretation of our lives. Of course, power exists as a force in the world, but so do charity, forgiveness, and love."[6]

Saying sorry has become unsafe. Instead we join the ranks of the defensive, fighting fire with fire, blame with blame. If I apologize, I lose. If I can shame you, I win.

At the very least, we must, like my friend Cathy, try to get inside the head of the other person, figure them out, and fix them. We are in danger of ceasing to see the person and instead see only issues. Where logic fails or ethics clash, we argue from the experience of suffering and vie for a position within the hierarchy of victimhood.

Should natural empathy not cause our opponent to hang his head, we pull out bigger guns: threats, intimidation, bribes, seduction, spin, and outright lies. It is a zero-sum game in which neither side dares lay down its weapons, for to do so would be the end of the world.

Like glue, these power plays hold together the fragile fabric of this world's economy and social infrastructure. It is manipulation, not money, that makes the world go round.

For example, tech giants such as Google, Facebook, and X (formerly Twitter) offer free services that are financed by advertisers who vie for our attention in the hopes of influencing our behaviour. Political factions,

---

[5] Murray, The Madness of Crowds, 53.

[6] Ibid.

forbidden by law from spreading false information, use media to hint at conspiracy theories and spread not just contagious ideas through memes but contagious emotions. Media startups launch with divisive content to generate public interest and ad revenue. It is in their best interest to provoke our outrage. Myriad books have been written about the psychology of the stock market, which is also applicable to the real estate market and other investment forums. Fear, greed, envy, lust, shame, nostalgia, national pride, affection, and despair can all be manipulated, and the means of that manipulation are of supreme market value. From global economic systems to the oppressive regimes of corrupt dictators to the brand of toothpaste we buy, our behaviour is driven not only by what *is* but by how we can be made to *feel* about what is.

The Church is no exception. Christ-followers should rightly be uncomfortable with the thought that we, too, use intimidation, seduction, and deception—the tools of the trade of manipulation—to control others. That discomfort does not negate reality. In fact, many of us unknowingly embrace a working theology which, in essence, argues that the ends justify the means. If a certain approach leads to what we consider to be an expedient result—be it increased giving, attendance, conversions, baptisms, or obedient children—then it must be good, and even be of God.

But is it really good? What good? For whom? What happens when we stop trying to persuade people for their own sake and begin to do so for our own? What happens when the rush of joy we feel at seeing someone give their lives to Christ is no longer enough, and we begin to seek instead the rush of personal power, the affirmation of our pastors, the assurance of our job security, or the satisfaction of the convert's gratitude?

None of us are beyond having our hearts' motives corrupted. It is hard to resist succumbing to worldly means of manipulation because, as pointed out, these methods *work*. It seems in our best interests to hone our persuasive skills in order to advance in social, professional, ecumenical, or ministerial spheres of influence.

For example, some ecclesial circles would argue that in order to win the lost, we must speak their language and be both relevant to and fluent in their culture. That's true, so far as it goes, but we can easily confuse the incarnational missiology of Christ with a kind of über-contextualized missiology that encourages us to adopt an inauthentic façade in order to be accepted and admired by the ones we are trying to reach. This is deception, yet it is a manipulation so natural, subtle, and apparently justifiable that we dismiss it.

Nonetheless, we are in fact practicing a dangerous and dehumanizing craft. As my friend Cathy says, we are "sabotaging free agency, demeaning the image of God, and effacing personhood."

How do we learn to recognize when we're crossing the line? How do we avoid it? Manipulation is a highly effective, socially accepted practice. Consider the subtle techniques of flattery, spin, selective camaraderie, and relational proof-texting. These are the softer skills of manipulation which, when practiced consistently, eventually stop yielding the results we hope for. Over time we turn to the coarser methodologies of outright deception, seduction, and intimidation. These are the tools of the trade.

Before we go any further, let's look at each one in turn, without flinching.

Deception can be active (lies) or passive (hidden truths), communicated through words and actions but also through silence and inaction.

Think of the racial tensions in the United States, notably during the initial stages of the Black Lives Matter movement. Microaggressions were not just about the speaking of racial slurs or promotion of racial stereotypes; they also occurred when these actions went unchallenged by others. Those who watched the trains roar by, filled with the haunting cries of souls destined for the ovens of the Holocaust, were equally complicit with the Nazis who knew full well what was going on. Bystanders who refuse to ask questions allow deception and other monstrosities to flourish unchecked.

Likewise, the refusal of many in the Canadian Church to acknowledge the need for a corporate, identificational confession for atrocities committed against First Nations peoples perpetrates an implicit lie, in effect saying, "You have no right to be angry at us." This is a gross dismissal of four hundred years of trauma.

Instead the Church ought to lead the way in owning the truth of their privileged colonialist past, saying, "I, too, am a part of this travesty. No, I was not there, but my people were. No, I did not oppress, but neither did I champion you. No, I did not know, but neither did I ask questions. No, it was not I myself who came to steal the land, but neither have I honoured its first stewards. I, too, bear the responsibility for your trauma. I, too, am a part of this problem."

Next, consider the manipulation of seduction. Seduction is not always sexual in nature. It involves the subtle art of wooing—winning over a heart for one's own purposes, garnishing support for a selfish cause, or creating a bond of intimacy for personal gratification. Seduction centres around our own image, carefully groomed to impress and attract. It can manifest through the intentional affirmation of another's image using the common social skills of courtesy, generosity, and politesse, but with self-serving intent.

"You look lovely today" (date me). "You seem like a smart, savvy person" (join my cause). "You are so good with children" (volunteer at my church).

What about intimidation? This can be blatant and obvious, as with ominous threats, or the physical and verbal abuse of a bully. But it can also be insidious and covert, where the practitioner intimidates by inferring an if-then scenario that benefits their motives. If you vote that way, our world will fall into neo-Marxism. If you disobey your parents, it will make them sad. If you tell our secret, I will stop loving you.

The line between altruistic persuasion and disingenuous manipulation is an easier one to cross than we might imagine. Our hearts may be in the right place, but our motives can quickly become self-serving when we seek to benefit our own lives and ministries. We may start out wanting to persuade the other for the sake of the other, then slide with near-imperceptible slowness into less noble motives: to be admired, to feel good about ourselves, to feel secure in our own shaky convictions, or simply wanting to be right.

Even when we evangelize, we may be unaware that we are using subtle forms of manipulation to convince the unsaved. What might this sound like to the hearer? Do this; go to heaven. Do that; hell awaits. Sign up; we'll be friends. Mess up; you're on your own. Volunteer; you'll belong. Sound familiar?

The reality is that manipulation—the intentional use of deception, seduction, and intimidation for self-serving gain—offers both the world and the Church a highly effective means of persuasion. One hopes that Christians would never resort to these methods, but such hope has been, and continues to be, deferred.

It is easier for us to spot this sin in others than in our own backyard. Our hearts are truly sickened by secular leaders who seek to influence others through gossip, slander, criticism, or the crass leverage of money. We are all outraged when we see politicians on social media who, through vitriolic vernacular, seek to bring to heel a fearful lost sheep in order to gain followers for their campaign.

But perhaps we are less likely to notice the cool clique of teenagers in our church youth group who, with inside jokes, BFF behaviour, and homogenous adherence to the latest fashions create an inner circle of social acceptance that excludes their misfit peers. In a culture that bases self-worth on affirming likes and tweets and memes, those who don't fit in pose a real threat to our self-worth; outsiders must be kept outside so insiders can feel special.

The Church, and we who call ourselves a part of her, practices manipulation and control just as much as the world does. Whether it is in the political rhetoric in our pulpits, the professional marketing of our church programs, the hipster staging of our worship, or the carefully affirming diplomacy of seeker-sensitive evangelism, all can be equally dishonouring to God, dehumanizing to those we manipulate, and destructive to our souls.

Too harsh?

Not really. To manipulate any person or group for personal gain is to demean the intrinsic value of a being created in the image of God. John Calvin urges us to "look to the image of God in them, an image which, covering and obliterating their faults, an image which, by its beauty and dignity, should allure us to love and embrace them."[7] Without this perspective, we are more inclined to see individuals, or even congregations, as a tool to be used rather than as image-bearers deserving of love, respect, and humble stewardship.

When the image of God is thus violated, we both dehumanize the other and ourselves, becoming something less than human. We erode and numb our desire for God and, in the end, completely lose the ability to love God as we ought—with all of our hearts, mind, and strength. We also become incapable of loving our neighbours as ourselves. We lose everything in our futile bid for power.

Feeling hopeless? Don't. We need no ominous prophetic oracle or spicy exposé of ecclesial corruption to convince us that the delicate tendrils of

---

[7] John Calvin, *Institutes of the Christian Religion*, Chapter 17:12. Date of access: October 21, 2024 (https://www.ccel.org/ccel/calvin/institutes.v.xviii.html).

deception, seduction, and intimidation have become entangled in our own hearts, lives, ministries, and churches.

We know.

No profound self-examination is required to reveal to us that we have been ourselves victimized by abusive authority figures and manipulative peers.

We know.

What we do *not* always know is how it happens, and how to prevent it from happening. What we need to know is that healing, freedom, and transformation are attainable.

First, however, we need to stop practicing witchcraft.

THE CURIOUS ARTS OF *PERIERGOS*

The Greek word περίεργος *(periergos)*, found only twice in the New Testament, is used to describe both the overt as well as the more subtle, socially acceptable methodologies of manipulation. Its literal meaning refers to any work or practice *(érgon)* which circumnavigates or "goes around" *(peri)* obstacles that prevent its progress.

Periergos and its cognates are translated in the Bible variously as magic, or sorcery, with the more literal translation being circuitous practices, or "curious arts." For example, in Acts 19:19 we read, *"A number who had practiced sorcery [periergos] brought their scrolls together and burned them publicly."*

But we might be surprised to see that this same term is used to describe those who engage in what we consider harmless social scuttlebutt. In 1 Timothy 5:13, the word *periergos* is used to describe the pastime of a bored housewife: *"Besides, they get into the habit of being idle and going about from house to house. And not only do they become idlers, but also busybodies [periergos] who talk nonsense, saying things they ought not to."*

Gossip, as sorcery?

While we might cringe at the thought that our casual, offhand comments made behind the backs of others could be labelled as a kind of witchcraft, the motivation behind both overtly occult practices and common gossip are inherently the same: to influence and use others for personal gain.

The use of the word *periergos* and its cognates is not limited to New Testament biblical sources; it was a trope of the times.

Greek philosophers like Philo coined this word to characterize women as busybodies, and American New Testament scholar Mariane Kartzow points out that Plutarch used this word to describe women who were inclined to participate in superstitious ceremonies. Gossip was, in this way, a gateway drug to the hard stuff.

Such pastimes were not always of malevolent intent. Women, universally disempowered then, as now, at times would have resorted to gossip and slander as a covert means of warranted social protest. Kartzow comments, "For those who lack the opportunity to openly challenge power structures, witchcraft may be a way to move beyond gossip and turn words into action."[8]

In a similar vein, social scientist James Scott, in his work *Domination and the Arts of Resistance: Hidden Transcripts*, writes of gossip as the forerunner to witchcraft, the next natural step in the escalation of social protest for "vulnerable subordinate groups that have little or no safe, open opportunity to challenge a form of domination that anger them."[9]

As an early form of social activism, however, the practice of *periergos*, justifiable as it may have felt, was widely perceived by the secular sector as being coercive and unethical. Societal reform was rarely the motive. At best, gossip served to give one a sense of greater social standing and increased self-worth; at worst, it was malicious—an intentional attempt to intimidate, humiliate, or discredit others out of base anger, jealousy, or ambition.

Paul simply called it sin.

To those of us who would excuse gossip as being relatively harmless when compared to other atrocities, Jesus would remind us that there are no *degrees* of sin. Name-calling is as the sin of murder; sexual fantasy is as the sin of adultery (Matthew 5:21–28). Gossip is just one more self-serving, idolatrous sin.

Then why do it?

---

[8] Mariane Bjelland Kartzow, *Gossip and Gender: Othering of Speech in the Pastoral Epistles* (Berlin, DE: Walter de Gruyter, 2009), 151–152.

[9] James Scott, *Domination and the Arts of Resistance: Hidden Transcripts* (London, UK: Yale University Press, 1990), 143–144.

Often the motive is fear. That fear may be legitimate, as in the case of oppressed and marginalized women or minority groups. More often the fear is less altruistic: we fear insignificance. There is within each of us the nagging anxiety that we do not matter, that we are lost in the shadow of those who shine more brightly than ever we may. There is a longing to belong to some safe, inner circle of important people, a longing for inclusion that ironically drives us to intentionally exclusive behaviour, offering *sotto voce* critiques from a lofty, morally superior perch.

This is not only natural behaviour, but also largely socially acceptable.

What does it look like?

Many of us walk uneasily into an unfamiliar social gathering. Clumsy attempts at casual chitchat may mask a racing heart as we cast about for some topic for conversation. The easiest way to establish mutual ease is to find common ground, and often that involves discussing some third party. It may start innocently enough: "Do you know so-and-so?" If we feel insecure, a little name-dropping flexes the conversational muscles. We may attempt to establish a social foothold with a mutual display of knowledge and opinion, made all the more credible (and intimidating) when laced with criticism. We find a topic, person, or ideology that triggers mutual disdain and bond over a common enemy, establishing a peculiarly potent—but false—comradery that is founded upon the sinking sand of an us/them dichotomy. Humour eases the conversation even more, especially sarcasm. Laughter diffuses our anxiety.

Later, we may compromise the confidentiality of other relationships, revealing personal details about friends or family members so the other person will be equally self-disclosing. Gossip can be cloaked in brotherly concern, sharing third-party "prayer requests" that allow us to appear spiritual. We use the details of our lives, or the lives of others, in a kind of social bartering, with information as a currency of exchange.

With an indifferent shrug, we discount this profound disregard for human dignity, forgetting that the details of a person's life, whether petty or profound, are the personal property of that person. They are the stories that comprise our sense of self. To extract them from one person and glibly offer them to another like an appetizer on a party tray is a kind of theft. It robs the owner of the story, delight, and right of telling it themself.

Many Indigenous cultures have an intrinsic understanding of the value of personal stories. When told, they are received with humble gratitude, preserved with reverence, and retold with sober care—but by permission only. The kind of casual swapping of intimacies which is normative in the West would be obscene in that context.

Having used someone else's stories to gain a firm social foothold, we then move to being selectively self-disclosing, choosing to share whichever personal stories of our own the other is most likely to approve of or identify with. It may even be to our advantage to confess some sin, admit to certain weaknesses, or share something from our times with God, pulling out his metaphorical love letter from where it has been fondly tucked beneath our pillow and casually handing it over to be read by someone we hope to impress.

At last we feel that we are on equal footing, having successfully created an artificial environment of feigned trust. Both parties can begin to relax.

We are in control again.

Gossip is only one, almost ludicrous, example of the curious arts that hold together the social, religious, economic, and political structures of our world, and the Christian Church is not immune to the attraction these arts hold. What draws us in? In our results-driven global culture, it is the fact that, for a time at least, these methodologies *yield results*. They work.

Take the example of gossip. Gossips are sought after, looked up to, and even feared. In the short term, there is a satisfying rush of power, the thrill of intimacy with those whom we draw into our circle of secret confidences. It is addictive. There is a satisfaction to be gained from honing this skill, researching new sources for the latest, raciest bit of information. We learn to embellish and adorn our stories and become keen observers of human nature, reading body language and microexpressions.

Another person's disinterest is a red flag; we are being too tame. And so we learn when to tease, when to demure, when to titillate, when to lecture, when to shock, and when to look shocked. Even as we see a veil of mistrust draw across the faces of our listeners, it does not dissuade us; it is true that no one trusts a gossip, but who needs friends when you can have fans?

In the end, of course, the scaffolding comes crashing down. Such is the fate of all who embrace rebellion and idolatry.

REBELLION, IDOLATRY, AND THE SORCERY OF SAUL

As we follow the life of King Saul, the themes of rebellion and idolatry are painfully present. His tragic story reaches a climax when his cumulative acts of self-serving rebellion result in his having the kingship torn from his hands. If his life were ever to hit the big screen as a movie, the trailer would likely show the prophet Samuel, furious and grieving, shouting his words of judgment on this power-hungry dictator. "Your rebellion is as the sin of witchcraft! Your arrogance is idolatry! Because you have rejected the word of the Lord, he also has rejected you as king!" (1 Samuel 15:23, paraphrased)

Wait. There is that word again. *Witchcraft*?

The Hebrew word here is *qesem*, and it refers broadly to any practice of soothsaying, necromancy, or divination in which a person consults with the spirits of the dead or with demonic powers.

At this point in Saul's story, ignoble as it may be, there is nothing to suggest that he has consulted with spirits, diviners, demons, or the dead (yet). What then did Samuel mean in saying that Saul's rebellion was "as the sin of witchcraft"?

Some translations assume a connecting phrase that does not actually exist in the Hebrew, adding the words "like" or "is as" or "as bad as" to the text. A more literal version would simply be, "Rebellion, sin of witchcraft; arrogance, evil of idolatry."

So what is Samuel implying here? Is Saul's rebellion against God simply "as bad as" the sin of witchcraft, or is it *in its essence* somehow the same?

For many Christians, the word "rebellion" conjures up the image of a stubborn child refusing to carry out his parent's commands. But rebellion is not merely the passive abstinence from the pursuit of God's will. It is the active seeking of our own desires regardless of the will of God.

Rebellion, like its counterpart repentance, is *active* rather than *passive*. It involves an active turning away, a changing of trajectory. To repent is to turn and move towards God, thereby worshipping rightly. To rebel is to turn and move away from God, thereby worshipping wrongly, idolatrously.

Rebellion and idolatry cannot be separated any more than one can separate the act of flipping down a light switch from the ensuing darkness that falls. When we rebel, we become idolaters. It cannot be otherwise, for the nature of man is to worship something. It is the purpose for which we were created. We cannot cease from worshipping God without by necessity turning to the worship of self.

And, as said, the only way to succeed in self-worship is through controlling others, an illicit pursuit of power and control for the sake of personal gratification. The curious arts of manipulation—seduction, deception, and intimidation—so evident in King Saul and in the lives of many other prominent biblical figures, offer the only real means of acquiring this power. They are, in a sense, akin to spells.

Rebellion → Idolatry → Witchcraft

Samuel recognized this sequence; Saul did not. Later, the disgraced king resorted to the kind of classic witchcraft we associate with secret incantations, sacred amulets, and magic potions. But his collaboration with a practitioner of the dark arts was nothing compared to his skills at deception, seduction, and intimidation. These are the original, ancient, and most effective of all spells, the ones that truly bind and blind. In the end, however, it is always the manipulator that is bound and blinded.

TWO
THE KING WE DESERVE

PERHAPS NO OTHER biblical character epitomizes quite so clearly the inevitable, downward spiral faced by those who choose to pursue power through manipulation and control as does the character of King Saul. His is the infinitely sad tale of a good man gone very, very bad.

Chosen by God through the judge and prophet Samuel, Saul's story begins like a classic fairy tale, but there is unfortunately no happy ending. This ending was forecast, right from the start; God adjures Samuel to solemnly warn the people that their clamouring for an earthly king is in fact a rejection of their God (1 Samuel 8:7). Knowing this, Samuel is not overly enthusiastic or optimistic about his appointed task. He describes to the people what the consequences will be of choosing to move from their theocratic tribal confederation to a political monarchy:

> This is what the king who will reign over you will claim as his rights: He will take your sons and make them serve with his chariots and horses, and they will run in front of his chariots. Some he will assign to be commanders of thousands and commanders of fifties, and others to plow his ground and reap his harvest, and still others to make weapons of war and equipment for his chariots. He will take your daughters to be perfumers and cooks and bakers. He will take the best of your fields and vineyards and olive groves and give them to his attendants. He will

> take a tenth of your grain and of your vintage and give it to his officials and attendants. Your male and female servants and the best of your cattle and donkeys he will take for his own use. He will take a tenth of your flocks, and you yourselves will become his slaves. When that day comes, you will cry out for relief from the king you have chosen, but the Lord will not answer you in that day. (1 Samuel 8:11–18)

Samuel is no idealist. Yet, encouraged by the Lord that there was a bigger picture and ultimate, divine plan that even the Israelites could not thwart, he searches for a king. The Lord instructs him to anoint a man who, by the standards of the nations the Israelites envied, fit the bill exactly. Saul was young (under thirty), strong, tall, handsome, charismatic, filled with the Holy Spirit (1 Samuel 10:10), and having a reputation for successful military forays (1 Samuel 11:1–11). He also belonged to a tribe of renowned warriors, valiant to the point of rash, risky impetuousness: he was a Benjaminite. Saul seemed a perfect choice and the people were unanimous in choosing him to be their king.

Sadly, Israel got not only the king they asked for but the king they deserved.

This is not only a spiritual principle but a political reality. Os Guinness, in his book *Last Call for Liberty*, writes ironically of the political crisis in the United States which some associate with the installation of one man or another into the presidency. Guinness writes that an elected leader, regardless of policy, is not the real issue; he is neither the cause of the current crisis, nor can he be the solution: "The president did not create America's crisis. The crisis created the president…"[10]

We see this dynamic in the story of Israel, although they cannot claim not to have been forewarned. Despite this, they turn a deaf ear and optimistically,

---

[10] Os Guinness, *Last Call for Liberty: How America's Genius for Freedom Has Become Its Greatest Threat* (Lisle, IL: InterVarsity Press, 2018), 24.

stubbornly, insist upon having their own way, that they might be like all the other nations surrounding them. Both the prophet and God consent... and let them have their own way.

Chosen, anointed, publicly proclaimed, and wildly popular with the people, Saul had no cause for insecurity. God was with him; who could be against him?

But from the very first it becomes evident that Saul has no such inner assurance. Rather than trust in God's promise of support, he repeatedly goes to great lengths to seize and hold on to power and control. It is apparent very early in his career.

Saul's earliest recorded military action involved calling the Israelites to join him in fighting against the Ammonites. He had already encountered Samuel, and the anointing oil poured over his head could barely have dried. Rather than trust in the Lord's affirmation of his calling as leader of Israel, Saul chooses to enlist the support of the Israelites through a horrific act of intimidation. We read that Saul *"took a pair of oxen, cut them into pieces, and sent the pieces by messengers throughout Israel, proclaiming, 'This is what will be done to the oxen of anyone who does not follow Saul and Samuel'"* (1 Samuel 11:7).

The threat was hardly necessary. The Lord was with him. Samuel had publicly recognized him before cheering throngs of supporters. The battle was foreordained to be won.

But we begin to see that Saul was not content with those assurances; he needed to take matters into his own hands. In the end, it was to be his undoing.

Few will argue that Saul was wrong in his attempt to rule through coercion, manipulation, and eventually overt witchcraft. But is all control sinful? In an imperfect, sinful world, do we not need police, legislative control, the rule of law? Owners of businesses need to have control of their business, and teachers and parents need to exercise control in order to train children's behaviour and both protect and socialize them. Pastors, priests, and rabbis may seek to exert influence over those under their care, seeking to shepherd with wisdom and responsibility and even sacrificial love.

The question then arises: what is legitimate control, and what forms of control are illegitimate in God's eyes?

The answer is that the *form* of control is not the issue. One can hold the legitimate office of political, parental, or ecclesiastical control and yet rule through self-serving power rather than godly authority. It is a question of *motive*.

THE ETHICS OF CONTROL

Other-centredness is at the heart of the gospel. Jesus tells us that *"the Son of Man did not come to be served, but to serve, and to give his life as a ransom for many"* (Matthew 20:28), and Paul warns that *"for those who are self-seeking and who reject the truth and follow evil, there will be wrath and anger"* (Romans 2:8) and to do *"nothing out of selfish ambition or vain conceit. Rather, in humility value others above yourselves…"* (Philippians 2:3) When we find ourselves in a rightful position of authority over others, any control we exercise must always be for the highest good of the other, for whom we take personal responsibility. To do less is to diminish both our own humanity and theirs.

All men, women, and children bear God's image. Those who sit in positions of authority over them must have this image in their minds, honouring, respecting, and guarding the best and brightest aspects of their humanity. This kind of legitimate control could well be defined as *pastoring*.

Legitimate control is selfless in character; it seeks to serve and nurture. It is a function of relational oversight as opposed to administrative control. Pastoral rule most closely parallels parental rule, aside from the fact that most of us have had a somewhat dysfunctional experience of being parented! Earthly rulers are meant to reflect the perfect rule of a loving, heavenly Father. All rule—or legitimate control, if you will—is meant to spring from a heart that reflects this loving father. Parents, politicians, priests, and employers should rule for the highest good of those under their care. This is what it is to be a man (or woman) after God's own heart.

But many of those who rule over others do so with a different goal; they are more concerned with efficiency, productivity, and profit, those things which will reflect on them and paint them as either successful or unsuccessful in their roles. In this case, their motive may not be to serve but rather to manage, manipulate, and climb the ladder to prominence. At this point, control is no longer for the benefit of those under one's care; it is for the benefit and convenience of the ruler.

The moment that rule becomes self-serving in nature, we relinquish the ability to draw upon the true authority we have been given by God and must therefore resort to manipulation in order to maintain power. We have already seen that this ultimately robs us of our agency and leads to a power addiction that is destructive and evil.

Jesus deplored the worldly leadership models of his day. True authority, he told his followers, comes not from exercising power but from serving for the sake of others. He tells his disciples,

> But you are not to be like that. Instead, the greatest among you should be like the youngest, and the one who rules like the one who serves. For who is greater, the one who is at the table or the one who serves? Is it not the one who is at the table? But I am among you as one who serves. (Luke 22:26–27)

Serving others when what we really want most is to serve our own interests calls for excruciating self-control. But it is possible, especially so for the Christian.

The spiritual gift of self-control is not control *of* the self *by* the self; it is when God, by his Spirit, is invited to be sovereign in his rule over our lives. God will cover us again with his mantle of authority, and extend it into our own spheres of influence, but only when we restore all control back to him. Though we talk much of being yielded and submitted to God, most of us have no idea how little control we actually ascribe to a sovereign God, perhaps because we do not understand his sovereignty to begin with. Most of us keep our God in a box with the lid firmly shut.

SOVEREIGNTY, SUFFERING, AND THE HEAVENLY SLOT MACHINE

"I was so scared," Carmelita told me, shuddering expressively. "These vaccines, who knows? Maybe they are good, but maybe COVID is not so bad as they say. It is so hard to know what to believe!"

"But you went ahead?" I asked. "You and the kids got vaccinated anyway?"

"Si, but first I claimed the Blood of the Lamb!" She lifted her head proudly. "Nothing can hurt us if we have faith. God will answer my prayers. He will protect my family from the pandemic, and from the vaccine, too!"

Then she faltered in her confidence, glancing nervously at her children, and then back at me.

"Right?"

What could I say? Should I crush her confidence by pointing out that we are all going to die of something, someday? Should I point out how prosperity doctrine had invaded her Latin American culture, embedding itself in her Pentecostal church? Should I tell her that her beliefs were formulaic and not so different from the way she had once lit candles and kissed icons to come under the protection of Catholic saints?

I took a deep breath and gently touched her hand. I could not promise what God would do in answer to her prayers, only who he would be.

"He loves you, amiga," I said with assurance. "Whatever happens, he will always be with you. Don't be afraid."

It was not what she wanted to hear. Walking away from me, Carmelita came as close to crossing herself as her Protestant ethic would allow.

***

Can one manipulate and control a sovereign God? Well, one can certainly try. When we decide to seize control, running our lives as we see fit, we soon discover that to retain that control requires us to also control others. It's an exhausting, never-ending battle—and it reaches a fever pitch when, faced with the terrifying prospect of a sovereign God, we find ourselves trying to control him as well. Chances are, we may not even be aware that we are endeavouring to do this.

In speaking about God's sovereignty, every culture has its maxims. "God is in control," some say. "God must have a plan," others agree. "Man proposes; God disposes" is a rough translation of a similar saying in Spanish that I frequently hear from those in my small group fellowship. Then there is another: "Everything has a reason."

For those who care, this is a version of instrumentalism, similar to the Irenaean soul-making theory that asserts God to be the originator of evil for the purpose of perfecting us, his creatures. This requires every unfortunate happenstance to have been sent deliberately by God in order to sanctify us.

Carmelita and other friends of mine clung to this belief with the advent of the COVID-19 pandemic. Somehow believing that God had sent the disease for our benefit seemed preferable to believing that it was a natural consequence of poverty and overcrowded living conditions in China.

"God created fire," I would argue. "Does that mean he is responsible for your house burning down?"

"One day we will understand why he did this," they assured me.

This did not assure me in the least.

While sounding suitably submissive, deep down I knew that Carmelita and some of the others were reeling from helplessness, terror, impotence, and rage. It is not surprising that she would embrace a theological stance that gave her a sense of purpose. Would good come of COVID-19? Indisputably. It already has. In terms of global mission, online outreach has been revolutionary in scope. Does that mean God sent the virus?

These are not easy conversations, as one might imagine.

What does sovereignty even mean? Does God's control mean that whatever happens on this planet is either ordained by him or permitted by him? This is, unfortunately, a common view of the sovereignty of God and leads to inevitable disillusionment and heartache. In this view, when we experience suffering we must draw one of four conclusions.

1. God is punishing us for some sin, and we must repent.
2. God wishes to refine and sanctify us through suffering, and we must endure without complaint.
3. Satan and his minions are attacking us, and we must fight back with more prayer and greater faith.
4. There is no God, and we must accept that fact.

For much of the developing world, influenced by millennia of colonial dominance with Catholic overtones, as well as for nations soaked in the heresy of a prosperity doctrine, which claims that those who have enough faith, pray enough, and please God will never suffer, these are bleak options to choose from when bad things happen to good people.

Views on the nature and extent of God's sovereignty are closely tied to various perspectives on suffering. It is usually when some misfortune or illness befalls us that we first ponder the divine sovereignty of God, because we develop a vested interest in it. When things go wrong, when we face injustice, and when we hurt, we look for the theory that offers us the most comfort. Are we being punished? Is this suffering meant to sanctify us? Is this a demonic attack? Is it time to rebuke Satan, proclaim the promises, plead the blood, and declare our healing?

All these views of suffering appear to have biblical precedent. The early Church was alternately told to endure trials, flee tribulation, count it all joy, pray for deliverance, and rejoice whether they were rescued or not. In the Old Testament, God sent plagues and other trials to confront and correct the sins of Israel or other individuals—always, it is to be noted, with a clear explanation of what was expected of them in order to alleviate the suffering.

The early Christians, as evidenced in the book of Acts, found that any or all of the aforementioned responses to their suffering brought them into a deeper relationship with God. For example, Paul and Silas in prison, the Christians in the diaspora, Steven the martyr, etc.). Why is it then that none of these views yield in us that same sense of intimacy or joy today? It may be that we are missing the point.

Let's look at each view in turn and examine how they tend to impact us when life gets tough.

GOD IN A BOX

Nothing makes us yearn for control like pain. When we cannot relieve it, we must explain it, even if our proposed explanations only make the pain worse. Those who endure suffering, believing it to be a punishment for their sins, often find that, in the words of C.S. Lewis, it "exhausts the mind as well as the body. The invalid gives up the struggle and drifts helplessly and plaintively into a self-pitying despair."[11]

Many face a sense of abandonment in which God seems distant, disapproving, and aloof. Should they repent and still suffer, this sense of God as cold, demanding, and punitive can become intolerable. They may even give up their faith altogether when they find, like Job's so-called friends, that God does not fit neatly into this box.

The book of Job, a poetic epic purported to be one of the oldest books of the Bible,[12] violently shakes the foundations of many mainstream, seemingly stable views on suffering and the sovereignty of God. Yet within these volatile pages we learn invaluable lessons regarding how an insufficient theology inevitably leads us into a posture of trying to manipulate and control God.

Job loses everything, including his health, wealth, children, and the respect of his wife and peers. All are systematically stripped away. Whether this is by God's direct hand (divine determinism)[13] or Satan's, with God's permission, the tension of the story is that God seems to be venturing outside the parameters we normally apply to his moral and ethical sovereignty. Good people who trust God are not, one protests, supposed to suffer *for no reason*.

Yet throughout the book, right to the very end, God offers no justifiable reason for Job's suffering. Many, even Job's friends, speculate the reason, including the possibility that God withdrew his presence from Job so he would recognize the wretchedness of life without him, a view espoused by Pascal.[14]

Ultimately God does not, in fact, explain himself. So what's the deal with Job?

Job apparently did nothing to deserve his sufferings. Quite the contrary, in fact. He is referred to as a righteous man in scripture, *"blameless and*

---

[11] C.S. Lewis, *The Problem of Pain* (New York, NY: Harper Collins, 1944), 162.

[12] Katharine M. Dell, "Job," *Eerdmans Bible Commentary*, eds. James D.G. Dunn and John William Rogerson (Grand Rapids, MI: Eerdmans Publisher, 2003), 337.

[13] Derk Pereboom, "Free Will, Evil, and Divine Providence," *God and the Ethics of Belief: New Essays in Philosophy of Religion*, eds. Andrew Dole and Andrew Chignell (Cambridge, UK: Cambridge University Press, 2005), 77–98.

[14] Thomas V. Morris, "The Hidden God," *Philosophical Topics* 16(2), 1988, 5–21.

upright; he feared God and shunned evil" (Job 1:1). He is the epitome of ancient Hebrew morality, measured according to the way of goodness, or *zedeq*, in Hebrew.[15]

God himself commends Job for his goodness (Job 1:8), which is reflected in his devout attention to God, family, and community. We read,

> I rescued the poor who cried for help, and the fatherless who had none to assist them. The one who was dying blessed me; I made the widow's heart sing… I was eyes to the blind and feet to the lame. I was a father to the needy; I took up the case of the stranger. (Job 29:12–13, 15–16)

Despite his righteousness, Job suffers unthinkable tragedies. Why? While his friends, *"miserable comforters"* (Job 16:2) though they may be, insist there must be some sinful causality yet to be exposed, by the end of the book God himself refutes this, saying that these friends don't speak the truth. Job is not then suffering because of his sins. All evidence to the contrary, he stands fast in this conviction that the horrific trials befalling him cannot possibly be a manifestation of God's retribution for his own sinfulness. Buffeted by the criticism of his friends, Job maintains this stance to the bitter end, denying that he is being punished.

Some commentators cast Job as a proud, angry man bent on stubbornly defending himself, but Job is in fact a radical thinker, centuries before his time in his understanding of suffering and the sovereignty of God. His refusal to entertain the idea that he is being punished for his sins is not arrogance but a manifestation of the very integrity for which God had already commended him.

Webster' s Dictionary defines the word integrity as "firm adherence to a code of especially moral or artistic values… the quality or state of being

---

[15] Gerhard von Rad, *Wisdom in Israel* (London, UK: SCM, 1972), 75.

complete or undivided."[16] Millard J. Erikson defines it as a "cluster of attributes" that include genuineness, veracity, and faithfulness.[17]

A person of integrity then is one who refuses to abandon a stance or conviction but instead remains singlemindedly committed to living wholly in accordance with a perceived reality, the veracity of which one is absolutely convinced.

Job, we are told, was just such a man. He says to his accusers,

> I will never admit you are in the right; till
> I die, I will not deny my integrity. I will
> maintain my Innocence and never let go
> of it; my conscience will not reproach
> me as long as I live. (Job 27:5–6)

For Job, having integrity meant that he would live according to what he truly believed—that God would not punish anyone for sins without making clear exactly what those sins were—even when he couldn't reconcile his current experience with those beliefs. In Job 13:22–23, he pleads with God: *"let me speak, and you reply to me. How many wrongs and sins have I committed? Show me my offense and my sin."* Job believed that God was just and that he himself had done nothing to deserve his current afflictions. Throughout the book, he stands upon these two conflicting truths. The resulting tension is unresolved and agonizing. He cries out, *"And after my skin has been destroyed, yet in my flesh I will see God; I myself will see him with my own eyes—I, and not another"* (Job 19:26–27). "The day will come," Job seems to be saying, "when I will argue with you face to face. I may die without an answer, but while I live, I am never going to stop asking."

This posture, far from incurring wrath, pleases God. Job wrestles boldly with the Almighty, demanding answers to questions with a near-hostile phraseology that makes the reader cringe, yet God is not threatened by this; on the contrary, in the end Job is commended for his brashness and refusal to put God into a box.

---

[16] "Integrity," *Merriam-Webster*. Date of access: October 21, 2024 (https://www.merriam-webster.com/dictionary/integrity).

[17] Millard J. Erickson, *Introducing Christian Doctrine* (Grand Rapids, MI: Baker Books, 2001), 5.

That box is familiar, and still present today. It is the box of an extreme theology of divine retribution.

One well-known advocate for this doctrine was J.C Ryle, first bishop of Liverpool. When a cholera epidemic swept the land in 1865, he wrote a tract called *The Hand of the Lord*, claiming that this was a sign of divine retribution, since "cholera, like every other pestilence, is a direct visitation from God"[18] Later, when another virus followed the cholera, he reiterated this position: "He it is who has sent this scourge upon us. It is the finger of God."[19]

This kind of extremism over divine retribution insists upon an absolute predictability of one's fate and presumes a legalistic control over one's God. It is, in many ways, a kind of karmic philosophy: you reap what you sow; what goes around, comes around; tit for tat; cross the Almighty and you're hooped.

Is this biblical? To a degree, yes.

Divine retribution was understood by ancient Israel as the process through which God meted out requital according to merit, punishment for sinful actions and reward for good behaviour. This teaching is both explicit and implicit throughout the Torah, most particularly in those passages of Deuteronomy 28 which deal with the blessings of obedience contrasted with the curses that follow disobedience.

This rigid interpretation of scripture, embedded in the mindset of Israel, is seen in Jesus's confrontation in John 9, where he is asked, *"Rabbi, who sinned, this man or his parents, that he was born blind?"* (John 9:2) Yet here is where the doctrine hits the skids, as Jesus proceeds to blow the karmic perspective of divine retribution out of the water. He answers, *"Neither this man nor his parents sinned… but this happened so that the works of God might be displayed in him"* (John 9:3).

What does he mean? Throughout the gospels, Jesus affirms the concept of divine retribution; our sinful acts will indeed have consequences, and blessings and rewards will most certainly come to those who live in accordance with God's ways.

---

[18] J.C. Ryle, "The Hand of the Lord!" *Being Thoughts on Cholera* (London, UK: William Hunt, 1865), 5.

[19] J.C. Ryle, "This Is the Finger of God," *Being Thoughts on the "Cattle Plague"* (London, UK: William Hunt, 1865), 4–5.

Consider Matthew 13:41–43:

> The Son of Man will send out his angels,
> and they will weed out of his kingdom
> everything that causes sin and all who do
> evil. They will throw them into the blazing
> furnace, where there will be weeping and
> gnashing of teeth. Then the righteous
> will shine like the sun in the kingdom of
> their Father. Whoever has ears, let them
> hear. (Matthew 13:41–43)

How does this fit with the man born blind, and Christ's insistence that his state was not evidence of divine retribution? In the teachings of Jesus, divine vindication, like divine retribution, is an ultimate consequence, one which is realized in the age to come. In Mark 10:28–30, Jesus assures those who follow him that there will be both rewards and persecutions (suffering) in this life, but that eternal life awaits as an ultimate reward for their faithfulness.

Where does that leave us? Are we helpless, passive victims of circumstance, injustice, natural and human evils, left to flounder as best we can without God's intervention until we die? Not at all. Do we embrace the claustrophobia of a paradigm which believes that "every particle of dust that dances in the sunbeam does not move an atom more or less than God wishes"?[20] With no offense meant to Spurgeon, who penned these words, that perspective on sovereignty can lead to an extremely self-defeating brand of fatalism. It is the kind of messaging that was, and in some places in the world still is, used to repress and control the masses and convince them that their misery and servitude are God's will and their suffering makes them holier. This message was spread by invading Spanish troops, employing Catholicism to keep the Indigenous peoples of Mexico from rebelling. It is also the reason my friend Carmelita was so eager to convert to being a Word of Faith Pentecostal.

---

[20] C.H. Spurgeon, "God's Providence," *The Spurgeon Center*. Date of access: December 17, 2024 (www.spurgeon.org/resource-library/sermons/gods-providence/#flipbook).

In God's kingdom, we are not meant to be pawns but participants. While our eyes remain firmly fixed upon the age to come—when God will finally set all things as they should be—we are to see that God is not only a very active participant in our lives in the here and now but also inviting us to collaborate with him in the act of setting things right here upon the earth, and in our own lives. What does that look like?

While theologians wrestle with trying to reconcile suffering and sovereignty—do we lean into determinism? compatibilism? libertarianism?—the apostle Paul offers a viewpoint that gives us courage to not just survive our own unanswered questions regarding suffering but to have both hope and strategy.

In Romans 8:28, we encounter a well-worn verse that is often extended to those who are suffering and seeking answers. At worst, it is quoted to imply that God has sent or caused this and every trial while working out some good albeit hidden purpose for us; we must accept the suffering, grit our teeth, and wait for the silver lining in the storm cloud. Those who adhere to this interpretation usually mean that God's purpose for us is at least *pleasant*, a blessing that will be recognizable, personal, beneficial, and agreeable.

As mentioned before, this kind of false teaching is convenient for oppressive colonial conquerors seeking to keep the populace in meek submission: serve your masters, tithe to the Church, and carry your burden without rebelling; God will reward you.

But what does this verse actually say? It reads, *"And we know that God causes all things to work together for good to those who love God, to those who are called according to His purpose"* (NASB). Is this saying that we need to accept and endure every evil happenstance that befalls us? What if no good seems to come of it? Are we then to assume that we are not loved by God, not called according to his purpose?

The potential for misuse of this scripture is appalling. How many have fallen by the wayside, their faith shattered, because they failed to experience some recognizable blessing in their pain?

It helps to look at both the context and specific verbs used here.

The context for Romans 8:28 is found in part in the previous verses (and chapters), which speak of the renewed creation of the age to come. Paul contrasts present suffering with future glory, without promising immediate deliverance. We read,

> I consider that our present sufferings are not worth comparing with the glory that will be revealed in us. For the creation waits in eager expectation for the children of God to be revealed…
>
> Not only so, but we ourselves, who have the firstfruits of the Spirit, groan inwardly as we wait eagerly for our adoption to sonship, the redemption of our bodies. For in this hope we were saved. But hope that is seen is no hope at all. Who hopes for what they already have? But if we hope for what we do not yet have, we wait for it patiently. (Romans 8:18–19, 23–25)

Romans 8:28 then draws our focus to consider God's dealings throughout history, towards generations of those who were called and beloved. He speaks of the evil and suffering that entered the world because of sin, then encourages us to play the long game: to take heart, for the redemption of the entire cosmos is on the way.

This passage is not about a meticulous divine determinism of all events, and it does not argue that God causes suffering for some hidden good purpose. Instead it presents a glorious picture of a creative God who, regardless of the evil or futility created by man or thrown at us by the enemy, catches up each ugliness in his hands and proceeds to re-create it into something supremely, eternally good. With a joyful flourish of pure artistic inspiration, he takes our tragedies and cries out to us, "Watch this!" And the canvas is breathtakingly transformed.

Somehow God fits each sorrow, loss, and injustice into a breathtaking mosaic. Beauty for ashes, love for hate, life for death, victory for the cross. This is what redemption is. This is our destiny. We are, as Ephesians 2:10

says, God's handiwork, his *poiema*, his masterpiece. He is writing lyrics that will resolve all which is discordant and does not now rhyme or harmonize in our lives—and then he will sing us.

So the redemption of all our suffering is assured in the ultimate sense. Like redemption, it is also a daily, dynamic experience. As we bring each of our sorrows to God, he *"causes all things to work together"* (Romans 8:28, NASB) in order to create something new. The active phrase used here derives from a single Greek verb, *sunergeó*, which describes a collaboration and partnership. God works together with us,[21] and with whatever we bring him, as a weaver might weave unlikely threads to fit some beautiful, ever-evolving pattern.

This is what we see in the passage where Joseph, having risen to power in Egypt, confronts the brothers who sold him into slavery, saying, *"You intended to harm me, but God intended it for good…"* (Genesis 50:20). This verb is the Hebrew *chashab*, which connotes far more than motive or intentions, and far less than divine determinism; it means to skillfully craft, design, and create. God worked together both with Joseph and the tragic events of his life to bring about a great good. He works together with *whatever we bring to him*, and he also works together with *us,* as he did with Joseph, leading us to be active participants in the redemption of our experiences of evil and suffering. We cooperate with God to weave these experiences into tangible evidence of our ultimate future hope, the hope of seeing all of creation renewed in glory.

We have a role to play. While clearly it would be unwise and unfair to curse God or accuse him in anger, neither are we meant to be passive in our suffering, pursing our lips and clenching our fists and squeezing our eyes shut while muttering, "I'll be good, I'll be good, I'll be good…" Nor should we declare that our suffering is actually good in its essence, sent by God and meant to be greeted with joy; we are told in 1 Thessalonians 5:18 to give thanks, not *for* all circumstances but *in* all circumstances. Nor are we to be flagrant triumphalists, naming and proclaiming a victorious end to our pain and waving an ambitious faith flag to impress the Almighty and manoeuvre him into rewarding us with ever greater prosperity and comfort.

---

[21] N.T. Wright, *Into the Heart of Romans* (Grand Rapids, MI: Zondervan, 2023), 261.

Each of these extreme views and postures regarding suffering and the sovereignty of God is an attempt to manipulate and control God. They lead not only to sinful idolatry but to a kind of madness.

James R. Edwards puts it this way:

> [Romans 8:28] does not mean that all things are good. They are not, and to call evil good is a grievous error under any circumstances. It means that for those who love God no evil may befall them which God cannot use for their growth and his glory … This verse testifies to God's sovereignty, not to the beneficent outworking of circumstances. God does not will all things, but he is at work in all things.[22]

Here we see God not as the initiator of all our pain but as the one who, together with us, can redeem absolutely anything. Any lesser viewpoint on suffering and the sovereignty of God results in the kind of destructive, reductionistic theology of the sort that Job's friends espoused. It insists upon casting God as the sovereign author of suffering, and in the same breath it presumes to manipulate God. If we just say and do the right things, he will have to remove our suffering; those are the rules.

When this innately coercive attitude meets with a painful event that does not fit tidily within this theology, it results either in panic and a more frenzied attempt to control God or else a complete deconstruction of our faith altogether.

Perhaps Job, deep down, knew that.

TO LOVE FOR NO REASON

In Job's day, it would have been unthinkable to conceive of suffering as being separate from divine retribution for sin; that would be undermining the

---

[22] James Edwards, *Romans: Understanding the Bible Commentary Series* (Grand Rapids, MI: Baker Books, 2011), 218.

very foundation of an ancient paradigm which insisted that every act of God toward man must be either a reward for our goodness or a punishment for our sin.

While Job affirms the general principle of moral law (Job 27:11), he insists that divine retribution for sin does not apply to his case. He does not claim to be sinless (Job 9:2, 20), but neither does he agree with his friends' accusation that his current suffering is a punishment for his sin. For him, that would have been hypocritical.

God, Job points out angrily, has gone way off-script. Job's portrayal of God is frightening to Job's friends, allowing for a sovereign God that can commit inexplicable deeds. It is no wonder they flinch and come back with ever harsher accusations and more circular arguments. Their world is being turned upside down by Job's insistence that God is outside their box, period.

God, it would seem, was inviting Job to get out of his own box, too.

Satan does a great job of describing that box. In the first chapter, he challenges God by asking. *"Does Job fear God for* nothing?" (Job 1:9, emphasis mine) In essence, Satan infers that Job is no different from any other self-serving mortal; he is only revering God for the sake of expediency and personal profit. So long as God protects his household and his herds, Job will honour him.

"He doesn't really love you," Satan is arguing with God. "He is *using* you! Take it all away and he will drop you like a hot potato and curse you to your face!"

God's response to this challenge is to affirm the core of the relationship he enjoys with his noble servant Job. God is not Job's employer, this is not a meritocracy, and theirs is not a relationship of transactional convenience; it is a covenantal vow.

God's love exists irrespective of any external evidence of blessing or hardship, and Job is invited to wrestle with this profoundly disturbing truth. The prosperity doctrine, had it been articulated back then, would have been shattered.

God was also offering Job the opportunity to exercise his own free will outside the theological constraints of either divine determinism or moral consequentialism. He was being invited to fear, serve, and love God *"for nothing"*—to worship without reward, to engage without evidence, to refuse to curse God regardless of pain, to remain in passionate, intimate dialogue with God over his torment and go to the mat with the Almighty, grappling and arguing and railing and flailing and never, never, ever walking away.

And in utter integrity, this is exactly what Job does.

In the end, God does not explain himself to Job. Yet he affirms Job for refusing to place formulaic limits or legalistic parameters on divine sovereignty. By Job 42:7, he is publicly vindicated, commended by God for having spoken rightly, while three of his companions are rebuked by God: *"I am angry with you and your two friends, because you have not spoken the truth about me, as my servant Job has"* (Job 42:7). What is the rightness of Job's speech? He insisted that God is free to act outside our own prescribed rules for him, acknowledged that love does not always comfort, and agreed that God welcomes, perhaps even provokes, our audacious clamour for justice, clarity, and understanding as a natural part of a healthy, dynamic relationship. God wants us all—outside the box.

In contrast, Job's three friends are warned by God that the intercessory prayers of Job will be their only hope for turning away the wrath of God that is about to be poured upon them *"according to [their] folly"* (Job 42:8). What exactly is this folly? It is the folly of those who seek to manipulate God with a neat theology of suffering that tries to keep his divinity in check.

On the surface, Job's friends appear to be defending the honour of the Almighty, whom they believe Job to be slanderously accusing of injustice. Beneath their apparent righteous indignation, however, lurks the consuming fear of every manipulator: what if God does not play according to their rules? Job's claim to innocence terrifies them. If Job is telling the truth, the universe as they understand it is undone. In Job 6:20–21, we read our protagonist's keen insight into their dilemma: *"They are distressed, because they had been confident; they arrive there, only to be disappointed. Now you too have proved to be of no help; you see something dreadful and are afraid."* Job's claim to innocence is horrific. Perhaps it is not with a tone of arrogant confidence that they protest but one of flustered anxiety.

Eliphaz says, *"Consider now: Who, being innocent, has ever perished? Where were the upright ever destroyed?"* (Job 4:7). And then, from Bildad: *"…if you are pure and upright, even now he will rouse himself on your behalf and restore you to your prosperous state"* (Job 8:6). Finally, Zophar says, *"…if you put away the sin that is in your hand and allow no evil to dwell in your tent, then, free of fault, you will lift up your face…"* (Job 11:14–15) It seems they cannot bear the thought that Job may, in fact, be innocent.

Elihu alone seems to have a higher view of God's sovereignty. He sees that God may indeed allow suffering for reasons other than in divine retribution for sin, saying, *"Whether for correction or for his land or for love, [God] causes it to happen"* (Job 37:13, ESV). At least this one man can envision disasters and suffering as being for some ultimate good, perhaps even for some demonstration of mercy and lovingkindness, as with Christ's explanation of the blind man in John 9:2–3.

Notably, Elihu appears to escape the anger of God in the final chapter (Job 42:9). Unlike the others, he hesitates to claim that he has figured God out. The other three go where Job has all along been loath to go and presume to speak for the Almighty. Never a good idea.

Job's refusal to *"[c]urse God and die"* (Job 2:9) portrays him as clinging stubbornly to what turns out to be a true premise: a sovereign God can in fact act outside our understanding of divine norms. It is not easy for Job to take a stand on that mountain; it almost kills him. He tries valiantly to restrain himself and not *"sin with his lips"* (Job 2:10). But pushed to the limit by his grieving wife, insensitive friends, and the satanic agenda itself (Job 1:12, 2:7), he reels through moments of intolerable despair. His bitter reflections lead to a heart-rending expression of his deepest fear—that God does not care. He cries out, *"Why do you hide your face and consider me your enemy?"* (Job 13:24)

Even in this agony, Job is not trying to manipulate God with his own pain; he is howling for relief, begging for some response from the one who once seemed so near. It is raw, it is real, and it is for some of us achingly familiar: "God, why is this happening? What are you doing?"

We are reminded of the disciples in the storm, their boat close to capsizing with the wind and waves, and Jesus curled up, asleep and oblivious. "Teacher, don't you care?" they cry out. "Don't you care if we drown?"

In the same way, Job is driven to cry out, "God, where are you? Why don't you come down and answer me?"

And God comes in a thunderous roar of self-declaration, finally and absolutely, as he always will. He comes not to answer Job's questions, but to be in himself, by his very presence, the stilling of all questions, fears, and doubts.

Job and his friends cower before the presence of God, listening in awe to this earth-shaking proclamation of holiness. Job bows his head to the dust.

Yet even while his heart quakes to hear God say, in effect, "Do you have any idea who I *am*?" there must also have been, for Job, profound relief. He may have thought to himself, *This is the one I have been waiting for! This is the God who cannot be manipulated, bought, bribed, or cajoled! This is a God worth worshipping, no matter what happens to me.*

Was Job expecting to be struck down? Possibly. Did he care? Probably not. He had been longing for death throughout this entire time of affliction.

Death does not come, though, nor do the answers he seeks. He also is not given the chance he had been demanding to argue his case face to face. All Job gets in response to his impassioned cries for justice is… God.

And it is enough.

On September 25, 2015, Miroslav Volf, the founding director of the Yale Center for Faith and Culture, delivered a chapel message on Job 12:1–12 at Biola University entitled "On Loving for No Reason." During this talk, he explained that if you love someone not for what they can give you but simply for who they are, you have touched upon the true mystery of love. He says, "The whole point of Job is that if you love God for nothing, you don't end up with nothing."[23] To love for nothing is to get *everything*, because we get God.

Job has spoken, and now God speaks. That itself is a spectacular affirmation of their relationship. It is not what God says that matters at this point to Job, but that God speaks at all. For it is this flow of "response, answer" that is the primary vehicle of all relationship.[24]

The relationship between God and Job, repeatedly dashed against the rocks of suffering and silence, survives because Job does not merely clamour for rescue or relief from physical pain; it is God himself he wants, some reassurance that he is being heard and seen, that he matters. He cries out,

---

[23] "Miroslav Volf: Loving for No Reason," *SparkBible*. Date of access: March 19, 2021 (https://sparkbible.com/r/biola-university/miroslav-volf-loving-for-no-reason-biola-university-chapel).

[24] Robert Alter, *The Art of Biblical Narrative* (New York, NY: Basic Books, 1981), 69–70.

"You will call and I will answer you; you will long for the creature your hands have made" (Job 14:15).

So it is for all of us. Whatever the torment, it is not an explanation but a *person* we long for.

God's response to the suffering of his people in Egypt was to bring them into his presence. According to Volf, "God's response to suffering is liberation, not explanation."[25] The responding nature of God, not just the nature of his response, heals Job. It will heal us all. Job's vindication lies not in the *content* of God's answer. Job was persistent in his cry for relationship and refusal to turn away from God in sullen, defeated silence. And it is God's presence, not his explanations, that stills that cry.

Job rightly acknowledges the sovereignty of God while still exercising his own agency in the midst of suffering. He does so without any attempt to manipulate, placate, or threaten the Almighty, but he remains at every turn engaged, honest, and emotionally vulnerable. In short, Job believes that God desires to be in relationship, and that he welcomes conversation, even argument, from his children.

While vehemently rejecting this painful, unjust chapter of his life, Job still believes there is a bigger story, a divine metanarrative, and he will dog his creator until he understands, until he is dead, or until God comes.

Remaining in relationship with God to the very end, despite pain, confusion, and despair, defines his rightness.

Celebrated Austrian psychiatrist and Holocaust survivor Viktor Frankl writes, "In some way, suffering ceases to be suffering at the moment it finds a meaning…"[26] Job demanded an explanation for his suffering; instead God gave meaning to his suffering by revealing not some mysterious, previously hidden agenda but by showing up. God's presence provides Job with the sense of meaning he sought: the willing response of a self-disclosing God that one cannot bribe, bully, manipulate, program, or control.

Like Job, we can only seek him ardently, knowing that our yearning is somehow met by God's yearning for us. The rightness of relational perse-

---

[25] Miroslav Volf, "Good, Evil, Suffering, and Silence," *The Table Video*. February 7, 2018 (https://cct.biola.edu/good-evil-suffering-silence-miroslav-volf-full-interview).

[26] Viktor E. Frankl, *Man's Search for Meaning* (Boston, MA: Beacon Press, 2006), 113.

verance will always be met with the person of God. He is himself the answer to every question.

Seen in this light, the added blessings of restored wealth, health, family, and status are not a reward for Job's endurance amidst suffering. The restoration of what was lost is not divine retribution but divine grace. When Job's fortunes are restored beyond merit, he realizes that the sovereignty of God is not abstract but that of an intimately involved personal deity.[27]

Job accepts the undeserved bounty just as he accepted the earlier trials, knowing perhaps that there was no formulaic correlation he could hold onto, no system by which he could manipulate God and guarantee his own future. Here, as at the beginning, his words would be no less true: *"Naked I came from my mother's womb, and naked I will depart. The Lord gave and the Lord has taken away; may the name of the Lord be praised"* (Job 1:21).

The Lord has now given; he may yet take away, but he will always come. For this reason, I will not resign myself to passive fatalism, I will not curse him, and I will never walk away. I will launch myself into the dark, again and again, until he catches me up in his arms.

But wait. What if the dark launches itself at *you*?

DRIVING THE DEVIL

"For the River People, stories are everything," Emerson shared with me while reflecting upon his travels along the Amazon River in Brazil. *"We spend hours listening to their stories, and sharing our own. This built trust. Then they ask us for spiritual advice. There are many in the tribe suffering from sickness, depression, and conflict in marriage. As animists, they attribute all these things to evil spirits.*

"One day, they brought to us a seven-year-old girl named Ana. Her parents were convinced that Ana was possessed by evil spirits and wanted us to cast them out. Ana was nonverbal, and barely made eye contact. They told us that she refused to play with the other children in the community and was aggressive. It was evident to us all that the girl was autistic, but in their worldview there was no place for this condition, only evil spirits.

---

[27] Sinclair B. Ferguson and David F. Wright, eds., *New Dictionary of Theology* (Lisle, IL: InterVarsity Press, 1988).

"The idea that their daughter was handicapped in any way was horrifying to Ana's parents. Why would the God whom we preached do such a thing to them? I encouraged the father, saying, 'I can pray for your daughter—and I will—but the most powerful prayers will come from you, her father. You need Jesus in your life in order to be the father that Ana needs.' These words found a place in the heart of that man, and he and his wife surrendered their lives to Jesus in that moment, and together we prayed for Ana.

"On the following day, the father came to us with wonder. For the first time, he shared, Ana had looked into his eyes and he had been able to hug his daughter! It was, for him, a miracle."

***

Notably absent in the book of Job is any consideration that the suffering he endured was directly attributed to Satan, despite the opening lines. God asks Satan in Job 1:8, *"Have you considered my servant Job?"* We, the audience, want to scream out for God to stop, to not draw fire in this way. It is clear from the text that this is no cosmic dualism, no pitting of the forces of evil and goodness against one another; God is clearly in charge, not directly controlling Satan but still governing him.

Early Hebrew readers had not seen *Star Wars*, and their concept of God would not have resembled Obi-Wan Kenobi. Today's reader, however, influenced as we are by skewed theologies of suffering and sovereignty and fifteen excruciating seasons of the television series *Supernatural*, might instantly assume a combative stance. "It's the devil making me sick," one may conclude. "I need to drive him away."

Like the tribal people my friend Emerson ministers to along the Amazon River, there are those who view all pain and suffering as being "from the devil." This perspective invites an antagonistic approach to all hardship and sickness. It keeps us constantly on the offensive, battling the evil forces that oppress us. We remain on high alert, which makes relationship with God virtually impossible. Any sense of God's presence in a close, loving way is eclipsed by an almost militaristic posture by which we can only relate to God as the authoritative commander who expects from us a soldier-like response. Hence the term *spiritual warfare*.

Immersed in a militaristic, transactional paradigm with God, proponents of this view of suffering may become harsh, impatient, lacking in mercy, and rather devoid of empathy or compassion for other sufferers ("You just need to fight harder"). This worldview meshes easily with the prosperity doctrine heresy which equates more vehement prayers with greater faith and argues that if only we have enough faith, we can influence God and achieve any goal. This claim is loosely pinned to scriptures such as Psalm 91, and verses where Jesus exhorts his disciples to believe that all things, including moving mountains, are possible to the one who has faith (Mark 9:23, 11:22–24).

Triumphalism, however, conveniently ignores the fact that one must pray *"in the name"* of Jesus (Matthew 18:19, 21:22, Mark 11:24, John 14:13); that is, in accordance with his known or revealed will, and in accordance with the values he represents. There is no magic formula where faith—or its cheaper substitute, enthusiasm—must equate with us getting what we want.

God is not a heavenly slot machine. Those who quote Philippians 4:13, claiming *"I can do all things through Him who strengthens me"* (NASB), mis-read it to mean that enough faith will enable them to achieve any goal. The actual wording in the original Greek is poignant, placing the emphasis not upon the doer of all things but upon Jesus and our position *in* Christ, argu-ably implying that one must be in a position of close communion with the ways and will of Jesus before doing anything at all. The Greek reads, rough-ly, "In him, in all, strengthening me, I am strong." This is not a statement about us and our goals. It's about Jesus and his goals being accomplished through us, as we abide in him.

It is also worth noting that Satan himself promotes this heresy, using the promises of Psalm 91 to tempt Jesus into naming-and-claiming his way to success. In the wilderness, the enemy urges Jesus to throw himself down from a precipice, because God will *"command his angels concerning you to guard you in all your ways; they will lift you up in their hands, so that you will not strike your foot against a stone"* (Psalm 91:11–12).

Along with the prosperity doctrine, the perspective on suffering being primarily a result of demonic oppression also leans us toward the dual-istic worldview mentioned earlier, which portrays a universe of equally powerful, corrupted beings at war with their creator. Think of Batman and the Joker.

In this view, Christians are told to directly rebuke Satan and his minions, to bring down the powers and principalities over demographical regions through direct engagement, sometimes involving a process called *spiritual mapping*.

This kind of direct engagement with Satan is often based upon a literal interpretation of Matthew 12:29, in which Jesus said, *"[H]ow can anyone enter a strong man's house and carry off his possessions unless he first ties up the strong man?"* Some well-known proponents of this teaching include C. Peter Wagner[28] of Fuller Seminary School of World Missions, John Dawson[29] of Youth with a Mission (YWAM), and novelist Frank Peretti.[30]

Valid concerns exist regarding the practice of initiating direct engagement of demonic entities, which is not modelled anywhere by Jesus—other than deliverance prayer in response to an obvious demonic manifestation in an individual. We are not meant to go digging for demons. As well, there may be genuine danger in initiating, outside God's specific mandate, a battle against spiritual entities (2 Peter 2:10, Jude 4–8, Acts 19:11–16). Scripture seems to point to the potential danger of such presumption and implies that one ought to take action against the demonic only when it manifests overtly in those to whom we are ministering, and only with a firm relational grounding in Christ.

Is there a battle to be waged? Most certainly. Spiritual warfare is most often based upon Ephesians 6:12–13:

> For our struggle is not against flesh and blood, but against the rulers, against the authorities, against the powers of this dark world and against the spiritual forces of evil in the heavenly realms. Therefore put on the full armor of God,

---

[28] C. Peter Wagner, *Engaging the Enemy: How to Fight and Defeat Territorial Spirits* (Grand Rapids, MI: Baker Group, 1995).

[29] John Dawson, *Take Our Cities for God: How to Break Spiritual Strongholds* (Lake Mary, FL: Charisma House, 2002).

[30] Frank Peretti, *This Present Darkness* (Nashville, TN: Thomas Nelson, 1993); *Piercing the Darkness* (St. Charles, IL: Crossway, 2003).

so that when the day of evil comes,
you may be able to stand your ground,
and after you have done everything, to
stand.

The early church had a concept of an active hierarchy of demonic beings opposing God (Romans 8:38, 1 Corinthians 2:6–8, 15:24, Ephesians 1:21, 3:10, 16:12, Colossians 1:16, 2:10,15, 2:8,20, and Galatians 4:3; 8–9) which was common in both Jewish and Gentile culture of that time. This was not dualism but a perspective on divine sovereignty in which God chose, sovereignly, to allow freedom of choice for all, including those angelic creatures that would rebel against him. God chooses not to control his creatures but allows them to initiate and determine aspects of their destiny. In some ways this could be considered a moderate form of open theism.[31]

In this view of God's sovereignty, it is over our ultimate destiny that God is ultimately sovereign. The same is true regarding evil. Demonic forces have an eschatologically inescapable fate; in the meantime, they are free to rebel just as we are and incur real casualties on the way to their eternal defeat. Satan, one might say, goes down fighting. And knowing that our own eternal victory is secure, so do we.

The Church is to oppose both the personal evil of transcendent beings as well as the systemic evil of unjust social structures. We are to displace evil with good, darkness with light (John 1:5). We do so by exercising our dominion—wise, loving, and responsible stewardship—in serving, tending, and protecting God's creation and creatures, recognizing that we may at times be called upon to speak truth to power (Mark 6:17–18, Acts 5:29) or actively confront spiritual entities.

In this battle, our primary weapons are relational in nature, practices which keep us close to the Captain of the Hosts. Revelation 12:11 tells us, *"And they overcame him [Satan] by the blood of the Lamb, and by the word of their testimony; and they loved not their lives unto the death"* (KJV). Victory over Satan comes through humble worship at the foot of the cross, through courageous obedience as we proclaim God's goodness (2 Chronicles 20:22)

---

[31] Open theism, recognized in most evangelical circles as heresy, has man both initiating and in ultimate control of his own salvation, as opposed to responding to God's initiative of grace.

and resist temptation (James 4:7), and through other-centred, sacrificial love, even unto death. This is our weaponry.

I enjoy reflecting on an early experience in the charismatic church movement in California back in the 1980s. A woman who was a recent convert to Christianity had hoped for instant healing and relief from suicidal ideation. Instead her situation worsened to the point where she heard audible voices telling her to harm herself. The best therapists and psychiatric prescriptions fell far short and she began to wonder whether she was afflicted with a demonic presence.

Upon asking church staff to exorcise the spirit, she was met with a less than enthusiastic response. This woman was under psychiatric care, on medication, suicidal, and possibly delusional. This degree of instability meant that the trauma of a direct spiritual battle could have done more harm than good. Instead she was told to get as close to Jesus as she could for the next two weeks, after which time they would reassess.

The woman decided to immerse herself in an atmosphere of worship, playing songs of praise from her first waking moments until she fell asleep each night.

The voices got louder.

One day, during the second week of this regime, she was singing along to a worship song while trying to ignore the voices and get some household chores done. Ironing a pile of wrinkled shirts, she suddenly stopped. The voices had gone silent.

Then, as clear as an audible bell, she heard them say, "We're not having fun anymore. We're going."

The voices, and the suicidal impulses, never came back.

We wage war with our worship, faithfulness, and sacrificial love. The atoning sacrifice of Jesus is to be apprehended daily as we confess our sins to one another and pray for one another to apprehend forgiveness and healing. The word of our testimony rings forth in thanksgiving for every mercy, proclaiming true things about God, to God, regardless of our circumstances.

And our faithfulness is lived out through a determined dying to self, a real and sacrificial love that opposes the systemic evil present in social structures through prayer, community development, and social activism—

for example, caring for the poor, speaking truth to power, and seeking to champion the cause of the oppressed.

We do have a mandate to collaborate with God's Spirit in setting right those aspects of creation that do not conform to the lordship of Christ, but we ourselves must do so under that very lordship, as servants—of God, and of each other.

We follow in the footsteps of our master, defeating evil in hand-to-hand combat, as Jesus did, healing the sick, and setting captives free, one by one. We may well look out over our communities and cities and rightly discern the oppressive clouds that hover, but rather than pull down the demonic strongholds we may instead sit as Jesus did, looking out over Jerusalem and weeping. If such love, the kind of grieving love that drowns our own tears, can blow up death from the inside by hanging on a wooden cross, it can also set our cities free.

When we apprehend that God is in ultimate control of this world, moving her inexorably toward the renewal and restoration of all creation, we are less prone to ask about the *why* of suffering; we will simply seek to alleviate it with love. Any other strategy places us squarely in the enemy's camp, using weapons of manipulation and control—Satan's own weapons—to try to gain the upper hand over God.

Fighting hate, we must never employ the weapons of hate ourselves. Resisting manipulation must never lead to the use of manipulation. Instead we are to come against evil in the opposite spirit. This is what Jesus taught when he spoke of loving our enemies and returning blessing for cursing (Luke 6:27). We win the war against evil when we *love well*— with self-restraint, kindness, thankfulness, generosity—rising above the reactive surges of our offended egos and defensive fears. This requires that we grasp the sovereignty of God, believing that in our suffering he can and will work together with us in all things, for our highest good, and for his glory.

HEY, CHECK OUT THESE SCARS

Most Christians are tied up in knots when it comes to the problem of suffering and tend to lean in one of the two extremist camps we've mentioned so far—either suffering is due to sin, and we must repent, or suffering is sent by Satan, and we must fight.

There is a third view, that suffering is sent by God on purpose to make us better. We are told to endure without complaint, or even to give thanks for pain. This view has ancient albeit somewhat twisted roots. Where did this idea come from, and when did it become popular?

Somewhere in early Church history, the concept of suffering, and the words used to describe it, became merged with our concepts of sickness and disease. As a result, we have interpreted, wrongly, most of the New Testament's words for suffering, affliction, trial, and tribulation to primarily mean illness, disease, and unfortunate happenstance. In actuality, the vast majority of these words are best translated as "the suffering of persecution," or simply "persecution," not sickness or misfortune.

Let's look at some of the most common words in the original Greek.

The word *pascho*, usually translated in English as "suffer," is used sixty-five times in the New Testament. In sixty-four of these occurrences, it describes persecution, and it is used one time to describe a case of epilepsy, which was the result of demonic oppression, arguably a persecution in the spiritual sense.

The word *pathema* is alternately translated as "suffering" or "affliction" and is used to describe the persecution suffered by Christ, whose suffering was a result of gross and deliberate injustice.

The word *thlipsis* literally implies being under "pressure." It is usually translated as "tribulation" or "affliction" and is used to describe the pressure of persecution, particularly the persecution that will be experienced in the end-times, as described in Revelation.

There are four other words less commonly used in the New Testament, usually translated as "trial," all of which refer to the testing of our faith through persecution.

The words used to refer to sickness are *astheneia*, *kakos*, *nosos*, and *malakia*. They are variously translated as "sickness," "infirmity," "disease," "weakness," or "unsoundness of flesh" and are used in the context of Jesus healing someone.

Somehow we have come to understand biblical suffering as referring mainly to sickness and misfortune, such as accidents and natural disasters.

Biblical verses meant to offer comfort and direction for those experiencing persecution are now frequently applied to those who suffer in any way, shape, or form. This view of suffering has infiltrated our theology and informs our daily responses to any hardship.

How did this happen?

Roman persecution of the Church in the second and third centuries precipitated a crisis of faith. Christians believed Jesus to have defeated the powers of sin and death upon the cross, and the injustice of persecution from dominant governing powers raised a question: if Christ is the victor, why is evil winning? Comfort and encouragement were found and extended through the teaching of the final words of Christ, such as those found in John 16:33, which assured his followers, *"In this world you will have troubles. But take heart! I have overcome the world."*

By the time of the Pauline letters, the suffering of persecution was not only assumed as normative but elevated to a place of honour. In Colossians 1:24, Paul writes, *"Now I rejoice in what I am suffering for you, and I fill up in my flesh what is still lacking in regard to Christ's afflictions, for the sake of his body, which is the church."* Persecuted believers found dignity and purpose in their suffering and saw in it evidence of the reality of their faith.

Over time, it became evident that persecution only served to cause the Church to grow in strength and numbers, as the blood of the martyrs indeed became, as Tertullian wrote, the seed of the Church.[32] During this time of frequent acts of violence against Christians, martyrdom was not feared but embraced. Those killed for their faith were called "confessors," often revered, and considered to have a higher standing in the afterlife.

Then, with Constantine sanctioning Christianity as a state religion, the persecution abruptly ended, and so did a familiar means of acquiring status through persecution. Believers actually became a privileged social class. Moral and spiritual standards dropped, and many Christians became complacent, lukewarm, and nominal in their faith. Comfort and affluence were not, it seemed, conducive to zeal.

In response to this embarrassing complacency in the Church, a new movement emerged. Asceticism through self-inflicted pain was adopted

---

[32] Tertullian, *Apologeticum*, 50.13.

to replace persecution. This included fasting, exposure to the elements, sleep deprivation, deliberate separation from family, spouse, and children, intentional neglect of personal hygiene, isolation, and denial of personal comforts.

What was the result of asceticism? A checklist for do-it-yourself martyrdom. This was supported by a Greek philosophy popularized by Plato, a body-soul dualism that taught that the spirit was what mattered, and the body was unimportant. Corporal needs came to be viewed with contempt by some ascetics; the body is corrupt and will pass away soon, so why take care of it?

Unsurprisingly, many self-made martyrs became ill and died, and this was seen as evidence of their higher spirituality. Sickness came to be seen as invaluable, even necessary, to one's sanctification. There was a marked decline in praying for the sick to be healed; in fact, within the Catholic Church there emerged a reinterpretation of scriptures such as James 5:13–18, which reads, in part:

> Is anyone among you sick? Let them call the elders of the church to pray over them and anoint them with oil in the name of the Lord. And the prayer offered in faith will make the sick person well; the Lord will raise them up. (James 5:14–15)

Passages like this one were recast to encourage prayer for the sick as a means of preparing the soul for death, birthing the last rites of extreme unction. Why pray for healing if the worse you got, the holier you were?

This attitude toward sickness and suffering seemed to survive the Reformation relatively intact. Although extreme unction was not practiced by non-Catholics, a general ambivalence towards the body remained. In the sixteenth-century edition of the Church of England Prayer Book, for example, direction is given on how to address the sick. The Office of Visitation reads,

> Wherefore, whatsoever your sickness is, know you certainly that it is God's

> visitation… [so that] your faith may be
> found in the day of the Lord laudable,
> glorious and honorable… or else it be
> sent unto you to correct and amend in
> you whatsoever doth offend the eyes of
> your Heavenly Father.[33]

Suffering was in; it was cool. If no one was persecuting you, you did your best to make it happen yourself.

Understandably, pain frightens us. It can make us feel out of control. In our fear, we resort to desperate strategies; if we just repent enough, believe hard enough, endure quietly enough, pray fervently enough, or rebuke Satan loudly enough, we can make it stop. When those strategies fail, we elevate suffering to the status of sanctification and call it good. Anything to feel in control again.

The fear is valid. While our ultimate destiny is secure, on earth nothing is certain. We will suffer. If not persecution, we will certainly encounter misfortune, injustice, sickness, and eventually death. What then? How do we face this looming threat without resorting to manipulative practices and attitudes that impel us to try to control God?

A first-tier response might be, as mentioned, to cease asking "Why?" and instead ask "What?" What should we do when facing suffering and sickness?

Well, what did Jesus do?

Bear in mind that most scriptures regarding suffering address persecution, whereas we in modern times have assumed them to address sickness and misfortune ("I broke my leg! I lost my job! Satan is attacking me! God is punishing me!"). This is an error.

Having said that, we know that there is overlapping truth. Sickness may in fact be caused by sin (John 5:1–14). It may be ordained or permitted by God (Luke 13:10–13). It may be a secondary result of a divine primary, as in God created fire (primary) and we are burned by fire (secondary). It may be the result of demonic oppression (Deuteronomy 28:58–60).

---

[33] "Church of England 'Office of Visitation,'" *Book of Common Prayer* (Gainesville, FL: Shanti Publications, 2020), 158.

But ultimately, we must surrender our obsessive need to know *why* and allow ourselves to be directed by God—his Spirit and his Word—in the *what* of our response.

What does the Spirit and the Word tell us? That there is always a legitimate need for us to repent and assume a posture of humble self-awareness. There is always a need for us to oppose overt manifestations of the demonic in our lives and the lives of others. There is always a justification for seeking healing because Jesus refused no one, whatever the cause of sickness and suffering. There is always an invitation to deeper relational intimacy. A child, when hurt, does not pause to question why a thing has happened; he looks for his daddy and runs into the nearest pair of arms.

And there is always a need to grow in patience and endurance, while exercising a far from passive faith in the *nevertheless* moments of our pain. We must not do anything to manipulate God, but that doesn't mean there is nothing for us to do.

DANIEL IN THE NEVERTHELESS

The posture of remaining steadfast amidst unanswered questions is one of extraordinary vulnerability. When we cease to demand to know the root of our pain, we relinquish control. If we are to have an honest relationship with God, free from attempts at coercion, we must be willing to embrace the discomfort of not having our questions answered yet still pursue communion with him in the midst of uncertainty, in the *nevertheless* of the fiery furnace and den of lions.

Daniel understood this. Faced with the threats of one of the most manipulative bullies the Bible presents us with, Nebuchadnezzar, he and his friends refused to panic. They refused to bow down to—or fear—the rulers and idols of the land.

When Daniel's friends were thrown into a fiery furnace for their blatant disregard for authority, they faced a horrible fate. The questions could not help but arise in their minds. Why was this happening? Why was God not addressing their injustice? Could God save them? *Would* he? If not, what then?

King Nebuchadnezzar taunted them with this question, and the response of Daniel's friends offers us insight into how to face the unthinkable:

> If we are thrown into the blazing furnace, the God we serve is able to deliver us from it, and he will deliver us from Your Majesty's hand. But *even if he does not*, we want you to know, Your Majesty, that we will not serve your gods or worship the image of gold you have set up. (Daniel 3:17–18, emphasis added)

To stand firm means to face our own worst-case scenario without flinching and obey God regardless of the outcome. Like Jesus in Gethsemane, Daniel's friends prayed for the cup to pass them by, but they were willing to confront the possibility of suffering and death with a resolute *nevertheless*. They did not try to dictate to God what he must or must not do in order to rescue or heal them.

Can we do likewise? Believe in and proclaim God's love, despite all evidence to the contrary, and face what comes? This is the opposite of control; this is to yield control and trust in a loving heavenly Father. This is to acknowledge that our repentance, faithful obedience, patient endurance, valiant spiritual battles, and vehement prayers neither earn us merit nor coerce God into action. And yet we choose to repent, obey, battle, and pray nonetheless. We may draw strength from the knowledge that the God to whom we pray also embraces the *nevertheless* of his own covenantal love for us, ever scanning the horizon for the return of the prodigals.

Prayer in and of itself has no power whatsoever. It is God who is all-powerful, yet he invites our prayers, not to manipulate his decisions but to enhance our friendship. Without apprehending this truth, we will be driven by fear to try and manipulate those around us, and our prayers will become little more than another grab for power.

Back to Saul.

THREE
MEANS TO AN END

IN 1 SAMUEL, we see just how far Saul is willing to go in his determination to maintain his control over the Israelites. Shortly after the new king was anointed, Samuel instructed Saul to go to Gilgal and to wait for him there. This was to be the time and place of Saul's public coronation, a sacred gathering to affirm him as the first king of Israel. Saul's instructions were crystal clear:

> Go down ahead of me to Gilgal. I will surely come down to you to sacrifice burnt offerings and fellowship offerings, but you must wait seven days until I come to you and tell you what you are to do. (1 Samuel 10:8)

Perhaps Saul intended to obey these instructions. However, some rather intense circumstances led to a rather spectacular failure on his part.

Previous battles initiated by Saul's son Jonathan—with Saul's approval, see 1 Samuel 13:3–4—had provoked the rage of the Philistines and they wanted revenge. Their irate troops came out in force and Saul and his men found themselves in a tight situation. His men began to panic, and so did he. We read,

> The Philistines assembled to fight Israel, with three thousand chariots, six thousand charioteers, and soldiers as numerous as the sand on the seashore. They went up and camped at Mikmash, east of Beth Aven. When the Israelites

> saw that their situation was critical and that their army was hard pressed, they hid in caves and thickets, among the rocks, and in pits and cisterns. Some Hebrews even crossed the Jordan to the land of Gad and Gilead.
>
> Saul remained at Gilgal, and all the troops with him were quaking with fear.
> (1 Samuel 13:5–7)

Waiting longer than he had expected for Samuel to come and offer the burnt offerings at Gilgal, Saul noticed that his men were beginning to sneak away and desert him. His control over them was slipping, a situation that was, for Saul, intolerable.

Rather than risk waiting any longer, Saul took up the knife himself. Justifying himself, he later told Samuel, *"When I saw that the men were scattering, and that you did not come at the set time… I felt compelled to offer the burnt offering"* (1 Samuel 13:11–12). In effect, Saul was acting in the role of priest at this point, both to impress and further intimidate his followers into submission.

Perhaps this is when Samuel first perceived that Saul's career as king was destined to be short-lived. Saul had sabotaged himself by needlessly using wrongful means to grasp the very thing God already wanted to give him: authority.

Instead Saul chose to pursue power.

There is a fine line, remember, between authority and control. The world teaches us that control over others is what gives us authority. Yet true authority—of the kind that can command the elements of wind and wave and cause demons to flee—has little to do with imposing control over others. Jesus taught us that real authority comes through service.

> Jesus called them together and said, "You know that those who are regarded as rulers of the Gentiles lord it over them, and their high officials exercise

> authority over them. Not so with you. Instead, whoever wants to become great among you must be your servant, and whoever wants to be first must be slave of all." (Mark 10:42–44)

True authority was manifested as Jesus removed his outer clothing and attired himself in his skivvies to wash the disciple's feet. He knew who he was, but he had nothing to prove. He also knew the sovereign dignity and authority he was about to assume on the cross.

Without doubt, Jesus was their Master. Knowing this, he did what masters do *not* do, and what we shrink from doing ourselves for one another. Yet he made it clear that only in serving is God's authority released to operate through us (Luke 22:25–26).

Authority is that which we only receive from God as we walk in humility and obedience. Power is that which we strive to take.

Saul was offered authority, but he wanted power.

Faced with hostile Philistines, he used threats and coercion to secure his men's loyalty in battle.

In 1 Samuel 14, Saul takes a vow of fasting, then binds his men to this same vow. He seeks to secure their support in battle by threatening death to those who eat before they have defeated their foes.

> Now the Israelites were in distress that day, because Saul had bound the people under an oath, saying, "Cursed be anyone who eats food before evening comes, before I have avenged myself on my enemies!" So none of the troops tasted food. (1 Samuel 14:24)

Saul essentially uses his power to try to bully others into obedience, including his own son.

NOT HIS FATHER'S SON

"Like everyone else, my life has been a journey," my friend Tim said. "When my path underwent a significant trajectory change from what my parents had hoped, the result was that they cut me out of their lives completely, forbade my siblings from having anything to do with me, was convinced that I would become a pedophile, told me that I would be condemned to hell for all eternity, and said that I was demon-possessed. I was not.

"I was just gay.

"Growing up, I was taught every Bible verse there is about homosexuality. Mom and Dad quoted them to me, to ensure that I would not be gay, and to make sure that I knew to treat gay people with contempt. As far as Bible exegesis was concerned, they had quite the double standard: divorcees, murderers, liars, fornicators, shellfish-eaters, and those who wore cotton-polyester blends could all go to heaven; gay people could not. When in my teens I finally came out to them, they said, 'God only gives us what we can handle. He wouldn't give us a gay child,' and then made me destroy all my Elton John albums.

"How did this become all about them, I wondered? They kept saying that they loved me. Love? Would love refuse to empathize, refuse to accept someone for who they are? Would love manipulate, bribe, threaten, reject? That was not love. That was control."

***

Tim's parents were convinced that their son's life would go on to be a shipwreck. They withdrew their affection and (considerable) financial support before telling him to get out. I still recall that chilly fall evening when he showed up at our house in pyjamas, bathrobe, and slippers, with his cell phone in one hand and his wallet in the other.

Despite their dire predictions, Tim went on to enrich his life with post-secondary education that he funded himself with part-time restaurant jobs. He established a meaningful career and deep, lasting friendships, including with my own daughter—not to mention a loving, monogamous partnership with another fine young man. Even with our definitive theological differences, we remain friends.

His journey, he says, is now "planets away from where it started, but it is filled with love." To date, his parents have never set foot in his apartment—to them, it is "unholy ground"—and they refuse to speak to him.

Tim bears these scars but has not gone on to become a bitter, manipulating Christian-basher. In fact, when rants on his Facebook page once got a little too toxic, he reminded his community that there are Christians out there who, unlike his parents, have never stopped loving him.

Tim is not the boy his parents wanted him to be. He is not his father's son. Neither was Jonathan.

Unlike his father Saul, Jonathan was not interested in winning personal glory, but he had a determination that God's name should not be dishonoured by the uncircumcised men who humiliated them.

Unbeknownst to Saul, Jonathan ventured out with his armour-bearer to provoke and attack the Philistines on his own. It was a brash and bold move, and completely outside of his father's authority. Jonathan launched himself into a battle where he was hopelessly outnumbered, yet the Lord was with him and the Philistines were thrown into a panic.

Meanwhile, back at camp, Saul called for the priest to bring the Ark of the Covenant and consult the Lord regarding battle strategy (1 Samuel 14:18).

But when Saul heard the earth-shaking noise of fighting in the Philistine camp below, he apparently changed his mind. The battle was already in progress!

"Withdraw your hand," he barks at the priest impatiently (1 Samuel 14:19). His eagerness to join the foray must have made it seem like a waste of time to pause and consult the Lord. There was no time, he thought to himself, and ran into the battle to catch up with a victory already being won by another man's hand.

Saul's lust for power blinded him. It caused him to threaten his own men, to dismiss as irrelevant the priest who sought God's will for the people, and to react with visceral envy when he realized a battle was being won by someone other than himself.

Perhaps this is the moment when Jonathan began to see the cracks in his father's fragile ego, and the dangerous lengths to which the king was willing to go in order to make himself the hero, or tragic victim, of every story.

Like my friend Tim's parents, Saul somehow managed to make everything about himself. He would later deeply resent his son's autonomy, seeing it as a personal betrayal.

When Saul later proposed yet another attack, the people supported him but the priest apparently found it necessary to interfere, suggesting that Saul first consult the Lord. Was the priest perhaps becoming all too aware of the fact that Saul was acting more and more on his own initiative?

> Saul said, "Let us go down and pursue the Philistines by night and plunder them till dawn, and let us not leave one of them alive."
>
> "Do whatever seems best to you," they replied.
>
> But the priest said, "Let us inquire of God here."
>
> So Saul asked God, "Shall I go down and pursue the Philistines? Will you give them into Israel's hand?" But God did not answer him that day.
>
> Saul therefore said, "Come here, all you who are leaders of the army, and let us find out what sin has been committed today. (1 Samuel 14:36–38)

Why did Saul assume that the Lord's refusal to speak to him must be because of another man's sin? Desperate to maintain control of his men, and control over his own image, Saul was unable to consider that the offence may have been his own dismissive indifference to consult the Lord the first time, as well as the fact that his prayer was simply a grab for power.

Previous action had made it clear that Saul, although willing to seek guidance for the sake of his own success, was not really interested in having a guide. He did not seek the Lord so much as any advantage he could get, any edge on the competition. To that end, he was willing to curry favour with the Almighty, to manipulate God into granting him success in battle. God was there to help and serve him, not the other way around.

Christian Smith, in his book *Soul Searching: The Religious and Spiritual Lives of American Teenagers*, describes this kind of attitude as "moralistic therapeutic deism,"[34] a view that sees God as being largely irrelevant unless one needs him to resolve a problem. He writes that for many people

> God is something like a combination Divine Butler and Cosmic Therapist: he is always on call, takes care of any problems that arise, professionally helps his people to feel better about themselves, and does not become too personally involved in the process.[35]

This was how Saul approached God—not as Lord, but as a resource. For Saul, it was not about surrendering control to an omniscient God, it was about staying in control with the help of an omniscient god.

This becomes clear when he automatically assumed that someone— someone other than himself, of course—had committed a sin and incurred God's wrath. Saul was convinced that someone else was to blame for God's embarrassing silence. In the end, he blamed his own son, the young man who had just become a legend and hero in the eyes of his people.

Hungry and faint after his surprise attack on the Philistines, Jonathan had already broken his father's vow that day in ignorance—by eating honey. When warned by his companions, Jonathan made it clear that he was opposed to his father having bound them all to a rash and unnecessary oath.

> My father has made trouble for the country. See how my eyes brightened when I tasted a little of this honey. How much better it would have been if the men had

---

[34] Christian Smith, *Soul Searching: The Religious and Spiritual Lives of American Teenagers* (New York, NY: Oxford University Press, 2005), 163.

[35] Ibid., 165.

> eaten today some of the plunder they took from their enemies. Would not the slaughter of the Philistines have been even greater? (1 Samuel 14:29–30)

When Jonathan arrived back in the camp, Saul was casting lots to determine who the culprit was. Jonathan was exposed before them all and confessed that he had disobeyed his father.

King Saul showed no mercy; he declared that his son must be put to death.

To the king's horror, his own men opposed him vehemently. The obedience he had sought to ensure through threats failed him and his men cried out in protest:

> Should Jonathan die—he who has brought about this great deliverance in Israel? Never! As surely as the Lord lives, not a hair of his head will fall to the ground, for he did this today with God's help. (1 Samuel 14:45)

The men rescued Jonathan and Saul was forced to concede mercy. But he must have seethed inwardly that his own troops preferred Jonathan over him.

The rift between father and son may not have begun at this precise moment, but it was doomed to become, for Saul at least, an uncrossable chasm of jealousy and hate.

By now, Saul had less and less interest in seeking God—and when he did, it wasn't for God's sake. God had become a means to an end. Consulting the Ephod, casting lots, offering sacrifices… all were done not to seek out and draw near to God but to get heavenly support for his own desires.

When we give in to the craving for control, even our prayers become a bid for power.

THE "POWER" OF PRAYER

Realistically, most of us only pray in times of need. We gravitate to a default setting from which we view prayer primarily as a means to an end. In this way, we may seek to profit off our relationship with God. That profit may be tangible, like the moneychangers in the temple, or more intangible, perhaps entailing a sense of personal significance. It is usually the former which impels us to become, at best, efficient getters-of-things-done. In the case of the latter, we become opportunistic narcissists who are only in it for the buzz.

Prayer which is seen primarily as a means to an end devolves into a grocery list where God is the shopkeeper and we his clientele. "I would like a bike please. Blue and silver. With a red bell. In Jesus's name, amen."

Or perhaps it becomes a way of offering God a bribe, pitching him as a miserly merchant and ourselves as the if-then hagglers. "If you give me a bike, then I promise to tithe, read my Bible, and attend church."

Power-tripping can happen, too, where God is the audience and we the performers trying to impress him ("Just look at all the good works I am doing. If only I had a bike, I could do so much more"). If that fails, we may begin to see God as an indifferent tyrant before whom we must grovel in order to earn his favour ("I know I don't deserve a bike. Have mercy").

With an agenda-driven prayer focus, we can slide toward trying to lay guilt trips on God ("Don't you care that my feet hurt? I need a bike!") or even threaten him ("I can't do this anymore! If you don't give me a bike, I will never speak to you again").

As with Saul, we might find ourselves clutching at the hem of God's garment in a pathos of panic, begging for what we want ("Please, please, oh please give me a bike just this once!").

If prayer is not meant to be a means to an end, what is it? Despite most of the Hebrew and Greek words used in connection with prayer being translated as "supplication" or "petition"—in other words, to ask for some-thing—there is much to be gained by unpacking the original meaning of these words. In doing so, we will see that prayer is meant to be far more than a grocery list.

One of the most common words used in the Old Testament is the Hebrew word *palal.* This is a rich and complex compound word that incorporates the sense of going low, or bowing down. For example, consider the posture of worship such as was assumed by the Jews before the fiery pillar of smoke in the wilderness of Sinai.

The word also conveys a sense of coming before an authority to listen and speak. It implies both reverence and daring.

A common Greek word used for prayer in the New Testament is *proseuchomai*, another compound word that carries a lot of freight. It includes the concept of turning, drawing near, and meeting with another. This implies a face-to-face encounter and suggests an expression of some desire, and an interactive response.

To pray, then, means to enter into a relational conversation which, despite the presence of an agenda, is not driven by that agenda. We approach God for who he is, not just for what he might do for us, as we turn toward, draw near, bow down, worship, desire, express, speak, hear, discern, and respond.

Is this our vision for prayer? Or are we so intent on getting what we want that God is diminished in our eyes, eclipsed by the urgency of our own wants and needs? If the latter is true, we run the risk of trying to manipulate the one we ought to be worshipping, of "using" the one who wants to ravish our hearts with his love.

We cannot manipulate God. There is poignant beauty to be seen in the knowledge that we are deeply loved by one who refuses to be influenced by either our goodness or badness. At our core, we all want to control love, to earn it, increase it, or even reject and destroy it. With God, we can do none of these things, and yet we still try.

It has always been this way, ever since Eden.

DAMAGED DNA: WHAT HAPPENED IN EDEN

In eternity past, Satan launched a frontal attack on the God of heaven. He lost. What could have provoked him to such a suicidal act?

In Ezekiel 28, a description of an ancient king of Tyre morphs into a description of the satanic power behind this king. And then it becomes a description of Satan himself. We read of his surpassing loveliness, as *"the seal of perfection, full of wisdom and perfect in beauty… in Eden, the garden of God"* (Ezekiel 28:12–13).

In another passage, one deemed by most commentators to have dual overtones of an earthly king and supreme and evil being, we read of how Satan's beauty and relationship with God were not enough to satisfy him; he wanted autonomous power:

> How you have fallen from heaven, morning star, son of the dawn! You have been cast down to the earth, you who once laid low the nations! You said in your heart, "I will ascend to the heavens; I will raise my throne above the stars of God; I will sit enthroned on the mount of assembly, on the utmost heights of Mount Zaphon. I will ascend above the tops of the clouds; I will make myself like the Most High. (Isaiah 14:12–14)

In this series of prideful and assertive "I will" statements, we see the roots of Satan's power lust: jealousy and ambition. He did not merely want to be raised up; he wanted to be *above* the stars of God, enthroned above God, above the clouds. In his rebellion against authority and subsequent play for power, he became bound to his own bitterness, blinded to the horrible trajectory of his own fate.

Ezekiel 28:16–17 tells us that he was expelled from God's presence and thrown to the earth. There, he meets Eve.

In his serpent form, he launched his plan B. If he could not displace God and rule the cosmos, he could and would seduce, deceive, and intimidate God's image-bearers into a rebellion that would cause them, too, to lose the freedom they enjoyed under the authority of the Most High.

Satan became the first recorded instance of manipulation, tempting humans with a false promise of power. It would be, for Satan, a double victory over his divine foe. Satan would wrest these humans from God's hands and have them forever in his power—wild with disappointment, corrupt with insatiable cravings, cringingly fearful, and crippled with eternal shame. Satan would rule over the very creatures who bore the divine image of his archenemy. Mankind would worship him, heed his word, and obey him… and then he would win the kingdoms of this world as his own personal power base.

What was Eve looking at when she met the serpent? What did she see? She saw a creature over which she and her husband were to have dominion. We think of the serpent as Satan, but Eve would have seen it as a subservient creature over which she had authority—at that point. In her mind, the serpent would have had no connotation of danger, none of the associations we have in retrospect.

Yet the danger was there. Adam and Eve were about to lose the authority they had been given as stewards over all creation. Their dominion was about to be forever fractured.

The serpent, we are told, was crafty (Genesis 3:1). Craftiness carries the connotation of manipulation, the *modus operandi* of the enemy.

He began by posing a question, cleverly designed to plant both seeds of doubt and the first stirrings of jealousy and ambition. In the garden, he said to the woman, *"Did God really say, 'You must not eat from any tree in the garden'?"* (Genesis 3:1) This opening remark combined a subtle attack on Eve's trust in God's word with a pretence of ignorance. "Did God *really* say…? Surely what you thought you heard couldn't be what he actually meant!" Satan never comes right out to directly impugn God's character, but the subtle process had begun of undermining Eve's confidence and awakening her to the glittering but false promise of power. It is Satan's standard approach.

The serpent faked naivete, adopting the pose of an inquirer humbly inviting instruction. He was acting dumb and flattering his victim while simultaneously undermining her trust in God.

Nothing about his form rang any alarm bells in Eve, and perhaps it appealed to her to be able to impart information to a subservient creature who was in the wrong. She replied,

> We may eat fruit from the trees in the garden, but God did say, "You must not eat fruit from the tree that is in the middle of the garden, and you must not touch it, or you will die." (Genesis 3:2–3)

Eve was quick to correct Satan's feigned misinformation. Perhaps she felt magnanimous towards him, even pity for his ignorance. An initial bond of trust was successfully formed, leaving her unprepared for his arrow. It shot straight into her heart.

> "You will not certainly die," the serpent said to the woman. "For God knows that when you eat from it your eyes will be opened, and you will be like God, knowing good and evil." (Genesis 3:4–5)

Not only did he raise doubts in Eve's mind about God's words, but he also slyly implied that God was holding out on her. Satan pretended to have secret knowledge of God, and implied, "God knows something he is not telling you! He fears competition. He is threatened by you, his creatures, and jealous of any attempt to dethrone him. He is hungry for power."

And it worked.

Eve and Adam had been given clear directions by a God with whom they had a close, intimate relationship. They had walked together in the cool of the day, naked and unashamed. Now their relationship with him was shadowed, full of doubt and suspicion.

Therein lies the germinating seed of all temptation to sin: doubt about the true nature of God. Is he truly wise? Does he really love? Can he possibly know what is best? Should he be trusted? And so we slide down a slippery slope into increasing confusion and darkness.

Temptation to sin presents us with a choice: either we take our doubts and fears *to* God or we retreat *from* him. Eve and Adam chose the latter.

Hope lies in the assertion that God never stops pursuing those of us who cower, naked and shivering and resentful, in the weed-infested world of our own rebellion. Satan's lie, though, is just as powerful and beguiling as ever it was.

The enemy presents us daily with a false promise of power and control independent of God. In eating of the tree, Eve and Adam gained nothing, certainly not the self-determination they were promised. Instead they lost control. In rebelling against God's authority, they came under the control of the ruler of this world. Their one free choice—a choice of masters—resulted in the loss of all free choice. The garden became dangerous. Should they eat from the tree of life also, they would gain an immortality that made them like Satan, doomed to eternal exile. Their only hope for salvation lay in their own finite mortality, facing death, so God might himself one day incarnate his sovereignty in finite mortality and conquer death for them.

Knowing the inevitability of this redeeming work of Christ only adds to Satan's teeth-gnashing spite, though he carefully suppresses it under a polished guise of friendship as he fattens us for the slaughter.

Readers of Don Richardson's *Peace Child* encounter the Sawi people of Irian Jaya. He describes their cultural practice of using flattery with treacherous motives, pretending friendship where bitterness and hostility exist, and employing subtle manipulation to lure others to their deaths. In their tribal language, the words *tuwi asonai makaerin* mean to fatten with friendship for the slaughter. Their pseudo overtures of friendship conceal their real purpose: to control a victim's feelings and attitudes if they have total confidence in the enemy.

The lurid practice of cannibalism has been said to have a benefit that is startling to those of us who are familiar with the Genesis story. Richardson writes, "In the day each individual ate of that flesh, it seemed to him that his eyes were opened to know both good and evil."[36] Satan, like the villagers of Haenam in Richardson's true account, fattens us with friendship for the slaughter, then trains us to do the same with one another. We become his apprentices in the craft of manipulation.

What Satan did to Eve was crueller than cruelty itself. It was murderous. Suavely, with feigned outward friendliness—can serpents smile?—he ruined her life so he could control her. The despicableness of his actions should sicken us.

Yet many of us know the story too well. Its vileness no longer causes us to shudder. This is because we are now also prone to practice Satan's craft. As we give in to the practice of manipulation, it numbs our consciences and dulls our senses. We lose judicial discernment, our empathy fades, and the one emotion which overrides all others becomes that of fear—fear that we will be exposed, that we will be replaced, that we will lose control over our

---

[36] Don Richardson, *Peace Child* (Bloomington, MN: Bethany House, 2005), 40.

circumstances, fellow man, and God. We blame everyone and refuse to take ownership of our own actions. Reactive, defensive arguments erupt spontaneously from our lips at every turn, and even our smooth, coercive tones mask a stark panic.

Just like Saul.

THE BLAME GAME

Saul's lust for power continued to corrode his soul. After the humiliating events at Gilgal, he was anxious to reassert himself as a king, soldier, and man. When next the prophet Samuel spoke to him, it was to tell Saul that the Lord was calling him to fight against the Amalekites. Saul's heart must have leapt at the chance to redeem himself and become, again, the hero he longed to be.

However, we soon realize that his motives had little to do with protecting his own people, and everything to do with protecting his own image. The longer one indulges in manipulation, the more difficult it becomes to feel anything other than narcissistic resentment and envy.

God's instructions for Saul were very precise: *"totally destroy all that belongs to [the Amalekites]. Do not spare them; put to death men and women, children and infants, cattle and sheep, camels and donkeys"* (1 Samuel 15:3). Unfortunately, it seems that Saul took these commands as mere suggestions, to be ignored when they conflicted with his own self-serving agenda.

Saul did indeed attack the Amalekites, according to the Lord's mandate, but he disregarded God's command to utterly destroy this people and all they had; instead he chose to spare their king, as well as the best of the sheep, oxen, lambs, fatlings, and *"everything that was good"* (1 Samuel 15:9). Pleased with himself, he proceeded to set up a monument in his own honour (1 Samuel 15:12).

When confronted by Samuel, Saul let slip that his disobedience was due to fear and his obsessive need to control his men. His leadership style involved not just threats but also bribes. Saul had hoped to secure the loyalty of his troops by giving them the booty of the defeated Amalekites. The men were won over.

But the prophet was not. Saul's actions earned him harsh condemnation from Samuel. Defensively, Saul blamed his men, refusing to take responsibility for his actions. He said to Samuel, *"The soldiers brought them from the Amalekites; they spared the best of the sheep and cattle..."* (1 Samuel 15:15, emphasis mine). Saul claimed to have carried out the Lord's instructions, yet it was clear, amid the bleating of sheep and the lowing of cattle, that he most certainly had not.

This was Saul's pattern, rationalizing his sin, making excuses, and blaming others. As a result, he merely succeeded in digging himself into a deeper and deeper hole, until he could no longer see truth, much less admit it. Like the infamous Cat in the Hat who guiltily tried to get rid of a stain before it was discovered, and only managed to make it grow, we could say of Saul, "Oh the things that they did! And they did them so hard, it was all one big spot now all over the yard!"[37]

Samuel's response to these weak excuses was harsh and absolute; the king had crossed the line one time too many and his utter disregard for the Lord and consistent efforts to secure his own power through intimidation now had severe consequences: God removed him from his position as king. The very thing Saul had strained to hold onto was to be taken away from him.

Yet even then, Samuel tried to bring him to his senses. The prophet grieved that Saul had become so calloused and blind that he could not see the heinous nature of his own actions. Samuel, by his choice of words, may have hoped to shock Saul back into sanity:

> Does the Lord delight in burnt offerings and sacrifices as much as in obeying the Lord? To obey is better than sacrifice, and to heed is better than the fat of rams. *For rebellion is like the sin of divination, and arrogance like the evil of idolatry.* Because you have rejected the word of the Lord, he has rejected you as king. (1 Samuel 15:22–23, emphasis mine)

---

[37] Dr. Seuss, *The Cat in the Hat* (New York, NY: Random House, 1958), 52.

What exactly did Samuel mean by this? Rebellion, divination, idolatry? Even while Samuel hoped to use these words to drive home the severity of Saul's sins, this was no last-ditch effort to avert consequences. Were Saul to repent now—unlikely, since he was probably past the ability to feel genuine remorse—judgment would still have already been decreed (1 Samuel 13:14). This only served as a final confirmation that Saul had irrevocably lost the kingdom.

Rather than present a reprieve, it would seem that Samuel was prophetically defining the nature of these sins that brought about the downfall of this rejected king of Israel. Saul's rebellion was an effort to control and manipulate God; he had practiced divination in order to know the future and thus stay one step ahead of fate, contrasting with the Israelites practice of *inquiring of the Lord*. Divination has no relation to God's will. It's only about gaining valuable information to use for one's own benefit.

Rebellion involves the idolatry of Self, and Self must be served. This can only be done by seeking to control God and others. Manipulation and the pursuit of power reap dire consequences, since judicial blindness and bondage to sinful cravings only increase. Inevitably, the controller becomes the controlled. The deceiver becomes the deceived. Saul heard the words of Samuel but had become incapable of taking them to heart. He was deaf and blind to his own bondage.

Saul had once been given every reason for confidence. God had appointed him and Samuel had anointed him. There had been undeniable prophetic promises. Yet he could not help himself from doing everything in his power to make sure those promises came to pass.

Perhaps we think that if an angel, prophet, or God himself spoke promises over us, we should be content to wait for their fulfillment. Such is not the case.

Since Eden, we have all been trained in the art of manipulating God and others. It is a kind of family business. Consider the life of Jacob, where the craft was passed down from mother to son.

JACOB: LEARNING THE FAMILY BUSINESS

"I was once told, 'Girls were not made to take care of themselves,'" Cynthia told me. "At twelve, I listened, wide-eyed. But at twenty-five, I wondered

how much longer I was expected to live at home. I found myself wondering, at some point should I not take responsibility for my own life?

"When I broached this with my mother, it did not go well. 'We have done everything for you! How could you be this ungrateful?' she said, 'You will live at home under the authority of your father until that authority passes to a husband. If you never marry, that authority will eventually pass to your brother. Do you know what would happen to a girl living out from under authority? Your house would be marked by evil men! And one day they would come for you… they would break in… No, don't try to speak. This is how things are.'

"I was almost thirty before I sensed God releasing me to finally leave home. I knew I was facing possible excommunication; I had seen it happen with other family members. Incredibly, they let me go. I moved into a house of my own, and for a long time I checked under my bed and looked in every closet before I slept. I double-bolted the doors, barred them with wood, locked my bedroom door, and slept lightly. The evil men might come.

"There was that tattooed, motorcycle-riding neighbour. But then, the day I set my house on fire, he brought me water and stood by my side until I was all right. There was also that scary, gruff old man across the street. He fixed my lawnmower and smiled when I brought him cookies to thank him."

***

Cynthia's experience was somewhat extreme, and she is grateful for God's grace in helping her to navigate the difficult passage of separating from her mother. She has multiple younger siblings, almost all girls, and now sees her mother struggling to untie some of the more unnecessary knots in the apron strings. Cynthia admires her for that. She encourages her sisters to be patient, kind, and respectful while helping them learn some of the basic life skills they woefully lack as they, too, move toward individuation.

"Remember, Mom was always there for us while we were growing up," she tells them. "We could depend on that. Now is the time to learn to depend on God."

In Genesis 25, we meet Jacob who, like my friend Cynthia, was very much tied to his mother, dependent upon her for direction and approval.

This was exacerbated by the fact that his father Isaac seemed to prefer his other son, Esau. This would cause a boy like Jacob to cling even more to his mother for comfort, affirmation, and identity.

In every way that mattered in his day, Jacob felt eclipsed by his brother. Esau was the stereotype of a man's man—hairy all over (Genesis 25:25), skilled at hunting (Genesis 25:27), and with a hearty appetite. He quickly became his father Isaac's favourite son (Genesis 25:28), to a large degree due to their shared love of food.

Again like Cynthia, Jacob felt bound to his mother, a powerful and dominant force in his life, and he bowed to her wishes. Yet he appears to have not been entirely content to be tied to those apron strings forever. He envied Esau's freedom to roam, hunt, and enjoy all the privileges and promises of a firstborn son.

Jacob's apparent envy of Esau comes through in the following story.

One day Esau, weak with hunger after a hunting expedition, begged for food from his brother. Jacob, perhaps on account of being *"content to stay at home among the tents"* (Genesis 25:27) handled the cooking. Esau came in from the open country, smelled the lentil stew simmering over an open fire, and exclaimed, *"Quick, let me have some of that red stew! I'm famished!"* (Genesis 25:30)

The story goes on:

> Jacob replied, "First sell me your birth-right."
>
> "Look, I am about to die," Esau said. "What good is the birthright to me?"
>
> But Jacob said, "Swear to me first." So he swore an oath to him, selling his birthright to Jacob.
>
> Then Jacob gave Esau some bread and some lentil stew. He ate and drank, and then got up and left.
>
> So Esau despised his birthright. (Genesis 25:31–34)

It was a con. Consider the seduction of the savoury stew, the deception of implying that the meal's value was comparable to that of a sacred birthright, and the intimidation of an if-then scenario to manipulate Esau while he was in a weakened state.

Jacob's self-serving power grab was also an insult to the God who had decreed the birth order in the first place, and a rebellion against the divine ordination of primogeniture. Did Jacob care at that moment? No. He wanted the birthright, and he got it.

Years later, Isaac sensed his imminent death and called Esau to his side. He told his oldest son, *"[G]o out to the open country to hunt some wild game for me. Prepare me the kind of tasty food I like and bring it to me to eat, so that I may give you my blessing before I die"* (Genesis 27:3–4). Blessings were prophetic utterances pronounced by a paternal authority on their deathbed, and they were greatly valued. Esau obviously didn't tell his dad that he had actually sold his birthright and forfeited any blessing of primogeniture. Perhaps Esau had never taken it seriously in the first place.

But Jacob had.

Their mother Rebekah heard of her husband's plan and told Jacob about it. Clearly there was a special bond here, not just a natural one of mother and favoured child, but a bond between two people intent on controlling others. A dominant mother, a neglectful father, a jealous son; they were all made for each other.

Rebekah favoured Jacob and wanted greatness for him, and Jacob felt small and weak next to his manly older brother. If this story were to take place today, Jacob might have gone the way of the passive, insecure adolescent desperate to be a superhero, retreating into the fantasy world of online gaming. That avenue of escapism—a means for chronically disempowered kids to feel in control—was not open to him. There was, for Jacob, no escape.

Mom had a plan and offered to help Jacob trick Isaac into pronouncing the blessing of the firstborn on him rather than Esau. They disguised Jacob, both in appearance and scent, to deceive the blind old man. At this point in the story, some men might roll their eyes, muttering about the manipulative ingenuity of women. Do they have a point?

Control is no more important to a woman than to a man, but historically it has been much harder for women to attain. Perhaps it is not that women are more innately manipulative than men but that centuries of disempowered women have felt limited in influencing their own destiny and that of their children. Around the world, women are seldom in a position to manipulate others through physical force or intimidation; they often have to rely instead on more subtle means. Over generations of patriarchal domination, it is reasonable to assume that these skills would be passed down from mother to daughter as a means of survival.

In many parts of the world today, much of a woman's life remains outside her control, even biologically. It is difficult to overcome hormonal and lunar cycles, and many cultures still forbid the proactive use of any form of birth control—or, for that matter, choosing to remain single. Marriage is mandated for many women, and this is often accompanied by the loss of personal freedom and property.

The frustration at such social injustice can be extreme and leave women with few options. Where open revolt can lead to beatings, ostracization, imprisonment, or even death, what choice does a woman have? It should not surprise us that mothers who feel impotent would dominate their children through guilt or covertly manage their husbands through seduction or deception. I say this not to justify these means, but to explain the way in which one form of manipulation (aggressive male dominance) leads to another. Women who have lost hope of achieving equality and justice resort to whatever means of self-determination is left to them.

Was this what drove Rebekah? Possibly. She seems here to have hedged her bets to ensure that God's promises regarding her son Jacob would come to pass. She trusted no one, not even God, and took matters into her own hands, ready to pay the price. There was, for her, no real guarantee that even God could be trusted to take care of her son, despite the prophetic word that had been given at Jacob's birth, when the Lord had said to her, *"Two nations are in your womb, and two peoples from within you will be separated; one people will be stronger than the other, and the older will serve the younger"* (Genesis 25:23).

Maybe, she thought to herself. But maybe not. Better to be safe than sorry.

We could speculate that Jacob spent a lifetime unwittingly learning the habits of manipulation from his doting mother. She pushed an unresisting Jacob into a deceptive scheme to secure his fortune.

It is a heartbreaking story, including a blind old man who is made to appear foolish. Who would play tricks on the sightless? Had Rebekah hardened her heart? Had their marriage become cold or competitive? Had the daily exposure to Isaac's crass favouritism of Esau become intolerable for her? Many marriages fracture over parental neglect.

Rebekah dressed Jacob in Esau's garments and covered his smooth arms with a hairy animal skin. Thus disguised, Jacob brought his father his favourite meal, prepared as Esau would have prepared it.

At first Isaac was puzzled. This son sounded like Jacob but looked, smelled, and felt like Esau. Jacob reassured him: *"I am Esau your firstborn. I have done as you told me. Please sit up and eat some of my game, so that you may give me your blessing"* (Genesis 27:19).

Isaac hesitated but seemed to buy the deception. Did Rebekah, listening behind the tent curtain, cross her fingers? Did Jacob feel ashamed, or excited?

Isaac ate of the meat and then reached out his groping hands to his son. *"Come here, my son, and kiss me"* (Genesis 27:26). And then he spoke the blessing Jacob had longed to hear:

> May God give you heaven's dew and earth's richness—an abundance of grain and new wine. May nations serve you and peoples bow down to you. Be lord over your brothers, and may the sons of your mother bow down to you. May those who curse you be cursed and those who bless you be blessed. (Genesis 27:28–29)

The blessing, issued in a quavering and hoarse old voice, had already been spoken over Jacob by God. There was no need to trick Isaac. God had already purposed that Jacob and his descendants should know "heaven's dew," and "earth's richness." The nations would serve him and his own brothers would bow before him. Jacob didn't need to steal what God was already willing to give. But because he did, the blessing had a dark shadow cast over it. Even as the blessing was fulfilled, the consequences of Jacob's manipulation warped both his relationship with his own brother and the nation's future for generations.

When Esau came home with the stew his father had asked of him, it was too late. Isaac trembled violently when he realized the deception and Esau cried out with heart-wrenching grief and anger: *"Do you have only one blessing, my father? Bless me too, my father!"* (Genesis 27:38)

Isaac's spiritual sight, quickened perhaps by the loss of his natural sight, came up with a grim picture of what had happened. As Esau wept, Isaac proclaimed over him,

> Your dwelling will be away from the earth's richness, away from the dew of heaven above. You will live by the sword and you will serve your brother. But when you grow restless, you will throw his yoke from off your neck. (Genesis 27:39–40)

Animosity would become the hallmark of Esau's descendants, known in the Bible as the Edomites. Because of Jacob and Rebekah's actions, Esau's bitterness was passed down to his children, and their children, until the resulting nation was destined to become the archenemy of Israel. The Edomites, Esau's descendants, hated Israel, Jacob's descendants, with *"an ancient hostility"* (Ezekiel 35:5).

The die was cast for tribal war, and it likely began right here—at Isaac's bedside.

A murderous rage sprang up in Esau's heart. When Rebekah learned of it, she urged Jacob to flee for his life. She intervened with her husband as well, proceeding to manoeuvre Isaac into sending Jacob away. Her approach continued to be manipulative.

> Then Rebekah said to Isaac, "I'm dis-
> gusted with living because of these Hit-
> tite women. If Jacob takes a wife from
> among the women of this land, from
> Hittite women like these, my life will not
> be worth living." (Genesis 27:46)

But again it worked. So he sent Jacob to Paddan Aram to look for a wife from among the daughters of Jacob's uncle Laban (Genesis 27:46, 28:1–2).

Perhaps Jacob was relieved to escape Esau. More likely he was greatly dismayed at having to leave home. For a boy who loved the comfort of the tents, and anticipated coming into his father's fortune, this didn't go according to plan. It must have felt more like exile.

En route to Paddan Aram, Jacob had a disturbing dream: *"he saw a stairway resting on the earth, with its top reaching to heaven, and the angels of God were ascending and descending on it"* (Genesis 28:12). He was awestruck, frightened, and then astonished to hear God speak over him the same kind of promises that had been pronounced over his ancestor Abraham:

> I am the Lord, the God of your father
> Abraham and the God of Isaac. I will
> give you and your descendants the land
> on which you are lying. Your descen-
> dants will be like the dust of the earth,
> and you will spread out to the west
> and to the east, to the north and to
> the south. All peoples on earth will be
> blessed through you and your offspring.
> I am with you and will watch over you
> wherever you go, and I will bring you
> back to this land. I will not leave you
> until I have done what I have promised
> you. (Genesis 28:13–15)

For the first time in his recorded life, Jacob encountered God and was overwhelmed. Homesick, fearful, and likely disappointed at the turn his life had taken, Jacob heard God speak gracious, undeserved assurances of divine protection and presence, as well as a promise that he would return to his home. In mercy, God reached out to reassure Jacob of his divine plan and unending love.

How did Jacob react? With the kind of anxious wheedling that becomes part of any conman's repertoire.

Using an if-then proposition, Jacob tried to bribe the Almighty into guaranteeing the fulfillment of these attractive promises:

> If God will be with me and will watch over me on this journey I am taking and will give me food to eat and clothes to wear so that I return safely to my father's household, then the Lord will be my God and this stone that I have set up as a pillar will be God's house, and of all that you give me I will give you a tenth. (Genesis 28:20–22)

The practice of manipulation destroys faith, and Jacob's faith is here tentative at best. It's a let's-see kind of faith, the fearful cynicism of a manipulator.

It is also the faith of the average believer.

Making the decision to try and control God and others erodes trust. Liars become suspicious that they are being lied to. Bullies see bigger men as a threat. Thieves hoard their possessions fearfully, convinced that others want to steal from them. Those who seduce a partner into a relationship are apprehensive that their partner will be unfaithful.

As a person's character degrades in this way, others perceive the lack of integrity and react either by avoiding the manipulator or by scheming to beat them at their own game. It is a long, slow slide with a rough landing at the end, as Jacob would soon find out.

SLIDING DOWN THE LADDER

Arriving in Paddan Aram, Jacob met his uncle Laban—and in doing so, he also met his match. Laban was about to beat Jacob at his own game, for he was a more accomplished manipulator.

Derek Kidner, commenting on the relationship, says,

> In Laban Jacob met his match and his means of discipline. Twenty years (31:41) of drudgery and friction were to weather his character; and the reader can reflect that presumably Jacob is not the only person to have needed a Laban in his life.[38]

Laban thought he would have a tough time getting rid of his older daughter, Leah, who had some sort of vision impairment and was less than a stunning beauty. Seeing that his nephew Jacob was entranced by Leah's younger sister Rachel, Laban slyly agreed to give her hand in marriage after seven years of labour. At the end of that time, however, during the wine-infused blur of the wedding celebration, Laban slipped his daughter Leah into Jacob's bed. In the morning, Jacob was dismayed to discover the switch and objected vigorously. Laban insisted that it would be highly improper for the younger sister to be married off before the older sister. Faced with the threat of losing Rachel altogether, Jacob reluctantly agreed to take Leah as his first wife. Laban successfully unloaded Leah and secured seven more years of labour from his nephew.

Both Laban and Jacob vied for control, using manipulative means to secure an advantage.

In Genesis 30, we catch Jacob in what some people would call witch-craft, in the classic sense of the word. Laban himself was accustomed to practicing divination (Genesis 30:27) and may have passed this practice on to his nephew.

---

[38] Derek Kidner, *Genesis* (Lisle, IL: InterVarsity Press, 1967), 170.

After fourteen years of hard service, Jacob was done. He wanted out and told his uncle that he was ready to leave with his wives and children. Seeking to mollify the nephew he had tricked, Laban offered him wages.

Seeing the opportunity to gain the upper hand, Jacob struck a bargain to be paid in livestock. He requested to be paid in speckled or dark-coloured sheep, which were seen as less desirable than sheep of solid colour. Laban eagerly agreed, perhaps sensing Jacob's naiveté, then promptly saw to it that the speckled and dark-coloured sheep disappeared.

Jacob practiced a kind of folk magic, peeling poplar branches and placing them where the sheep copulated. The result was a steady stream of vigorous animals, both streaked and speckled, and all destined for Jacob.

Jacob grew very wealthy from this act (Genesis 30–31). Does that mean that the folk magic worked? It did, but only in the sense that stealing from a baited trap works; one may get the cheese, but only at the cost of freedom.

Jacob grew ever more insecure and fearful knowing his father-in-law was upset. This was probably a massive understatement: *"Jacob noticed that Laban's attitude toward him was not what it had been"* (Genesis 31:2). Angry at the way he had been treated, Jacob complained to his Leah and Rachel, hoping to garnish sympathy and support.

Fearing Laban's wrath, Jacob packed up his wives and belongings and headed for the hills. He did not march off proudly, with his head held high. No, he escaped with stealth and in shame—in the dark of night.

Yet the God who was determined to bless him, despite it all, relentlessly pursued.

CLING AND CONQUER

Laban discovered the deception and overtook Jacob and his retinue in the desert. The two men came to an uneasy truce, and Laban left Jacob to go on his way—although Jacob didn't know at first where to go.

Somewhere along this uncertain journey, Jacob encountered the *"angels of God"* (Genesis 32:1) and seems to have come to a decision: he would take his chances back home. But what about Esau? Had enough years passed for his brother's fury to cool?

Anxiously, Jacob sent messengers ahead to let Esau know he was returning. The messengers returned with an ominous report: *"We went to your brother Esau, and now he is coming to meet you, and four hundred men are with him"* (Genesis 32:6).

Hearing this, Jacob's blood ran cold. It was over. They were doomed. Esau was on his way with armed troops to kill them all.

Frantically, he divided his retinue into groups and sent them ahead with gifts, staggered so they wouldn't all encounter his vengeful brother at the same time. Maybe, just maybe, some of them would be spared.

Miserable and alone, Jacob stayed behind. We can imagine him pacing nervously up and down, biting his fingernails under the cold starlight. Fearful of the inevitable meeting with his estranged brother, Jacob would have wondered whether the placating gifts he'd sent ahead would be enough.

He was startled to see a man suddenly appear where no one had stood a moment before. We know now that this looming aggressor was the pre-incarnate Son of God, but Jacob had no idea—yet. A wrestling match ensued, between God and a human being. How was this even possible?

As one might imagine, the match was entirely uneven. Before Jacob had time to think, he was seized in powerful arms. His mind had already been full of spectres of enemies and now his heart pounded, adrenaline surging through his veins.

Panting and grunting from the effort, he fought to get his legs further apart and effect a wider stance. This mysterious enemy was strong! Jacob struggled in vain to throw him off-balance.

To Jacob's surprise, despite the imparity of strength, the stranger didn't finish him off. Perhaps the aim of the fight was different for the two opponents. Jacob fought for freedom; God fought to embrace.

With the lightest of touches, the Angel of the Lord inflicted upon Jacob the searing pain of a dislocated hip. Jacob cried out, sagging and clutching as waves of nausea washed over him. He was no longer wrestling to win; he was just trying not to faint from the agony that blurred his vision and threatened to loosen his bowels.

The fight should have been over, but the stranger didn't fling him off and hurl his helpless body into the dust. Instead he stood there and allowed Jacob to cling to him.

The extraordinary identity of his opponent began to dawn on Jacob; this was no ordinary man. Cowed before the awesomeness of this Angel he had been foolish enough to fight, Jacob hung on, wondering weakly what would happen next. Was this God? What was he doing? And why?

This struggle was the symbolic climax to a much longer and deeper wrestling that had been going on. God was determined that Jacob should receive his love. Jacob, though, had spent his life trusting only in his deceptive skill, eroding his capacity to trust. God wrestled with him because that was all Jacob would allow him to do. Now, helpless and clinging, he at last received the blessing and affirmation he had craved all along.

> Then the [Angel] said, "Your name will no longer be Jacob, but Israel, because you have struggled with God and with humans and have overcome." (Genesis 32:28)

Was God commending Jacob for his manipulative ways? By no means. The fact that God changed Jacob's name and spoke a blessing does not necessarily indicate approval but acknowledges reality. "Well, this is who you are, Jacob," the Lord might have said. "You've wrestled all along for the very things I wanted to give you. Don't you get it yet? You didn't need to struggle so hard. You are a prince in my eyes. I've always loved you."

Was the Angel of the Lord saying that Jacob had somehow defeated him? Had Jacob in fact won this wrestling match with God? Hardly. But then what does the word *overcome* refer to in Genesis 32:28?

In the New American Standard Bible, we read that Jacob "contended with God and with men, and… prevailed" (NASB). The word used for "prevail" and "overcome" is the Hebrew *yakol*, which does not carry the connotation of vanquishing a foe. Rather it means "to be able." Jacob might have grimaced wryly at the phrase, for it was quite evident that he could not prevail in this encounter with the Angel.

But in another sense, Jacob *did* prevail. He learned that the only way to "be able" was to hang on, to cling, to ask rather than take. He did not prevail in his own strength. He prevailed by realizing his helplessness and absolute dependency upon his creator. That made him a prince in God's eyes.

THE FACE OF GOD

The next morning, Jacob was fearful again, and in pain to boot. He still hoped that the plans he had laid the night before would work.

Following the train of appeasing gifts he had sent ahead, Jacob limped toward Esau. His wives and children had preceded him along with the gifts, serving as a shield to deflect any ire and malice his brother might still feel. Perhaps Esaw would see his family and think, "Aren't they adorable? Isn't she sweet?" This strategy certainly seems cowardly and unmanly, but it would take a long time to eradicate the habit of manipulation from his life, angelic affirmation notwithstanding.

The meeting could not be put off any longer, though, and Jacob finally encountered his brother at the head of four hundred men. The recognition between them was instantaneous.

Jacob prostrated himself seven times, which was probably agonizing given his out-of-joint hip. And while Jacob struggled to bow, Esaw broke into a run. He then seized Jacob in his arms.

At that point, something clicked in Jacob's mind, but there was no time for him to express it; Esau was pressing him for introductions and explanations. When these were done, Jacob said something significant: *"For to see your face is like seeing the face of God, now that you have received me favorably"* (Genesis 33:10).

Was this polite, manipulative flattery? For once, perhaps not. Jacob had just come from seeing the face of God, remember. He had expected to die but instead had been shown unexpected favour. Now his brother was showing him the same favour—one that he could not take, only receive.

The clinging of Jacob contrasts sharply with the clinging of King Saul. Jacob clung to God; Saul clung to his image.

IMAGE IS EVERYTHING

Having tried to retain control over his men through manipulation, the kingship was now being torn from Saul's hands. True to form, when facing the unrelenting Samuel, Saul tried to bargain. He grasped at straws, even clutching at the prophet's cloak.

This was a very different kind of clinging. Jacob clung because he knew, at last, his own powerlessness. He clung because he could do nothing else.

Injured, defeated, and all too aware that he was reaping the consequences of decades of willful, self-serving manipulation, Jacob begged for mercy, for a blessing he knew was undeserved.

Saul knew he had lost everything. But far from humbling himself, he grabbed hold of Samuel begging to be allowed to keep his public image intact. His highest priority was not to rule with truth, justice, and wisdom but to protect and maintain his own façade for as long as possible.

> Then Saul said to Samuel, "I have sinned. I violated the Lord's command and your instructions. I was afraid of the men and so I gave in to them. Now I beg you, forgive my sin and come back with me, so that I may worship the Lord."
>
> But Samuel said to him, "I will not go back with you. You have rejected the word of the Lord, and the Lord has rejected you as king over Israel!"
>
> As Samuel turned to leave, Saul caught hold of the hem of his robe, and it tore. Samuel said to him, "The Lord has torn the kingdom of Israel from you today and has given it to one of your neighbors—to one better than you. He who is the Glory of Israel does not lie or change his mind; for he is not a human being, that he should change his mind."
>
> Saul replied, "I have sinned. But please honor me before the elders of my people and before Israel; come back with me, so that I may worship the Lord your God." (1 Samuel 15:24–31)

Even his repentance contained an undertone of manipulation. Having lost the mantle of authority, Saul gathered the scraps of his shattered dignity and wrapped it around himself like a protective cloak.

But it was too late. Samuel shook himself free from Saul's grip, stricken with grief; like any prophet, he had hoped to serve a godly king. That dream was now dust and ashes.

Samuel retreated to the town of Ramah, mourning. And it would seem that in his mourning he shared the heart of God, who that day *"regretted that he had made Saul king over Israel"* (1 Samuel 15:35). Saul and Samuel parted ways and Saul never saw the prophet again.

At least not while Samuel was alive.

FOUR
DIVINERS DRIVEN MAD

TURNING HIS BACK on Saul forever, Samuel was sent by the Lord to find and anoint another young man to reign in Saul's place. God sent him to search among the sons of a man named Jesse, in Bethlehem.

At first Samuel feared that Saul would hear of this treason and seek to kill him, but in the end Samuel obeyed.

Sifting through the young sons of Jesse, Samuel saw potential. Each one was tall, strong, brave, and handsome. But God was adamant:

> Do not consider his appearance or his height, for I have rejected him. The Lord does not look at the things people look at. People look at the outward appearance, but the Lord looks at the heart. (1 Samuel 16:7)

The next king was to be a man after God's own heart (1 Samuel 13:14), and it was the shepherd boy David who was chosen to rule in Saul's place.

Saul, however, did not go down without a fight. Refusing to relinquish his position of power, he struggled for many years to maintain control of the kingdom. He used every means at his disposal, from laying guilt trips on his soldiers to attempting to murder his competition. His arsenal of manipulative weapons was impressive.

However, the one thing he no longer had was the assurance of God's calling. As a king, he had been fired. God was no longer with him. Whatever anointing he may have had was now formally lifted.

When the Holy Spirit came upon David, God removed his Spirit from Saul (1 Samuel 16:13–14). This is no mere metaphor. Whatever fragile hold

Saul had on his sanity was due to the grace of God. That has now been taken away.

A distressing spirit began to torment the rejected king. Scripture tells us this spirit was *"from God"* (1 Samuel 16:14). Does that mean God sent a demon to torture Saul? Or does it mean that the demons held at bay by God's hand of protection were simply released because Saul had finally pushed that hand away? It's not clear, but we can imagine sporadic bouts of intense anxiety, depression, and even unbearable guilt as a natural consequence, amplified by some gleeful satanic minion.

Ironically, the young shepherd boy chosen by God to one day take Saul's place as king of Israel ended up being asked to come to the palace and strum soothingly upon his lyre to bring Saul relief. Typically self-absorbed, Saul barely paid attention to the boy and didn't even bother to learn his name.

Not long after David was formally chosen and anointed by Samuel, the Philistine army attacked, challenging Israel with their reigning military champion, a giant named Goliath. The headline is a classic: Unknown Shepherd Boy Becomes Hero. David came to bring food to his brothers, who had enlisted in Israel's army. He proceeded to shame his brothers, Israel's warriors, cowering bystanders, and even King Saul himself by boldly and openly challenging the giant: *"What will be done for the man who kills this Philistine and removes this disgrace from Israel? Who is this uncircumcised Philistine that he should defy the armies of the living God?"* (1 Samuel 17:26)

Saul would have seen David as being full of righteous indignation, a noble youth rising up to offer to fight the enemy who dared malign Israel's God. Even then, he would have been consumed by jealousy.

So it is that when we read of the armour with which Saul first clothes David, we might wonder whether this was done less out of kind concern for David's well-being and more from an intent to humiliate the boy, knowing it would be far too heavy and cumbersome; David would look like the arrogant little upstart Saul believed him to be.

Either way, no one was prepared for David's impetuous shucking of this gear and snatching up a slingshot. When Goliath was then brought down with a single stone, the king was appalled. Before the cheering crowds of Israel, he was forced to praise his unlikely competitor. Perhaps this is when he narrowed his eyes in suspicion. Who was this boy? He looked vaguely familiar.

The Philistines were defeated, their camp plundered. It was a glorious victory all round.

As soon as David returned from killing the Philistine, the commander of Israel's army brought David before Saul, with David still holding the Philistine's head.

> "Whose son are you, young man?" Saul asked him.
>> David said, "I am the son of your servant Jesse of Bethlehem." (1 Samuel 17:58)

Suddenly, the identity of this obscure youth would have become all too clear.

Goliath isn't the one I need to worry about, Saul might have thought.

The king caught the looks of admiration and affection being directed towards David, son of Jesse. The admiration was not confined to the faces of the crowd; it was mirrored in the face of his own son, Jonathan. Jonathan took off his robe and gave it to David, along with his tunic, sword, bow, and belt. What his father Saul had done, likely in mockery of young David, Jonathan now did in open adulation and friendship. And this time, the clothes fit.

The honour done to David would have rankled Saul beyond imagining.

As his paranoia grew, he brought David into the royal palace to keep him close, perhaps to keep an eye on him and prevent him from committing any more acts of valour that might further win the people's hearts.

Sun Tzu, general, military strategist, and philosopher of ancient China, is credited with the phrase "Keep your friends close; keep your enemies closer." This was most certainly Saul's thought as well, as he felt the kingdom beginning to slip through his fingers.

Saul continued to employ David to play music from time to time, relegating the young hero to a role akin to the court jester. Indeed, the day after Goliath's defeat Saul's tormenting spirit returned with a vengeance and

David was brought in to play music in his court, as before. But whatever small comfort Saul had at first been able to derive from David's soothing music was now drowned out by the envy raging within. Saul was furious and hurled a spear, hoping to pin David to the wall.

David managed to escape harm but was surely dismayed by the king's increasingly erratic moods. Yet he showed no resentment. Instead he went on to display genuine concern for his king's well-being.

Such sincere solicitude, nobility, and selflessness would have driven Saul crazy. He sent David into battles against hopeless odds, hoping David would die at the hands of Israel's enemies.

It didn't work.

He then offered his daughter's hand in marriage, in exchange for a hundred Philistine foreskins, hoping David would die in the attempt to secure them.

No such luck; David got the foreskins—and the girl as well! This only served to increase David's popularity.

It is a painful irony that Saul's own son Jonathan betrayed his father with the intense love and loyalty he felt for David. Jonathan was a wild card, unpredictable and refusing to be governed by the unreasonable and unjust whims of his own father.

As Jonathan's friendship with David grew deeper, Saul couldn't help but gnash his teeth. This may have been another reason Saul insisted on bringing David back to court, in order to monitor the relationship between his rival and his son, assess the threat to his own power, and keep an eye out for possible treason.

Saul may have felt that the threat to his control as a father was even worse than the threat to his position as king. It was more than he could endure, and his mind began to break down.

SELF-PITY AND MENTAL DECAY

"It's as if, with each argument, she makes less sense," Bob said, shaking his head. "Her perception of reality keeps shifting, getting more and more distorted."

Listening to our friend speak about the breakdown of his marriage, I wondered whether self-pity can rot the brain. His wife Carla was becoming increasingly unstable and volatile. Counselling had long since ceased to be of any use.

"She blames everyone else for... well, everything," he went on. "She blames me for the fact that our son wants nothing to do with her. He won't even acknowledge her existence since he moved out, and he will only meet with me if I promise not to talk about 'that woman.' Carla refuses to take responsibility for the way she damaged him as a child."

Bob paused and looked up at us with a bleak smile.

"Is she going crazy? Or am I?"

***

Bob invested thousands of dollars over many years, going from counsellor to counsellor with his wife. Each time, the sessions were terminated when Carla perceived herself to be challenged to change in any way.

Their marriage was exhausting, expensive, and showed no sign of improvement. If anything, the longer Carla felt sorry for herself, the more entrenched she became in her behaviour. There were signs that her irrationality was getting worse, and she even went so far as to accuse her husband of being afflicted by demons, stridently insisting that they pay for an off-the-grid—not to mention off-their-insurance-coverage—faith therapist of dubious professional skill.

Eventually, Bob put his foot down.

So did she. The madness was relentless and eventually drove them apart.

Once a person has managed to convince themselves that they are a victim, it is very difficult to back up and assume any responsibility. To do so would be to admit that maybe, just maybe, some of the blame must fall on them. The longer one indulges in blaming others, the less one is able to see the other's point of view.

Carla reached that point, and it led her to make some very poor decisions.

They were nothing compared to King Saul's, though.

As Saul's fits of rage increased, he began to openly attack his rival and, in the face of Saul's violent behaviour, David fled for his life. Yet far from being released from his anxiety, Saul became even more paralyzed by fear, indecision, and bitterness.

By now, we can see evidence of growing mental instability. As with every committed manipulator, Saul slid into a morass of self-pity, leading to an inevitable moral and mental decline. It trapped him. He couldn't endure the howling sense of abandonment he felt when he realized that David had found refuge with the prophet Samuel.

Samuel! How could Samuel do this to him? *His* prophet, *his* seer, *his* advisor!

Unhinged by this betrayal, Saul spent months hunting David down, only for the young man to repeatedly escape. The king's hold on sanity was slipping; Saul was destined for madness. He began to accuse his own men, hurling guilt-laden slander and offering pitiful promises in an attempt to win them back.

> Listen, men of Benjamin! Will the son of Jesse give all of you fields and vineyards? Will he make all of you commanders of thousands and commanders of hundreds? Is that why you have all conspired against me? No one tells me when my son makes a covenant with the son of Jesse. None of you is concerned about me or tells me that my son has incited my servant to lie in wait for me, as he does today. (1 Samuel 22:7–8)

Finally, weighed down by the accusations, Saul's chief shepherd, Doeg, admitted to having seen David in the company of the priest Ahimelek, asking for food and a weapon. As a shepherd himself, Doeg may have resented David, a shepherd who had risen in the ranks at an astonishing pace, and hoped for him to be taken down a notch. Whatever the motive of his heart, Doeg wasted no time relating all that he had seen.

Enraged, the king sent for Ahimelech and condemned him to death, along with all the other priests.

Saul, reeling with jealousy, complained that no one cared about him, that everyone was conspiring against him (1 Samuel 22:8), and commanded his guards to slay the priests.

There was a moment of cold silence as no one moved. To strike a priest of the Lord was unthinkable. Saul then turned to his chief shepherd and barked, *"You do it"* (1 Samuel 22:18, NLT).

Doeg, thinking perhaps that his star was finally ascending, took a sword and plunged it into the nearest priest. It was a gruesome massacre, with eighty-five men slaughtered. Saul then ordered his men to put the entire population of the priestly city of Nob to the sword, killing not just the men, but the women and children, even the livestock.

Saul continued to search for David with murderous intent. During this time, the prophet Samuel died; all of Israel mourned him, yet it barely slowed Saul down. His obsession with killing David was all that mattered.

Twice David found himself near Saul, hidden and in a position to do the king harm—and twice he spared Saul. When this came to light, instead of softening the king's heart, Saul was consumed with shame and even more self-pity. It was intolerable that David should not only continue to elude him but publicly come off as the better man.

A day came when the Philistines, Saul's age-old enemies, gathered against him in full force, uniting thousands of men in a vast army to attack Israel. Saul was no longer the brave warrior king; he was weak and terrified. His obsession with maintaining power and control had eroded his mind, leaving nothing but fear.

With Samuel dead, Saul had no prophet to turn to. Too little, too late, he tried to seek God's counsel. We are told that when he *"inquired of the Lord… the Lord did not answer him by dreams or Urim or prophets"* (1 Samuel 28:6). God, whose guidance Saul had repeatedly spurned, was silent.

Now we see the black depth of Saul's hunger for power and control, his total disregard for any pretence of honour. It is with depraved wretchedness that he gave up on God and instead sought out a medium—a diviner, a witch—to help him. Saul had gone too far to come back from the brink. He was tumbling over the edge, mentally and spiritually. His lust for control sent him spinning out of control.

And neatly into the control of another.

NO MIDDLE GROUND

Earlier we saw how, in eating the forbidden fruit in Eden, Eve and Adam gained nothing. In taking control, they lost control. In rebelling against God's authority, they came under the power of the ruler of this world. Their one free choice—a choice of masters—resulted in the loss of all free choice. God's warning to them came to pass, and the pristine perfection of life was marred. The priceless gift of free will was forever compromised by sin, sickness, lunar cycles, unavoidable hormonal fluctuations, and blood sugar levels.

Our ancient forefathers made their choice just as Saul made his, and just as we make ours. There may be no audible clang as the iron-barred cell doors close, but the prison is nonetheless very real.

Bound and blind, Saul still refused to concede that he was no longer in control. Like many of us, he persisted beyond the limits of sanity in trying to hold on to something that was not his to grasp. His delusion is one we all face, that we can somehow retain free agency apart from God. Saul straddled the same fence we balance ourselves upon. A little obedience to God, a little self-determination; a little humility, a little idolatry. We teeter back and forth, unwilling to commit ourselves fully to a God we fear might strip us of our freedom altogether. In reality, by holding ourselves apart from God we abdicate the only freedom that matters.

God, who alone controls the universe, chooses to limit his control for the sake of allowing a voluntary love relationship to evolve between creator and creation. We are free to respond, or not respond, as we choose. If we choose to say yes to this relationship, he can work with us to direct our steps, redeem our misdeeds, and rewrite our stories with the kind of endings that bring divine plot twists to tragedies.

Remember, we are offered one truly free choice: a choice of masters. What does this mean? The theories regarding free will are confusing, to say the least.

Determinism states that all our so-called free choices are predetermined by a causality outside our control, such as God.

Libertarianism holds that all choices originate in a person's own will.

Compatibilism argues that any choice we make is the inevitable byproduct of external causes which do not originate with us—such as culture, socioeconomic status, family of origin—yet somehow we are also free agents, part of our own causal network.

These are dizzying philosophical issues, addressed in tomes such as thirteenth-century theologian Thomas Aquinas's *Summa Theologiae* and eighteenth-century philosopher David Hume's *Treatise of Human Nature*, all well beyond my comprehension.

What then?

That mankind is free to choose is implicit in biblical teachings on accountability. We will be judged; therefore, we must be in some way responsible for our own actions. The very nature of God would argue for a creator who creates beings that have free will. Just as the omnipotence paradox falls—can God make a stone too heavy for him to lift?—so too God, being love, cannot make a man who is unable to choose freely respond to that love. There is no such thing as choiceless love.

On the other hand, Jesus also seems to make clear that we are only judged according to what we know and understand of God's will, not just according to how well we fulfill it (Luke 12:47–48).

For example, in the ensuing brouhaha following the healing of the man born blind in John, Jesus responded to the outrage of the Pharisees by saying, "If you were blind, you would not be guilty of sin; but now that you claim you can see, your guilt remains" (John 9:41). All of this argues for the reality of our free will, and the consequences of our choices.

Perhaps it might be helpful to adopt a view which holds that our free will does exist but in a damaged state. Our will is whole enough to allow for one truly self-generated choice—God or Self. Should we choose God, our ability to perceive and desire his reality is progressively healed. We become less driven by our own selfish, sinful, and misguided impulses and more free to choose the good.

There is one free choice—a choice of masters, and only one intends to set us free.

If we turn away from God, we may think we are choosing self-determination, but we are actually turning our broken selves over to the corrosive influences of a broken world. Under this influence, we gradually lose all freedom, including the freedom to think our own thoughts clearly. The enemy, a very real and deadly contributor to our ensuing self-delusion, then steps in as a cruel and vicious taskmaster intent upon the destruction of our humanity.

Only in willingly yielding ourselves to a good and wise Father can we find true freedom. And freedom is what we all crave, even though few of us actually understand what it is for.

Os Guinness, in his book *A Free People's Suicide*, explains that we have a distorted understanding of what freedom really means. Despite having risen as the highest value and priority in a secularized world,[39] our understanding of freedom is based upon the negative—that is, we focus on being free *from* external restraints rather than on being free *unto* our best and truest selves, for the sake of a better and truer world.

Tim Keller puts it this way in his book, *The Reason for God*:

> A fish, because it absorbs oxygen from water rather than air, is only free if it is restricted and limited to water. If we put it out on the grass, its freedom to move and even live is not enhanced but destroyed. The fish dies if we do not honor the reality of its nature.[40]

When a teapot decides to accept being a teapot, the possibilities for delightful social interactions are endless. Should that teapot insist upon the right to pursue being a piano, its choices dwindle.

In a secular society, distaste for external restraints is coupled with disdain for self-restraint. Guinness writes that "choice itself, rather than the content of any choice, has become the heart of freedom. The result is that [we] value choice rather than good choice."[41]

The result? In casting aside any notion of either submitting to a master or mastering ourselves, we become our own gods. This idolatry of Self, far

---

[39] Os Guinness, *A Free People's Suicide: Sustainable Freedom and the American Future* (Lisle, IL: IVP Books, 2012), 17–18.

[40] Tim Keller, *The Reason for God: Belief in an Age of Skepticism* (New York, NY: Penguin Random House, 2008), 47.

[41] Guinness, *A Free People's Suicide*, 60.

from being full of high ideals and nobility, is rife with pathos. As Guinness says, "there is no greater folly than the masterless self" as we fail to realize that true liberty is not the "permission to do what we like, but the power to do what we should."[42]

The concept of "should" is unpopular in the extreme. In days long past, it meant sacrificing self for the sake of the other. Today, particularly in the secular West, "should" is the verb we use when we are insisting that others must respect our rights. This perspective comes from the merging of traditional Judeo-Christian values with nationalistic values of expressive individualism, democracy, and the right to bear arms. This is not bowing before God as king; it is using God to serve and defend our own agendas as we tell God what he "should" do for us. When God becomes utilitarian, he is no longer God.

In rejecting God's sovereignty, our only other choice is to serve self. There is no neutral territory, no middle ground. While self-service may seem to offer us freedom—with self-actualization being the means to attaining personal fulfillment—idolatry to Self always leads to a loss of freedom. We're at the mercy of our inconsistent, incoherent, and selfish desires, and we're increasingly at the mercy of the one who amplifies those desires.

When we choose the idolatry of Self, we gain an instant, eager, and evil ally.. His ways align seamlessly with our self-serving mindset. He is happy to help us succeed. With Satan cheering us on, money, sex, and power go from being satisfying pleasures to addictions in the blink of a bloodshot eye. As with any addiction, tolerance builds up over time, demanding greater and greater stimulation in order to achieve the same effect. This is the enemy's goal. The things we crave enslave us, and then they kill us.

Even knowing this, most of us persist in our willfulness, believing ourselves to be captains of our own souls. It does not take long for us to discover that the only way to control our own destiny, illusory as that control may be, is to control the lives of those around us. We scrabble to gain the upper hand, striving to surpass and dominate. When we succeed, the rush of power is intoxicating, deadly, and demonic.

As it was for King Saul.

---

[42] Ibid., 150, 152.

WHAT HAPPENED AT ENDOR

The Philistines had surrounded Saul, his son had given his heart away to his rival, David's star was rising, the men were defecting, God was giving him the cold shoulder, and the prophet Samuel was dead. Years of self-pity and blaming others had eroded his ability to perceive truth, assume personal responsibility, or change trajectory.

As with Carla, our friend Bob's wife, Saul had damaged his own rationality and could no longer think clearly or make wise decisions. Whereas Carla demanded that she and Bob consult a sketchy therapeutic spiritualist for marriage counselling, Saul turned to a witch.

Saul had only once, grudgingly, inquired of the Lord, and he had been met with absolute silence. With good reason! Inquiring of the Lord was not meant to be done in order to get information, it was to be done in order to *receive instruction*. Saul had no desire to submit to anyone, much less God. He didn't want to be told what to do; he wanted to be *in the know*, to have an edge over his enemies.

In the Old Testament, to inquire of God through a prophet was to say, "Command me." To consult a medium was to say, "Tell me what I need to know, so I can be in command." Saul wanted to know the future so he could be in control of it, so in 1 Samuel 28 he asked a diviner to summon the spirit of the deceased Samuel, hoping to receive some guidance to help him recover the upper hand.

This diviner was, in fact, able to reveal the future to him; there was real power there. Knowing the future, however, can still leave one in the dark. It is far worse than ignorance, for we are left to decide for ourselves what we ought to do.

And, as in the case of Saul, it can also paralyze us with despair.

Having persistently chosen to take matters into his own hands, Saul came more and more under the enemy's influence. He was not in control; he was being controlled. There had been a steady escalation in his manipulative efforts to regain control over others, and now there was no longer any pretence at subtlety. Threats and bribes hadn't been enough and Saul finally turned to a practice explicitly forbidden by God's laws (Leviticus 19:31, 20:6, 27; Deuteronomy 18:11). In consulting a medium, he crossed over into blatant witchcraft.

This was doomed to end badly. Commentators differ as to whether the medium Saul consulted actually conjured the spirit of the dead prophet Samuel. Regardless, the practice of consulting the dead was considered a sin; whatever wise advice Saul might have hoped for would have proved fruitless. Isaiah tells us what God thinks about such pursuits:

> I am the Lord, who makes all things,
> who stretches out the heavens all
> alone, who spreads abroad the earth
> by Myoolf; who fructrates the signs of
> the babblers, and drives diviners mad…
> (Isaiah 44:24–25, NKJV)

In the dark of the night, Saul disguised himself to visit the woman at Endor, a well-known medium skilled in necromancy. She greeted him and the séance began.

> Then the woman asked, "Whom shall I
> bring up for you?"
> "Bring up Samuel," he said. (1
> Samuel 28:11)

When the apparition was brought forth, the woman cried out in dismay. Somehow, with the appearance of Samuel, she recognized that her client was the king himself. She felt terrified to have been trapped by a sovereign who, at one time, had threatened all such spiritists with death.

That was then, Saul might have thought blackly. *This is now.*

From the earth emerged the ghostly figure of an old man in a long robe. Did Saul see the ghost? That is not clear. But he believed he was in the presence of the prophet and quickly prostrated himself before the summoned spirit.

> "I am in great distress," Saul said. "The
> Philistines are fighting against me, and
> God has departed from me. He no lon-

ger answers me, either by prophets or
by dreams. So I have called on you to
tell me what to do." (1 Samuel 28:15)

There is a heartbreaking poignancy in these words. Samuel—if in fact
it was he, brought up from the grave—would have winced. How long had
he endeavoured to turn Saul's heart to seek the Lord, in truth, humility, and
integrity? And here he was, using witchcraft rather than taking ownership of
the consequences of his years of wilful rebellion. There was no penitence in
Saul's tone, only desperation, a frantic grab for one last win.

We can imagine the bluntness of Samuel's response.

"It's too late," Samuel in effect told him. "What did you expect?"

Then, as the king inhaled to argue his case further, Samuel silenced him
with a grim pronouncement.

"Stop. You have lost the kingship. Tomorrow, you and your sons will be
with me. Dead."

Aghast, Saul fell to the ground, trembling with horror. It was over. He'd lost.

The next day, Israel was defeated by the Philistines at Gilboa, and Saul
and his sons were slain. In a final note of poetic irony, as Saul lay injured
on the battlefield, he asked his servant to deal the killing blow. The servant
refused. Grimly determined not to fall into enemy hands and endure slow,
agonizing torture, Saul did what he had always done: he took matters into
his own hands. Propping himself up, he fell upon his own sword, for even in
death he needed to be in control.

Perhaps, reading this tragic end to a twisted story, we feel a degree of
pity for the fallen monarch. Perhaps we think ourselves above him. We think
our manipulations are far less sinister. We might indulge, from time to time,
in a little gossip or harmless flirtation, perhaps embellishing a story or two at
the gym or pub, but we would never fall into occult practices.

The descent is easier than we might imagine.

Practicing manipulation fertilizes our own fears. Using others for our
personal advancement makes us edgy and nervous; we are constantly
on the alert, fearful that we ourselves might be likewise used. Over time,
we grow more and more wary. We trust no one, keep our affections in
check to avoid the risk of betrayal, and hold both people and God at

arm's length. The more control we think we have, the more we fear losing it. Eventually the more subtle forms of manipulation stop working, or at least we fear they will, and so we turn to cruder and more overt methodologies, such as threats, bribes, and outright lies. We become superstitious and obsessed with luck—a concept, incidentally, which did not exist in Hebrew culture.

For a while, we feel like we have the inside track, but it is never enough to abate our growing fear of losing control. More power is needed, the kind of power promised by supernatural forces.

BARLEY, BREADCRUMBS, AND BALAAM'S ASS

When Saul consulted the medium at Endor, it was the final madness in a man no longer able to surrender control. He could not cope with the heavens being brass; he was obsessed with finding some other option, some other means to both determine and secure his future. He had lost his anointing, his reputation, his son's love, and his position of power. What did he have left? His purse. Saul went to the medium because he could buy her services; it was the only leverage he still possessed.

We all want to know the future, so we can have a sense of control over the present. There was a fortune to be made in ancient Israel by those canny enough to discern what a person wanted to hear and offer to speak that word or blessing over them in exchange for a handful of barley and breadcrumbs.

Ezekiel 13 is a classic chapter describing the practices of false prophets. There is a reference to grain being used as a form of offering, alongside coinage or livestock, in exchange for a consultation (1 Samuel 9:78, 1 Kings 14:3). While true prophets at times received gifts, false prophets always charged a fee. Motive is crucial, differentiating between prophecy and witchcraft, because both practices may offer accurate predictions.

The medium at Endor may or may not have conjured the real Samuel—commentators disagree—but the prophetic words spoken by this apparition were true and came to pass.

A witch speaking a true prophetic word? This has disconcerting implications for those who believe, as I do, that the gifts of the Spirit, including prophecy, are still active today. Just how thin is the line between prophecy and divination, and how do we avoid crossing it?

First, let's look at the nature of true prophecy.

Prophecy is a message from God communicated by the Holy Spirit through a person (John 16:13, 2 Peter 1:20–21) or angelic being (Daniel 9:20–27). The message may also be communicated through visions (Ezekiel 1:1), dreams (Matthew 2:13), or some other spontaneous insight called by some a word of knowledge, as with Mary's cousin Elizabeth in Luke 1:41.

The message may be expressed in first person—*"The allies of Egypt will fall… declares the Sovereign Lord"* (Ezekiel 30:6)—or indirectly—*"[Agabus] stood up and through the Spirit predicted that a severe famine would spread over the entire Roman world…"* (Acts 11:28)—or even expressed through symbols: *"Now, son of man, take a block of clay, put it in front of you and draw the city of Jerusalem on it… This will be a sign to the people of Israel"* (Ezekiel 4:1, 3).

Prophecy in the Old Testament could be prognosticative (Daniel 9:24–27), often involved the giving of conditional warnings or promises regarding the future (Isaiah 66:12–24), and was intended to influence the behaviour of the receiver; in other words, it was directive or corrective.

Prophecy in the New Testament could also be prognosticative (Acts 11:28, 21:11), directive, and/or corrective, but most Pauline teaching seems to indicate that the prophetic gift, in the context of the new covenant, was to be employed primarily for the *"strengthening, encouraging and comfort"* (1 Corinthians 14:3) of the receiver.

In both the Old and New Testaments, prophetic words were to be tested. How? Accuracy was not the only test of a true prophet. The Old Testament taught that true prophetic words would come to pass and false words would fail (1 Samuel 3:19, 1 Kings 8:56, Jeremiah 28:9, Isaiah 41:21–24, 42:9, Ezekiel 33:33, Deuteronomy 18:22). However, Deuteronomy 13:1–5 also tells us that this was not the exclusive means of testing prophecy. It all boiled down to motive.

> If a prophet, or one who foretells by dreams, appears among you and announces to you a sign or wonder, and if the sign or wonder spoken of takes place, and the prophet says, "Let

us follow other gods" (gods you have not known) "and let us worship them," you must not listen to the words of that prophet or dreamer. The Lord your God is testing you to find out whether you love him with all your heart and with all your soul. It is the Lord your God you must follow, and him you must revere. Keep his commands and obey him; serve him and hold fast to him. That prophet or dreamer must be put to death for inciting rebellion against the Lord your God, who brought you out of Egypt and redeemed you from the land of slavery. That prophet or dreamer tried to turn you from the way the Lord your God commanded you to follow. You must purge the evil from among you. (Deuteronomy 13:1–5)

Even accurate, prognosticative prophetic words must take into account the reputation of the speaker, discernment of the community, and above all motive and trajectory of the prophetic word spoken.

The fulfillment of a prediction was never enough to attest to the true nature of the prophet or prophetic word. It was also expected that the words would not in any way contravene the revealed will of God.

The scriptures are our primary means of discerning God's will and ways. Deciding whether a specific prophetic word is in fact cogent with the whole of scripture (Acts 17:11, 2 Timothy 2:15) involves a community discernment process.

For example, the letters of 1 and 2 John, with their instructions to love, live righteously, obey, and test the spirits were corporate instructions written to a community. Prophecy was to be submitted to credible leaders and peers who were well-versed in scripture and wise in its application. This is still our best route for discernment.

Prophecy is also expected to be for *"the common good"* (1 Corinthians 12:7). If a prophetic word encourages isolation, promotes a critical spirit towards others, or creates barriers that divide the community of believers over something other than clearly salvific issues, it is to be suspect.

We see an example, again, in 1 and 2 John. These letters address a situation where members of the community had pulled away and were teaching false doctrine as itinerant prophets (2 John 10–11). The secessionists were labelled "antichrists." They had withdrawn, isolated themselves from the main body of believers, and actively attempted to teach and convert others. These actions are contrary to what the Word of God instructs (1 John 2:18–20, Matthew 7:21, Deuteronomy 13:1–5) and discount the credibility of anyone claiming prophetic insight.

Attitude is also important. The attitude of those who prophesy ought to be one of humility, love, mercy, patience, and joyful celebration—manifesting the fruit of the Spirit (Matthew 7:15–16, Galatians 5:22–23)—as opposed to a consistently negative, ominous, or critical attitude.

In 1 John 4:2 we read, *"This is how you can recognize the Spirit of God: Every spirit that acknowledges that Jesus Christ has come in the flesh is from God…"* This word acknowledges is a Greek translation of a Hebraism that means not just to agree, since demons can and do agree on who Christ is—and tremble (James 2:19); it means to celebrate, which demons cannot do.

For example, there was no praise or rejoicing in the Gerasene demoniac's acknowledgement of Christ as *"Jesus, Son of the Most High God"* (Mark 5:7). It was sheer torment.

A last test might be called the test of love. Since prophecy, as with all spiritual gifts, is not an impersonal force or power but a manifestation of a Person (1 Corinthians 12:7), the implication is that we do not own these gifts any more than we can own the love of God.

In recent years, it has been very popular to conduct book studies and take online assessments in order to find one's gift. But the gift does not belong to us; a better word might be the present participle "gifting." The moment we begin to think about a gift of the Spirit as being ours, we cross over into control, and love does not aspire to a position of power and influence; rather, it *"seeketh not her own"* (1 Corinthians 13:5, KJV).

It is not always easy to discern motives. Is the discomfort we feel about some prophetic word simply due to the person's unfortunate choice of vernacular? Or are they intentionally perverting a genuine prophetic gifting to turn it into an opportunistic, ego-gratifying tool?

We in the West often wonder why we see so little genuine prophetic gifting or healing. Perhaps it's because we have turned these spiritual gifts into a kind of parlour game, meant to impress and entertain, while for those in the rest of the world they are a genuine matter of life or death. Again, it could be a matter of our motives; like anyone, God does not wish to be used.

It may also be a case of faulty expectations as opposed to a lack of faith. Scripture seems to indicate that all spiritual gifts may manifest in and through all believers, at any time. If this were not so, we would not be encouraged to eagerly desire the gifts (1 Corinthians 12:31, 14:1), and especially that we might prophesy (1 Corinthians 14:1, 39).

But most of us have been led to believe that we only "get" one gift. This is ludicrous. Imagine a crowd of Christians gathered around a dying man at the scene of an accident; as he begs for healing, he is told, "Sorry. I only have the gift of tongues."

Along with faulty expectations, we often fail to discern the context. Like love, gifting manifests in response to specific needs. What is the need? How will the person be best loved by the giftings of the Spirit? Since the primary purpose of prophecy is the well-being not just of an individual recipient but of an entire community (1 Corinthians 12:7), we need to love in ways that fit each context. An older, conservative Mennonite congregation would not benefit from love being expressed through ecstatic tongues, for example. The clear injunction to the church of Corinth for orderliness in the use of the gifts (1 Corinthians 12:29–31) was an encouragement to *love well*.

We may also fail to consider those things which either nurture or impede the free flow of the Holy Spirit's love and giftings in and through us. Sin is an obvious impediment, as is pure selfishness or avoiding fellowship with God's people.

We would assume that only an intimate relationship with God will result in free-flowing gifting, yet Jesus acknowledged that the giftings could be operative in and through any who were open to them, regardless of their state. It hardly seems fair, we protest! Yet in Matthew 7:22–23, he says,

> Many will say to me on that day, "Lord,
> Lord, did we not prophesy in your name
> and in your name drive out demons
> and in your name perform many mir-
> acles?" Then I will tell them plainly, "I
> never knew you. Away from me, you
> evildoers!"

The final, penultimate test of prophecy is always that of relationship with Christ. The word used in this passage for "knew" is the Greek *ginőskō*, which means something far deeper than merely having information. It implies a kind of knowledge that comes through personal experience and firsthand acquaintance. It is a word of intimacy, used to also refer to sexual relations (Luke 1:34).

Many may operate in great spiritual power, making a positive impact on the Church and in the world, yet they may do so with empty hearts, devoid of passion for their Saviour. To counter this, Paul taught that while we should eagerly desire the spiritual gifts, especially prophecy, we must pursue love. What does that look like?

The word "desire" refers to an emotion—a jealous longing (Greek *zéloó*). "Pursue" refers to an action. The Greek word is *diókó*, translated in 1 Corinthians 14:1 as "pursue." But an even better translation would be "to persecute." Our pursuit of love is to be one of dogged, zealous, single-minded determination. The false prophet reverses the order, loving little while being devoted to the pursuit of the prophetic.

To be fair, prophecy offers a much bigger dopamine kick than love. Such people may be effective for a time, but they will not bear the most definitively important fruit of all: deep affection and love for Jesus and others. We would be wise to graciously decline their prayers, prophecies, and advice, regardless of their track record. As the passage in Matthew 7 tells us, exposure of false prophets, even those performing real miracles, is inevitable.

In both divination and the prophetic, there can be accurate spiritual insight. God can choose to give that insight to those he knows will abuse it, as we saw in Matthew 7 with those who cried out to the Lord. It may be, as in the Deuteronomy 13 passage dealing with false prophets, that God invests real gifting in false prophets so as to test us: *"The Lord your God is testing you to find out whether you love him with all your heart and with all your soul"* (Deuteronomy 13:3). In permitting an opportunity for deception, he also offers us an opportunity for growth, to be challenged and increase in faithfulness, wisdom, and righteous resolve.

The source of all true revelation is God alone; all power, even that which we or demonic beings choose to corrupt, comes from him. He alone is the creator of all things. It is not a case of divine power versus satanic power, which would be a form of dualism. It is a matter of divine power being satanically corrupted. Satan is a created being with no innate power of his own other than what was given him. He can only exercise his influence over us if we choose to enter his domain; in our pursuit of control, we cross the kingdom border and come under his oppressive rule.

This is what Saul did when he chose to resort to divination to secure his position rather than inquiring of the Lord. We have already seen that to use spiritual insight, even God-given gifts of prophecy, for personal gain moves us from the realm of the prophetic into something much darker, doomed to ultimately yield fruit which poisons the one seeking guidance as well as the guide. When we, like Saul, are desperate to glimpse future events to exert control over the present, we practice divination. This is true regardless of methodology; we can use our Bibles as if they were Ouija boards.

Divination and true, godly prophecy may both give an accurate portrayal of present realities and future events, but ultimately divination—prophecy which seeks to control for self-serving gain—will benefit neither the diviner nor the one who consults him.

Consider the slave girl in Acts 16:16–18. This fortune teller, possessed of a spirit, followed Paul and others, shouting, *"These men are servants of the Most High God, who are telling you the way to be saved"* (Acts 16:17). She was right.

In Mark 1:24, a demonized man likewise cries out, *"What do you want with us, Jesus of Nazareth? Have you come to destroy us? I know who you are—the Holy One of God!"* Again, right on both counts.

Neither of these people were prophets, yet their insights were accurate. Both had hearts bent on causing as much damage as they possibly could.

In Acts 8, we meet a magician named Simon Magus. Even after coming to faith in Jesus, being baptized, and joining with Peter and the disciples, he struggled to be free of the effect of decades of using spiritual insight for selfish purposes. Amazed at witnessing the impartation of the Holy Spirit through the laying on of hands, Simon offered money to the disciples to purchase this power for himself.

> When Simon saw that the Spirit was given at the laying on of the apostles' hands, he offered them money and said, "Give me also this ability so that everyone on whom I lay my hands may receive the Holy Spirit."
>
> Peter answered: "May your money perish with you, because you thought you could buy the gift of God with money! You have no part or share in this ministry, because your heart is not right before God. Repent of this wickedness and pray to the Lord in the hope that he may forgive you for having such a thought in your heart. For I see that you are full of bitterness and captive to sin."
>
> Then Simon answered, "Pray to the Lord for me so that nothing you have said may happen to me." (Acts 8:18–24)

Simon was *"full of bitterness"* and *"captive to sin."* Even as a baptized believer, he was still in some degree of bondage. There is no mention of demons or any suggestion that his conversion was a pretence; he was a real believer, in real trouble because of a lifelong career of manipulating others for profit.

What then? Ought we to covertly glance around our churches, looking to root out the false prophets in our midst and expel them? By no means. While we should be wise in discerning where the gifts of the Spirit are being abused, and both rebuke and restrain—even discipline—those involved, we are not to push them out of the Church.

In the parable of the wheat and the tares (Matthew 13), Christ sowed good seed while an enemy, Satan, sowed weeds. It was not until the seedlings sprouted that the weeds became apparent:

> The owner's servants came to him and said, "Sir, didn't you sow good seed in your field? Where then did the weeds come from?"
>
> "An enemy did this," he replied.
>
> The servants asked him, "Do you want us to go and pull them up?"
>
> "No," he answered, "because while you are pulling the weeds, you may uproot the wheat with them. Let both grow together until the harvest. At that time I will tell the harvesters: First collect the weeds and tie them in bundles to be burned; then gather the wheat and bring it into my barn." (Matthew 13:27–30)

This would have been rather unsettling for Jewish listeners, who were taught for generations that to remain pure required them to remain separate from so-called "bad seed." In this parable, a careful digging out of all the bad plants would have been impossible. Jesus was telling us that to try and yank out all the weeds would potentially unleash inconceivable harm on the wheat, pulling up good plants along with the bad. Both must be allowed to grow up together in the Church, and we must not assume that the one abusing power is therefore not saved.

As John Owen wrote,

> We may observe, in our way, that the Holy Ghost is present with many as unto powerful operations with whom he is not present as to gracious inhabita-

> tion; or many are made partakers of him
> in his spiritual gifts who are never made
> partakers of him in his saving graces.[43]

The problem of sorting weeds from wheat, saved from unsaved, true prophet from sorcerer, is one for God alone.

We must do more than merely watch out for a false prophet; we must do all we can to avoid becoming one ourselves. Like Peter, we must learn to recognize when we are practicing self-serving manipulation and confess it openly, and quickly. What is hidden cannot be healed. What we refuse to bring to the light will one day consume and destroy us.

Living transparently, open to accountability with our believing peers and leaders, is what provides the checks and balances needed for us to be effective in the giftings of the Holy Spirit, especially prophecy. And being effective means learning to express the gifts in ways that are helpful and loving.

Speaking in tongues without an interpretation is not helpful (except to the one speaking in private prayer). It isn't helpful to describe our imaginative mental images or vivid symbolic dreams in excruciating detail. Likely it is more a sign of our need to impress than our desire to edify. Excess emotion or drama are likewise not helpful. They often come from our own insecurity and get in the way of the Holy Spirit. We are there to communicate a word or administer a healing, not to bring conviction or to move someone to repent; that is God's job.

We need to stay in our own lane. Otherwise we will use these giftings as a means of control. That is how a genuine prophet of the Lord crosses over into divination.

That is what happened to Balaam.

THE WRONG SIDE OF THE MOUNTAIN

In Numbers 22, we are introduced to a Moabite king named Balak. Alarmed by the encroaching armies of Israel en route to their Promised Land, he formed an alliance with Midian to stop them. It was a tense time. Balak had

---

[43] John Owen, *The Works of John Owen, Volume VII*, Rev. William H. Goold, ed. (New York, NY: Robert Carter & Brothers, 1853), 26.

already heard of how the Amorites were defeated by this obscure people who had slipped their chains in Egypt. Moab had itself been conquered by the Amorites, and their defeat by Israel meant freedom for Balak and his people.

There was no sense of thankfulness, however. Balak assumed, wrongly, that Moab would be next. How had these vastly outnumbered Jewish troops won such outrageous victories? Could it have been magic? If so, he mused, the only way to destroy them was through that same means.

Balak sent messengers to a man named Balaam, a magician of great renown in those days, asking him to come to Moab to curse the people who threatened to overrun their lands.

We know little of Balaam, son of Beor, other than that he was a pagan prophet who lived in Pethor, likely near the Euphrates River in Aram Naharaim (Deuteronomy 23:4). Balaam described his home as being in the *"eastern mountains"* (Number 23:7) and historians speculate that this was several hundred miles north of Moab, not far from the Aram, where Abraham came from. The region would have been under the influence of Assyria and Chaldea at the time, both of whom embraced various magic practices, including divination, particularly through dreams. There was a venerated class of sorcerers with whom the gods were said to communicate; they were known as the Sabru and may have held a high social position, including priesthood.[44]

Chaldean magi were also called wise men, and we can safely assume that Balaam would have been considered not just a soothsayer but a sage.[45]

The political instability of northern Mesopotamia and the fact that Haran served as a crossroads for the slave trade meant that Balaam would likely have been exposed to multiple tribes, cultures, and nations. His propensity for gathering wisdom would have led him to want to become conversant with the religions of those he encountered and familiar with their gods.[46]

---

[44] Serafim, Bishop of Ostroh, *The Soothsayer Balaam: Or The Transformation Of A Sorcerer Into A Prophet, Numbers 22-25* (London, UK: Rivingtons, 1900), 90..

[45] Ibid., 96.

[46] Ibid., 100.

Over time, his broadminded tolerance for different views would increase, perhaps including even his doubts about the validity of one set of beliefs over another. Syncretism plus doubt plus the economic necessity of plying his trade to put bread on the table might have led to his choosing a career as a prophet for hire.

Within this syncretistic soup there also existed monotheists who worshipped God Most High, as evidenced by biblical figures like Abraham; Melchizedek, king of Salem (Genesis 14:18–20), Abimelech, king of Gerar (Genesis 20:3), and Laban, who apparently worshipped both the Lord and yet had household idols (Genesis 31:32–35, 50, 53). We can suppose that the god of the Hebrews would have been at least familiar to Balaam. He would also have known that the current threat being faced by the king who summoned him was, in fact, a result of the recent miraculous intervention of this god in delivering the descendants of Abraham, a former citizen of Haran, from slavery in Egypt. Word of the parting of the Red Sea, the plagues, and the appearance of manna and water in the desert would have spread this far, perhaps producing in this pagan seer an uneasy conviction that these monotheist Israelites were on to something. Perhaps there really was only one true God worth seeking, worth worshipping.[47]

Facing the advancing Israelite force, Barak sent a delegation of Moabite and Midianite elders from Kiriath Huzoth to Haran, about a two-week journey by foot. They were to ask for Balaam to come back with them to Moab.

> Now come and put a curse on these people, because they are too powerful for me. Perhaps then I will be able to defeat them and drive them out of the land. For I know that whoever you bless is blessed, and whoever you curse is cursed. (Numbers 22:7)

The elders took along a hefty diviner's fee with which to persuade Balaam, and it never crossed their minds that he might hesitate to accept it.

---

[47] Ibid., 106–113.

Balaam received the men but was reluctant to immediately receive the money he was offered.

> "Spend the night here," Balaam said to them, "and I will report back to you with the answer the Lord gives me." (Numbers 22:8)

It seems that Balaam was in fact consulting with the God of Israel. He used whatever methods of divination were normal for him, and the answer came in a dream, which was common among the Chaldean soothsayers with whom Balaam would have trained.

That God would deign to answer his inquiry is astounding.

In fact, Balaam heard from God with remarkable clarity. Was he a pagan priest at this point or a prophet of the one true God? It seems that he may have been straddling that fence. Nevertheless, God spoke to him. Why? Perhaps God was asking him to choose, and giving him a chance to walk in the right direction.

Balaam's life, like ours, was a journey. In any journey, the direction travelled matters more than the milestones reached. Like little Christian, pausing on the Hill of Difficulty in *The Pilgrim's Progress*, we are most in danger when, thinking ourselves safe, we stop moving.[48] Salvation is not merely positional; it is directional and dynamic. Balaam may not have been in the best of place with God yet, but that night he was at least facing the right direction, and he was moving forward.

Balaam invited the delegates to spend the night. He then presumably went to sleep to see what the Lord would say to him in a dream. Graciously, God came to Balaam with a question: *"Who are these men with you?"* (Numbers 22:9) Assuming this was an actual divine encounter, we know that God didn't need the information.

We might be reminded of other occasions when God asked a question he already knew the answer to. Moses, stopped in front of the Red Sea, was asked by God, *"Why are you crying out to me?"* (Exodus 14:15) Elijah,

---

[48] John Bunyan, *The Pilgrim's Progress* (London, UK: Hurst, Robinson, and Co., 1820), 44.

hunted by an evil king and hiding in a cave, was asked by God, *"What are you doing here, Elijah?"* (1 Kings 19:13). In the New Testament, Jesus asked a seemingly ridiculous question of a blind beggar named Bartimaeus, who had been crying out to him for attention: *"What do you want me to do for you?"* (Mark 10:51) And in Genesis 3:9, we read perhaps the most painful and poignant question of them all. While in the garden, looking for his companion, God asked Adam, *"Where are you?"*

In none of these instances did God actually need the information. Such questions are asked with some other motive. Why would God ask us anything? The answer can only be that his question is meant to provoke us to self-evaluation, to cause us to ponder, think, and perhaps learn something about ourselves.

Adam and Eve heard God's question as a plaintive cry, a lament of the Almighty at the loss of the close relationship he had enjoyed with his creatures. His question was not meant to make them feel guilty; it was intended to break their hearts. They would wonder, "Where *are* we that God should need to ask this? What have we done?"

Moses, at the Red Sea, had just finished telling the people not to fear the approaching Egyptian armies; God was going to fight for them. He had the staff in hand and had already received extensive instructions from God. God's question would have made him realize that he was hesitating to use the authority he had already been given, that perhaps his faith was not as great as it appeared, despite the assurances he had just given the people.

Elijah needed to understand that he was acting in fear and self-pity, and that God was telling him to gird up his loins for what lay ahead.

The blind beggar had been rebuked by the crowd for being disruptive, told to be quiet and not bother Jesus. He had been forced to shout even louder. Jesus seems to have meant to say, essentially, "I see you. I hear you. Never give up. Seek me with all your might. You have infinite worth, and I want everyone here to know that. I want you to believe that about yourself! Tell me, what do you want me to do for you?" This beggar received far more than sight that day; he received an epiphany.

And Balaam? The Lord prompted him to think more deeply. This was not just a job—to divine, curse, and get paid. Had his work as a seer become mundane? Had he stopped assessing the ethics of his actions? Had his ministry, like that of some pastors, simply become a job, another paycheck?

God asked Balaam, *"Who are these men with you?"* (Number 22:9)— and it was a loaded question. The delegates represented an unlikely union of two historical enemies, Moab and Midian (Genesis 36:35). They had been sent by a king, forming a powerful alliance in order to destroy the descendants of Abraham, the people who had been favoured by their God to a miraculous degree.

Note that the question was not merely "Who are these men?" but "Who are these men *with you*?" The question contained a rebuke: "What are you doing, Balaam? Why would you even entertain their request? Think about who they are. Think about who the Israelites are. Think about who I am!"

Balaam was then told by the Lord, *"Do not go with them. You must not put a curse on those people, because they are blessed"* (Numbers 22:12). As if Balaam needed a reminder that God's blessing clearly was upon Israel! Yet somehow he had grown dull and materialistic enough in his profession to stop asking himself the questions that really mattered.

It was an ominous foreshadowing here of things to come.

A RECKLESS PATH

The next morning, Balaam sent the officials on their way: *"Go back to your own country, for the Lord has refused to let me go with you"* (Numbers 22:13). We might wonder at the phraseology. Perhaps Balaam was disappointed. It's not that he wouldn't have wanted to comply with their request, but God was being difficult. The delegation, making the long trek back with bad news, might well have entertained the hopeful perspective that Balaam was simply bartering with them—and perhaps he was. It was customary to haggle over a purchase (Genesis 3:3–18, 2 Samuel 24:20–25). Maybe they just thought Balaam was playing hard to get.

King Balak's response was to send even more distinguished representatives and more cash. Again, Balaam's response was ambiguous. He refused them outright in righteous indignation but then suggestively mentioned money: *"Even if Balak gave me all the silver and gold in his palace, I could not do anything great or small to go beyond the command of the Lord my God"* (Numbers 22:18).

Then he invited them to spend another night while he inquired of the Lord one more time on their behalf, just in case.

This gets to the heart of the internal battle between those who genuinely want to honour God with their prophetic gift and the pull to turn instead to divination, which is prophecy for the sake of profit.

Balaam was seeking God on a matter to which God had already responded, and this time God instructed Balaam differently: *"Since these men have come to summon you, go with them, but do only what I tell you"* (Numbers 22:20). This confusing change is not indicative of God relenting or changing his mind. Rather, it is the have-it-your-way divine response to a hardening heart, similar to that which the Egyptian Pharoah of Exodus experienced as he repeatedly hardened his heart against Israel. Balaam had made a choice to disobey God, and God was going along with it.

The next day, when Balaam chose to accompany the men, God opposed him. This was not contrariness on his part but evidence that he had hoped Balaam would come to his senses and repent. This is the anger of grieved love, as a parent who acknowledges a child's right to choose but is sick with regret over the choice itself.

That the Lord cares about this spineless seer is seen in the next thing he does: he pulls out all the stops to make sure Balaam takes his warning seriously. Even a veteran magician would be taken aback by these outrageous events. There is an angel, an accident, and a talking donkey.

Three times the Angel of the Lord stood in Balaam's way, causing the seer's donkey to veer off the path, at one point crushing Balaam's foot against a wall. Three times Balaam punished the donkey and failed to recognize the theophany. Not until the donkey spoke did Balaam's eyes open to see the Angel. When Balaam fell on his face, the Angel spoke:

> I have come here to oppose you because your path is a reckless one before me. The donkey saw me and turned away from me these three times. If it had not turned away, I would certainly have killed you by now... (Numbers 22:32–33)

Seemingly abashed, Balaam prostrated himself before the Lord and said, *"I have sinned. I did not realize you were standing in the road to oppose me"* (Numbers 22:34). But was he truly repentant? No, not entirely. He was still waffling, wondering whether this was a both-and scenario in which he could honour God and yet turn a profit.

Knowing full well that he had been given a definitive "No!" as regards the cursing of Israel, Balaam still added, *"Now if you are displeased, I will go back"* (Numbers 22:4). If? There is no *if*. Clearly God was displeased, to the point of threatening to kill him. Was Balaam really that obtuse? Regardless, God shook his head and allowed him to go on, reminding the seer to only speak the words God himself gave.

Arriving at Balak's camp, Balaam was greeted by a grumpy king who asked him, essentially, "What took you so long?" And in the morning the king took Balaam up the mountain to observe the Israelites camped below, as though to say, "Look! Look at them all! This is a disaster. Curse them for us!"

Balaam instructed Balak to prepare an elaborate array of sacrificial offerings, a bull and a ram on each of seven consecutive altars.

Then Balaam went off to a barren height to listen, and God spoke to him clearly, saying that there was to be no cursing of a people he had blessed. Balaam was sent back down to disappoint his prospective client.

> How can I curse those whom God has
> not cursed? How can I denounce those
> whom the Lord has not denounced?
> From the rocky peaks I see them, from
> the heights I view them. I see a peo-
> ple who live apart and do not consider
> themselves one of the nations. Who can
> count the dust of Jacob or number even
> a fourth of Israel? Let me die the death
> of the righteous, and may my final end
> be like theirs! (Numbers 23:8–10)

Balak was not impressed and angrily rebuked the seer, in essence saying, "Clearly you are not seeing what I am seeing! Come with me to a different viewpoint. Then you will see more clearly what a threat these people represent to us all."

He took Balaam to a different height and prepared another seven altars. But Balaam's second revelation from God was no better than the first, and again Israel was blessed rather than cursed.

This time, Balaam began to understand that he was on a fool's errand. His skills would be useless against the Lord's anointed. He said, *"There is no divination against Jacob, no evil omens against Israel"* (Numbers 23:23).

This was not good for his business. If his curses were useless, there would be no reward.

Frustrated in the extreme, Balak dragged Balaam off to one more viewpoint, overlooking the wastelands. Surely this time, the prophet would see what he saw.

No such luck. Fourteen more animals were slaughtered in vain and only a blessing was given. We are told that *"the Spirit of God"* fell upon Balaam (Numbers 24:2), which in no way set him apart as a true, god-fearing prophet—no more than it had for Saul.

The grace shown to this stubborn seer is incomprehensible.

Joshua 24:10 implies that Balaam was pretty much pleading for God to allow him to curse Israel but God *"would not listen to Balaam."* Why would God still speak to him at all? It is hard for us to accept that the Spirit falls on those who will receive him, even the ones intent upon using his anointing for their own selfish purposes.

By now, Balak was done.

"I would have rewarded you richly," we imagine him saying. "Get out of here, you miserable excuse for a prophet, and go back where you came from!"

It may be that by now Balaam himself felt his heart sinking, as the chance at riches faded. Yet he prophesied one last time, and not just another blessing but one of spectacular, eternal import. His vision paralleled that of the apostle John, destined to prophesy two thousand years later: *"I am the Root and the Offspring of David, and the bright and Morning Star"* (Revelation 22:16).

In other words, Balaam saw Jesus.

The prophecy of Balaam son of Beor, the prophecy of one whose eye sees clearly, the prophecy of one who hears the words of God, who has knowledge from the Most High, who sees a vision from the Almighty, who falls prostrate, and whose eyes are opened: "I see him, but not now; I behold him, but not near. A star will come out of Jacob; a scepter will rise out of Israel. He will crush the foreheads of Moab, the skulls of all the people of Sheth. Edom will be conquered; Seir, his enemy, will be conquered, but Israel will grow strong. A ruler will come out of Jacob and destroy the survivors of the city." (Numbers 24:15–19)

We may find it shocking for God to allow a degenerate, soon-to-be traitorous prophet to receive such an exquisite vision. Again, we are reminded that both true, god-fearing prophets and false, merchant-minded opportunists may receive divine revelations.

We can imagine Balak and his leaders listening to this final prophecy, mouths agape. To their growing horror, Balaam went on to pronounce the doom of all who opposed this chosen people. His vision of the future was true, though his heart was far from faithful to what he saw.

Then the moment came for Balaam to make a decision. He knew sorcery would not work against the Israelites, and he had fulfilled to the letter his promises to God. He had completely blown his chances with Balak, who by now was apoplectic with rage.

Was there any other way to still turn a profit here? We know that Balaam *"loved the wages of wickedness"* (2 Peter 2:15), but just how far was he willing to go?

Revelation tells us what happened next. Unable to earn his fee in the usual way, Balaam pursued other means, and *"taught Balak to entice the*

Israelites to sin so that they ate food sacrificed to idols and committed sexual immorality" (Revelation 2:14).

Tragically, this worked. Numbers 31:16 tells us that the Midianite women collaborated by seducing the Hebrew men, and as a result a plague struck the people.

Balaam later chose to side with Israel's enemies while fierce battles were fought. In Numbers 31:8, we discover that he died on a battlefield alongside five Midianite kings—God's judgment falling upon a seer who had been given an opportunity to be a genuine prophet only to throw it all away for fame and fortune.

None of us who manifest prophetic giftings are above falling into divination, and none who practice divination are beyond God's reach. It is bewildering, humbling, and a sober warning for all who embrace the charismatic. Great anointing is not a guarantee of godliness, nor does apostasy always end outside his loving arms.

His sovereign grace is frightening and glorious.

As Christians, we abhor the occult, yet we toy with it all the time. There are no degrees of sin where the curious arts are concerned. The one who curses in anger is guilty of murder, Jesus said. The lustful glance is as bad as the act of adultery (Matthew 5:22, 27–28). Likewise, the innocuous eyeroll and covert wink are carefully timed to convey mockery, undermine credibility, and convince others of our superiority: this is rebellion, idolatry, and witchcraft.

Unless and until we take seriously the ways in which we are practicing manipulation, we will inevitably, incrementally, lose our ability to find a way back.

Like Balaam, we will become connivers, always looking for the loopholes in God's command. We will harden our hearts, a little at a time, until even an angelic visitation and speaking animal fail to move us.

Like Saul, we will jump at every crisis except the crisis of our own unfaithfulness, seek God in a panic when it is far too late, and be met with his silent grief. We will play with the powers of hell and call it prophecy. Seeping shadows will enter our minds and enshroud our hearts until we find ourselves taking up the trade of a satanic craft and sliding into insanity.

It can happen. It does happen. It is precisely what happened at Salem.

HIDDEN AGENDAS IN SALEM

Mankind has always been fascinated by the occult and the supernatural. Whispered rumours of dark and sinister rites hold us spellbound, literally. Christians may vehemently protest, but the Church, no less than the world, is drawn towards any manifestation of power. We may piously avert our eyes at the checkout stands of our local supermarket, turning our noses up at horoscopes and numerology. We compulsively mute and fast-forward through movie scenes dealing with satanic rituals or the demonic. We do our research and take a stance against the festivities of Halloween. The enemy will never lure us into his domain; we're on to his game, and we know his strategies.

Do we?

As crafty and cunning as our enemy is, do we honestly think his plan is to somehow seduce the Church through exposure to the coarse, grotesque, and horrific? Tabloid satanism is laughable, as much for its content as for its crass, sensationalistic presentation. Pictures of blood oozing out of glowing skulls are unlikely to tempt the average person into genuinely practicing occult practices. Do we honestly believe that Satan is so simplistic?

On the contrary, there is a frightening depth of sophistication in the enemy's strategies.

A few may in fact be snared by the exposé of cheap horror. But many more will be inclined to mock such caricatures and be lulled into a false sense of security, believing that real evil does not exist. Thousands more simply become desensitized through frequent exposure; what once might have been considered satanic will be permitted to continue unchallenged because it is paired with romance, humour, and a catchy soundtrack.

We roll our eyes at cheesy horror, thinking it two-dimensional and cheap, never suspecting that we are being led to think our enemy is a buffoon. He is not. There is a sinister hidden agenda whose aim is to slowly incite a kind of emotional cannibalism among us. Our enemy is indeed a prowling lion, looking to devour the unsuspecting soul (1 Peter 5:8), but his deeper purpose is to lead us to bite and devour one another (Galatians 5:15).

To lure a Christian into idolatry, witchcraft, and other satanic practices requires both subtle and deadly tactics. It also requires a brilliant decoy. While we are shaking our heads and snorting in derision at the gaudy distractions and fake blood, we entirely miss the enemy's real intent. Our very revulsion, recoiling at the bad acting, bad makeup, and high school scripts, herd us in the exact direction Satan wants us to go.

Seventeenth-century Salem presents a prime example of how the Church, in its fervour to abolish overt witchcraft, can fall into the practice of witchcraft in an almost unrecognizable form... and that form has flourished to the present day.

The popular view of the Salem witch trials comes from historical portrayals of rigid judges, influenced by religious bigotry, putting to death a few unfortunate and mildly deranged naturopaths. Alternately, one might espouse the view purported by the persecutors themselves: the community was in serious danger from practicing witches.

Both views are misleading.

There existed in Massachusetts at that time, as there exists now, sincere practitioners of genuine witchcraft who wielded very real power. But these were just the decoy. The enemy's hidden agenda was to encourage disproportionate fear and paranoia that led not simply to exposing the so-called witches but slandering, persecuting, and killing innocent women, destroying a community, and subsequently enslaving the populace to an even more insidious and despicable practice of witchcraft themselves.

Did it work? It did.

Cotton Mather was the grandson of New England's spiritual founders and rose to their esteemed reputation. He was educated at Harvard, received an honorary Doctor of Divinity from Glasgow University, and served as pastor of Boston's Second Church, becoming one of the most well-known Puritan ministers of the era. He published more than four hundred works touching on theology, history, politics, and science. In fact, his involvement in promoting ground-breaking inoculation against smallpox was renowned, despite the fact that it cost him the life of his son.

In short, the man had credentials that could not be ignored.

Prior to the Salem witch trials, Mather had published a study on what modern psychologists might refer to as the dynamics of mass hysteria. Two sisters who were afflicted with bouts of extreme, irrational, and disturbing behaviour had come to his attention as a minister. Mather studied and cared for these sisters, known as the Goodwin girls, even bringing the eldest girl, age thirteen, into his own home. In the end, he claimed to have cured them of their demonic possession through prayer and fasting.

Mather decided that the demonic affliction must have had a human agent involved. An Irish washerwoman, employed by the Goodwin family, was determined to have practiced witchcraft in such a way as to afflict the girls, and she was soon arrested, found guilty, and hanged.

Mather's subsequent publication in 1689, called *Memorable Providences Relating to Witchcraft and Possessions*, became the seventeenth-century equivalent of a viral social media post.[49] The seed of panic was planted and took root in New Englander minds; if these girls were possessed, every high-strung young lady was suspect. Suddenly, people's eyes narrowed in suspicion at their neighbours. Failed crops, sick children, convulsive fits, dead livestock, bad dreams, and miserable weather were all attributed to the devil and those who served him. There began a flurry of whispered gossip, and slanderous allegations.

The hunt was on.

AND SATAN LAUGHED

The satanic decoy worked perfectly. While genuine, intentional practitioners of satanic rituals no doubt existed, ironically almost all commoners in Massachusetts were now being drawn into practicing a more subtle form of witchcraft themselves—through the curious arts of gossip, slander, intimidation, and deception.

To be fair, Salem was a mess long before the infamous witch trials began. Rapidly expanding trade commerce had left farmers resentful, with disputes over land usage, taxes, and religious hierarchy. Many felt that the social order, which depended upon everyone accepting their station in life, was in grave danger. Brother was pitted against brother and a solution was urgently needed to bring unity again. As in Nazi Germany, the solution was that all must agree upon a common enemy.

Cotton Mather became a means by which a common enemy was identified. There is debate as to his motives. Was he devious, using religion as a

---

[49] Cotton Mather, *Memorable Providences Relating to Witchcrafts and Possessions* (Ann Arbor, MI: ProQuest, 2010). Paperback reproduction.

123

means of political manoeuvring? Or was he genuinely convinced that Satan was at work in his town?

Anthropologists Pamela Stewart and Andrew Strathern, who write of gossip as a covert form of witchcraft, point out the irony of Mather's frequent use of the scripture *"rebellion is as the sin of witchcraft"* (1 Samuel 15:23, KJV). Whether intentionally or not, this verse allowed him to broaden the scope of his accusations and condemn the merchants who threatened Salem's social order as being rebellious practitioners of the dark arts.[50]

The legally and morally approved pastime of witch-hunting caught on fast. It became a convenient means of dealing with fractious neighbours, rebellious children, lazy servants, and boring wives.

On May 27, 1692, the first case was brought before a special court convened to try witches. Bridget Bishop, broadly disliked by the community for her habits of self-assertion and promiscuity, stood accused of witchcraft. The accusation came from her second husband, who claimed that she was a bad wife and sat up nights with the devil. The court nodded sagely; Bridget was known to be a "pugnacious woman who quarreled bitterly with her mate."[51]

Obviously, it had to be demonic.

During Bridget's examination before the magistrates, girls in the courtroom shrieked as if being tortured. Others cried out accusations of Bridget murdering their children, seducing their men, and even bewitching their pigs. She denied all charges.

Bridget was found guilty and two weeks later became the first person hanged on what was later called Gallows Hill.

More would follow.

Fingers were soon pointing everywhere, at anyone. If no tangible evidence could be produced, accusations of supernatural visitation were flung at those suspected of being in league with Satan.

In a moment of stricken conscience, perhaps, Mather wrote a letter to the courts asking that such "spectral evidence" not be allowed. He was

---

[50] Pamela J. Stewart and Andrew Strathern, *Witchcraft, Sorcery, Rumors, and Gossip: Departure in Anthropology* (Cambridge, MA: Cambridge University Press, 2004), 165–166.

[51] Daniel Allen Hearn, *Legal Execution in New England: A Comprehensive Reference, 1623–1960* (Jefferson, NC: McFarland Publishing 2008), 65.

referring to a witness testifying that the accused person's spirit had presented itself to the witness in a dream or vision. Spectral evidence had so far
been deemed acceptable at the Salem trials, based on the widespread belief
that Satan was powerful enough to send these spirits to the pure in order to
lead them into sin. Mather's theology could not, apparently, embrace such a
weak and ineffective view of a sovereign God.

However, he too seems to have been swept along by the heinous trend.
In the thick of the Salem trials in 1693, Mather released *Wonders of the
Invisible World*, exposing what he saw as Satan's plot to overthrow New
England's churches.[52]

In this book, Mather wrote that he had set himself "to countermine the
whole PLOT of the Devil, against *New-England*, in every BRANCH of it"[53] and
demanded a spiritual reformation in which citizens would "do their utmost
in first *Reproving*; and, if it must be so, then *Exposing*, and so *Punishing* as
the Law directs,"[54] (79), for, he claimed, "The Devils having broke in upon our
World, there is great asking, *Who is it that has brought them in?*"[55]

Wonders of the Invisible World became, in effect, the weighty and offi-
cial defence of the New England court's persecution, arrest, torture, and
execution of those accused of witchcraft, no matter how circumstantial
or biased the evidence. In the book, Mather also included titillating details
of court proceedings, replete with supernatural curses causing boils and
burns in distant spectators and writhing physical contortions in the afflicted,
descriptions that would be read by some as having a forbidden and enticing
erotic subtext. Think of some sparkly vampire TV series, a dime-a-dozen
slasher flick, or a horror movie with swooning, voluptuous women in shred-
ded attire and the virile male monsters who desire them.

While Cotton Mather alone can hardly be held responsible for trigger-
ing the wave of mass hysteria and hatred so horrifically exemplified by the
Salem witch trials, it was respectable voices like his crying "Game on!" that
led ordinary people to practice witchcraft in order to catch and kill those they

---

52 Cotton Mather, *Wonders of the Invisible World* (Charleston, SC: Bibliolife, 2009). Reprint.

53 Ibid., 16.

54 Ibid., 79.

55 Ibid., 93.

feared. Fear amplifies our craving for control, remember, and the pursuit of control requires that we control and manipulate others.

While the practice of the occult may have been curtailed, the essence of witchcraft—manipulation and control—spread like a plague, fuelled by fear. The people of Salem were *using* witchcraft to *fight* witchcraft.

And Satan laughed.

NEOPAGANISM AND THE SEDUCTION OF RATIONAL EVIL

We have looked at the kind of tabloid satanism that existed in Salem, and that still exists today. We have seen how the enemy's strategy caused people to be so overcome with fear and hate that they exercised fanatical control over and condemnation of others.

What of the mature, rational, well-educated mind that refuses to be impressed by cheap sensationalism? For such a person, the trap must be baited with something that appeals to their intellectualism and social sensitivities. That "something" finds its expression in a contemporary form of witchcraft known as Neopaganism.

Neopaganism is a form of witchcraft practiced by middle class dilettantes. It incorporates many classical occult practices but turns its nose up at cruder examples such as ritual abuse or blood sacrifice.

One of the first notable works on neopaganism was published by Tanya Luhrmann in 1989, an anthropological study of a magical community in London into which she integrated herself in the 1950s. Her question was how normal, middle class people could come to believe in magic.

In her book, *Persuasions of the Witch's Craft*, Luhrmann describes seeing a process of "interpretive drift"—the slow, imperceptible shift in the way a person interprets reality as they become more involved with a particular activity.[56]

What once would have been shrugged off as superstitious nonsense, or else condemned as heresy and sin, could appear to become quite rational and socially acceptable.

Luhrmann writes,

---

[56] Tanya Luhrmann, *Persuasions of the Witch's Craft* (Oxford, UK: Blackwell, 1989), 312.

> Magicians are ordinary, well-educated, usually middle-class people. They are not psychotically deluded, and they are not driven to practice by socioeconomic desperation. By some process, when they get involved with magic—whatever the reasons that sparked their interest—they learn to find it eminently sensible. They learn to accept its core concept: that mind affects matter, and that in special circumstances, like ritual, the trained imagination can alter the physical world.[57]

This is what neopagans believe. It is also what many in today's first world believe. Educated Westerners believe that the mind has power to alter the physical world, whether it is to lose weight, win friends, revive a wilting plant, or break an addiction. They laugh, however, at the outdated notion that this is accomplished by the empowerment of demonic forces.

Having faith in the power of one's own mind is a slippery slope. It is a smaller step than it looks from charming one's boss to get a promotion to bending a spoon, cursing an ex-wife, or launching into astral travel.

Luhrmann only examined the beginning of neopagan and Wiccan groups in North America. It was a relatively small but rapidly growing movement whose popularity is today based on its apparent rationality. Neopagans emphasize the normality and ordinariness of their beliefs and practices. The low-key sanity of neopaganism is seductive, but then all evil is.

Luhrmann writes of small groups called covens that would meet from time to time, with occasional conferences and special interest seminars. The process of acceptance moved at a slow pace, so members felt comfortable in establishing mutual trust.

For the well-educated and socially conscious, intellectualism is admired. It is an effective lure. They feel flattered by the attention and are likely to

---

[57] Ibid., 7.

crave more as time goes on, participating in certain activities that might have at first been uncomfortable. Attention is addictive. Once certain acts have been committed, particularly during the rites of initiation, a bond of intimacy is established between members and novitiates.

INTIMATE BONDS OF SHAME

There are many appealing aspects to neopaganism. Some people are attracted to its environmental concern. Many of those interviewed said that neopaganism is a response to a planet in crisis. Indeed, almost all pagan traditions emphasize reverence for nature. Neopagans claim to practice a neutral form of magic—that is, neither black nor white—which is in tune with nature, much in the same way as some Indigenous groups communicate with, and receive guidance from, various spirits of animals and the elements. Women may be drawn to the neopagan high view of their sex, as some neopagans invoke a Mother Goddess figure, the recipient and nurturer of seed. Many ancient cultures followed this motif, worshipping Artemis, Astarte, Melusine, Aphrodite, Diana, Brigit, etc. Many Wiccans worship a Mother Goddess in her three aspects of Maiden, Mother, and Crone.

Others are drawn to neopaganism because of its prime concern with the arts: beauty, vision, imagination, and the pursuit of artistic and intellectual self-expression and personal growth.

Still others are attracted by the promise of power, such as the power to banish forever their feelings of inadequacy and insecurity.

For some, the attraction is freedom and escape from what is seen as the stifling rigidity of monotheism.

In her book *Drawing Down the Moon*, journalist and self-proclaimed Wiccan Margaret Adler writes of the intoxicating experience of listening to an initiation tape of neopagan ritual:

> A feeling of power and emotion came
> over me. After all, how different was this
> from the magic rituals of my childhood?
> The contents of the tape had simply

given me *permission* to accept a part
of my own psyche that I had denied for
years—and then, extend it.[58]

Then there is the appeal of animism, the cohesive vitality and life force of all things; pantheism, where divinity is inseparable from nature; or polytheism, with its tolerance for multiple and diverse gods and religious practices.

Neopagan sexuality also has great appeal, with its lure of the prohibited. Introduced gradually, and in the right ambience, sexuality in worship can feel undeniably right. Initiation rituals can be performed naked, in groups, where the nakedness builds an intimate bond of secrecy (or shame), which in turn exerts enormous pressure to continue.

Further initiation takes place over the course of several years. Through it, one becomes the equivalent of a god or goddess, the ultimate in power and control. In neopaganism, Eve and Adam have no regrets. Eating the forbidden fruit, having their eyes opened, being like God, is worth the loss of one's soul.

NO NEUTRAL MAGIC

What, one might ask, is wrong with exercising a concern for women's rights, holistic self-care, sex, religious tolerance, or environmentalism? Nothing, so far as they go. Good things, however, can easily become idols that enslave us.

Tim Keller, in *Counterfeit Gods*, writes that

> internal idol worship, within the heart, is universal… the human heart takes good things like a successful career, love, material possessions, even family, and turns them into ultimate things. Our hearts deify them as the center of our lives, because, we think, they can give

---

[58] Margaret Adler, *Drawing Down the Moon: Witches, Druids, Goddess-Worshippers, and Other Pagans in America Today* (New York, NY: Penguin Books, 2006), 20.

us significance and security, safety and
fulfillment, if we attain them.[59]

When a good thing becomes an idol, no good comes of it. No master other than the God of Judeo-Christian faith promises freedom. All other gods, all other idols, all other masters enslave us. Neopaganism, with its suave, persuasive arguments of ancient wisdom, is simply another taskmaster.

There is no neutral magic. Neopagans may boast of harmonic resonance with the cosmos, but the freedom they claim to experience—a freedom from external restraints of narrow-minded religiosity—is a progressive enslavement to self: narcissistic self-expression, promiscuity, and pride. Whether it is to bow before the ancient gods or claim to become a god, the neopagan exchanges true freedom for the ever-tightening bonds of self-worship.

The mind, focused on its desires, does not alter any reality except the reality of its own state of being. To focus with all our heart, mind, soul, and strength on the true God brings us freedom, joy, and eternal life. To focus on altering our reality, internal or external, in order to fulfill our own desires is idolatry. It brings bondage, fear, and death.

Neopagans, and others like them, focus their minds and wills on altering matter, events, people, and themselves. We all, in different ways, similarly devote our energies to altering reality to conform to our desires. Self-help manuals, the power of positive thinking, the false theology of the prosperity doctrine, and the latest phone apps… they all promise us control. In devoting ourselves to the pursuit of power, we are, without realizing it, bowing before ancient idols.

---

[59] Tim Keller, *Counterfeit Gods: When the Empty Promises of Love, Money, and Power Let You Down* (London, UK: Hodder and Stoughton, 2010), xiv.

FIVE
UNMASKING ANCIENT IDOLS

EMILE CAMMAERTS, IN his book *The Laughing Prophet: The Seven Virtues and G.K. Chesterton*, quotes G.K. Chesterton's famous fictional character, Father Brown, in which the priest detective asserts that "the first effect of not believing in God [is] that you lose your common sense. It's drowning all your old rationalism and skepticism, it's coming in like a sea; and the name of it is superstition."[60] Cammaerts then summarizes this pithily, saying that the "effect of not believing in God is to believe in *anything*."[61]

So it is that when we turn from the one true God, we face a confusing and bewitching display of glittering idolatrous options, all vying for our attention, all equally empty of real power. Like starry-eyes shoppers at a discount sale, we are eager to grab onto whatever promises to satisfy our craving.

Which idol offers the best means for attaining power and control? In Salem, the road to power lay in either a practice of the occult, or in the brutal extermination of those suspected of practicing it. For neopagans, the path to power runs through communion with the spirits of nature and in ancient pagan rituals. For the twenty-first-century millennial, power and control lie in defiantly self-expressive individualism, as seen with the current debate over gender fluidity. For the diehard modern hedonist, it is about freedom—unrestrained indulgence in sex, food, and fun (with the high and lofty ideal of securing enough disposable income to play hard until we die).

Which ancient idols are represented here? All of them.

---

[60] Emile Cammaerts, "The Laughing Prophet: The Seven Virtues and G.K. Chesterton," *Chesteron. org*. Date of access: January 9, 2025 (https://www.chesterton.org/wp-content/uploads/2020/04/The-Laughing-Prophet_ACS-Books.pdf), 230. Emphasis mine.

[61] Ibid.

Christians today might recoil at the suggestion that they've sold out to the worship of Baal, Nebo, Mammon, Astarte, and the like. Yet that is precisely what we are doing. There are no new idols, only new clothes worn by ancient ones. They promise, as they promised our ancestors before us, power and control through money, sex, knowledge, beauty, fame, and positions of influence, and they demand that we practice deception, seduction, and intimidation—the curious arts of manipulation—in their service.

MAMMON AND THE GODS OF EGYPT

Money and material goods offer the most tangible form of earthly power. Wealth offers us more control over our circumstances, including our own bodies. Rich people can afford to eat better, live longer, look prettier, and be admired for being more successful. Success is often measured with a dollar sign, and in a world where scruples count for little and consciences are numb we pursue success by any means available, ruthlessly dealing with those who get in the way, or using people to get ahead, only to discard them afterward.

Christians are more likely to rationalize their pursuit of money, even going so far as to create a theology that allows guilt-free pursuit of wealth: if a shady business venture yields profits, it clearly must have God's blessing on it. A winning lottery ticket is his reward for our faithfulness. The echoes of the prosperity doctrine heresy have crept into many churches, equating wealth and worldly success with righteousness. Those with no worldly success to speak of, or in financial or physical distress, must be in sin.

Martyrs would cringe at this pat, reductionist formula. While money, possessions, and health may indeed come from God, they are not the primary litmus test by which we are to judge whether we are in favour with the Almighty. Satan is also quite capable of making sure we win the lottery.

When we follow the maxim of "whatever works must be right," we fall into the worship of the ancient gods of Egypt. How often did the Israelites cry out in the desert to return to Egypt, complaining that if God had really wanted them to leave and cross the desert he would have made it easier, safer, and far more comfortable? The exodus was not "working" as far as they were concerned; they were hungry and thirsty all the time, and in Egypt they had never gone hungry or thirsty. And look at those Egyptians! They had unlimited leeks, onions, and melons—everything they could possibly want. Egypt must be doing something right. "Let's go back!"

How many times do we wonder at the apparent injustice of seeing the wicked prosper while we do not? Scripture is full of those who wrestle with this question.

> There is something else meaningless that occurs on earth: the righteous who get what the wicked deserve, and the wicked who get what the righteous deserve. (Ecclesiastes 8:13)
>
> You are always righteous, Lord, when I bring a case before you. Yet I would speak with you about your justice: Why does the way of the wicked prosper? Why do all the faithless live at ease? (Jeremiah 12:1)

And the psalmist cried out, *"How long, Lord, will the wicked, how long will the wicked be jubilant?"* (Psalm 94:3)

The prophet Habakkuk foresaw the rise of Babylon and argued vehemently with God over this. He railed, *"Why are you silent while the wicked swallow up those more righteous than themselves?"* (Habakkuk 1:13)

Then there was Gideon, hiding from the Midianites, when the angel of the Lord appeared to assure him, *"The Lord is with you, mighty warrior"* (Judges 6:12). It is not a stretch of the imagination to hear the exasperation in Gideon's voice when he replied, *"Pardon me, my lord... but if the Lord is with us, why has all this happened to us?"* (Judges 6:13)

Success does not always equate with God's favour. He often allowed wicked nations to prosper so as to bring judgment upon other, equally wicked nations, or to discipline his chosen people, to their shame. In the moment, it can feel unjust. It can also feel like a waste of time to pursue righteousness if there is no immediate profit to be enjoyed. It can be very tempting to give up and imitate the worldly ways of those whose lives seem so much more secure, comfortable, and glamorous. If we are honest with ourselves, we all face moments when it would be tempting to, metaphorically speaking, go back to Egypt.

But if we look closely at the way in which the Egyptians worshipped their gods of success, we glimpse a parody of the miserable rat race of their idolatry.

In Egypt, there were lesser and greater gods, all of whom needed to be appeased. It consumed the people's lives. The Egyptian cult of the greater god followed one general pattern, though: they treated him like an unpredictable human who needed constant coddling, like a child. This god needed to be reminded of his duties, as well as to be awakened from sleep each morning with song while his image was washed and dressed for the day. An extensive sacrificial system required that he be given regular meals—morning, midday, and evening—before retiring for the night. To fail to provide in any way for his comfort was to court disaster.

This god might forget about you completely. You could not for a second relax in your duties. It was expedient to neglect your other duties, your own health, and even the well-being of your own family in order to meet the needs of this capricious god. The people's health and prosperity depended upon being at his beck and call, 24/7.

Sound familiar? When we substitute this Egyptian idol for the idol of our own careers, the picture becomes clear. Devotion to the pursuit of money and success takes us back to Egypt, in shackles. When money is pursued for the sake of power and control, it becomes a god—the idol of Mammon.

The term *Mammon* was used by Jesus when teaching about the greedy pursuit of wealth. Although some commentators suggest that it references a Syrian god of riches, there is little evidence that this is so. Regardless, Jesus seemed to have used the title as a personification of the idol of money.[62] He said, *"No one can serve two masters. Either you will hate the one and love the other, or you will be devoted to the one and despise the other. You cannot serve both God and money [Mammon]"* (Luke 16:13).

Paul, in 1 Timothy 6:10, called the love of money the *"root of all kinds of evil."* Wealth in and of itself is not evil. How can we tell if we have crossed the line into the idolatry of money? One way is to watch how we

---

[62] "Matthew 6," *Bible Hub*. Date of access: April 9, 2021 (https://biblehub.com/commentaries/barnes/matthew/6.htm).

react when we think that our money is being wasted. Judas condemned what he perceived as the extravagant waste of expensive perfume, poured over the feet of Christ by Mary in John 12:3. When he exclaimed that it should have been better sold, and the money given to the poor, he was not moved by a passion for social justice but by his own obsession with wealth. He had already been stealing from the disciples' common coffers, and it rankled him to see this potential profit drip between someone's toes to be lost in the dust.

Judas's love of money ate away at his integrity, and in the end it led him to betray his Lord for a few silver coins. His idolatry may have started out as casual thriftiness, perhaps a need to control the purse strings, but it ultimately controlled him.

This is the fate of all who worship the idol of Mammon.

Consider Eugene Peterson's interpretation of some lines from James 5:

> Your money is corrupt and your fine clothes stink. Your greedy luxuries are a cancer in your gut, destroying your life from within. You thought you were piling up wealth. What you've piled up is judgment.
>
> All the workers you've exploited and cheated cry out for judgment. The groans of the workers you used and abused are a roar in the ears of the Master Avenger. (James 5:2–4, MSG)

What is the purpose of money? Why would God enrich us? He gives us money because, in his divine extravagance, he wishes to impart to us some of his own extravagant nature. Even knowing we will never eradicate poverty, through giving we tear this idol of Mammon down in our midst. Jesus said, in Matthew 26:11, *"The poor you will always have with you..."* This was not said to discourage giving but to *commend* it. Jesus was quoting from a well-known passage in the Torah:

> If anyone is poor among your fellow Israelites in any of the towns of the land the Lord your God is giving you, do not be hardhearted or tightfisted toward them. Rather, be openhanded and freely lend them whatever they need... There will always be poor people in the land. Therefore I command you to be openhanded toward your fellow Israelites who are poor and needy in your land. (Deuteronomy 15:7–8, 11)

Mary's extravagant gift, done in worship, was far from a waste. It was a model for all generous giving. Where poverty is endemic in this sinful world, for any of us who can help, it should be our duty and delight to aid the poor as an act of worship and compassion.

Instead we categorize them, deeming those who might be a drain on society—because of addictions and immoral lifestyles—to be a poor investment. We focus less on meeting needs and more on wise portfolio planning and wealth management. Christians do this as much as the world, ostensibly under the label of good stewardship, conveniently forgetting that all stewardship is meant to be for the sake of others, not our own self-interest.

In the face of global pandemics and looming recessions, we would do well to remind ourselves that, in God's eyes, the Church, not the government, ultimately bears the responsibility to care for the poor.

In Acts 4:33–35, we read of a context in which there was great need, and we may face that in our own lifetimes:

> And God's grace was so powerfully at work in them all that there were no needy persons among them. For from time to time those who owned land or houses sold them, brought the money from the sales and put it at the apostles'

feet, and it was distributed to anyone
who had need.

Sell our house? Give away our retirement fund? Although it may sound
like a Marxist ideology, it is in fact a strategy for a time when survival may
depend upon such radical generosity. It must come, we are told, from God's
grace, *"powerfully at work in [us] all."* We are called to give, not because it
will eradicate poverty but because it is a reflection of the Father's heart.

His is a heart of sacrificial love. Can we not also give sacrificially to
those in need, even if it means we are forced to eat a few more boring meals
of manna? If we refuse, Egypt will be happy to welcome us back, and we will
retreat to our all-inclusive prison resorts with cold and selfish hearts, forever
in bondage to the idol of Mammon.

These are aspects of Mammon worship which apply broadly to the individual. What of the corporate? The Church as an institution would never
openly advocate money for money's sake. Wealth, we would argue, is only
a means to the altruistic end of global evangelism, effective discipleship
programs, and comprehensive pastoral care.

That's true, so far as it goes.

But none of us are immune to the pull of personal ambition and pride.
Who does not want to be part of a church that is seen as successful, thriv-
ing, and alive? Money is needed, we argue, to create programs that will
attract the lost. In the name of relevancy, we take cultural contextualization
of the gospel one step further and the lines begin to blur. Instead of being
about the mission, we are about messaging. We obsess over contemporary
branding of the gospel. We become propagandists.

GOEBBELS, GOOGLE, AND OTHER PROPAGANDISTS

Marketing has been around forever, but it has not always been recognized as
a legitimate professional field. In the West, marketing came into its own with
the advent of psychology, promoted by entrepreneurial thinkers like Edward
L. Bernays, nephew to the father of psychoanalysis, Sigmund Freud.

Born in Vienna in 1891, Bernays grew up in New York, where he applied
the principles gleaned from his uncle's lectures to public relations and
advertising. In his 1928 book *Propaganda,* Bernays theorized that by under-

standing the group mind one could manipulate people's behaviour without their even being aware of it:

> The conscious and intelligent manipula-
> tion of the organized habits and opinions
> of the masses is an important element in
> democratic society. Those who manip-
> ulate this unseen mechanism of society
> constitute an invisible government which
> is the true ruling power of our country.
> We are governed, our minds are molded,
> our tastes formed, and our ideas sug-
> gested, largely by men we have never
> heard of… It is they who pull the wires
> that control the public mind.[63]

His hypothesis was tested when he was hired by the president of the American Tobacco Company to launch a public relations campaign to increase the sales of cigarettes. Specifically, Bernays targeted women.

They didn't stand a chance.

He consulted with New York's leading psychoanalyst of the day, Dr. A.A. Brill, who told him that women saw cigarettes as being symbolic of male power and sexual promiscuity; both were considered taboo. With one brilliant stroke, Bernays capitalized on the lure of the forbidden and began to promote the cigarette brand Lucky Strikes as "torches of freedom."

The launch of this campaign took place during an Easter parade in 1929, where a number of debutantes were convinced to smoke openly in the public square of Fifth Avenue, flaunting freedom and proclaiming their emancipation from the constriction of outdated male mores in a first wave of the women's liberation movement.

Coco Chanel, who had already been stretching her feminist wings with clothing designs that tossed the corset and mixed traditionally male and female fashions, became an iconic, trousered, suntanned model for

---

[63] Edward Bernays, *Propaganda* (New York, NY: IG Publishing, 2005), 37. Reprint.

the modern woman, brandishing a smouldering cigarette in her elegantly extended hand.

Bernays's campaign was a huge hit. Smoking was sexy.

The Third Reich sat up and took note. During the 1920s, Joseph Goebbels took an interest in the successful marketing campaigns of Bernays and added these techniques to his arsenal of persuasive weaponry as Minister of Propaganda for Adolph Hitler.

In 1933, Bernays learned that his insights were being applied to garner public support in Germany for the genocide of the Jewish people. He was appalled, but not surprised.

After World War II, propaganda was not a word that evoked anything but hostility and mistrust; consequently, it became known as public relations, and Bernays was the undisputed expert in this field. His impressive list of clients included not just the American Tobacco Company, but General Electric, Proctor & Gamble, Calvin Coolidge, and CBS.

By the time of his death in 1995, aged one hundred, he had helped create the American consumer and sales culture. Job security after World War II was anchored in the mass manufacturing of desirable, well-marketed goods, creating a situation in which production soon exceeded actual demand. The answer? More PR.

Inevitably, society changed from a needs-based to a wants-based economy. Consumerism birthed a vast array of new careers. With the advent of the world wide web, there was explosive growth in the field of marketing through media. Bernays just missed his greatest opportunity by a few years.

What began as a shoestring project in the dorm rooms of two graduate students at Stanford University in the late 1990s—using cheap, used, and borrowed personal computers bought on maxed-out credit cards to construct a novel server network—became the global phenomenon known as Google. This ubiquitous search engine forms the backbone of the modern internet, with an estimated 3.8 million queries being typed into Google per minute.

Google steadfastly insists that it does not use its many products in opportunistic or manipulative ways but relies solely upon objective and autonomous algorithms and data usage information, employed without any human bias or economic or political consideration.

Many remain unconvinced. Information is, after all, a fast track to power, and Google has amassed information about its users at a colossal pace. Every search is tracked, recorded, and can be analyzed for patterns. Pop-up ads mirror with uncanny and chilling accuracy personal preferences, whether in shopping, entertainment, or sexual proclivities. Users of the internet's myriad free products and services go from being customers to being a commodity. Our browsing information and social media activity are used by giant corporations to generate billions of dollars in targeted sales. When a high-tech monopoly marries a consumeristic society, the potential for global dominance is staggering, shaping how we search, organize, value, and perceive information in every arena of life.

As one might imagine, conspiracy theories abound, including the accusation from right-wing Republicans that the left-wing ideologies they perceive in Google were used to manipulate voters in recent elections, a debate which refuses to die. Those who are convinced that they are the victims of online economic surveillance take actions ranging from boycotting all social media to constructing their own personal Faraday cages. Parents who believe that tech corporations take advantage of the addictive tendencies in their children are desperate to block or at least monitor their children's time online.

In her book *Caught in the Net*, psychologist Kimberly Young shares the results of her three-year study of internet abuse, telling stories of those whose lives have been destroyed by addiction to online activities. Young is the founder of the Center for Internet Addiction and an advocate of a therapy that promotes a kind of digital detox. Young is determined that "internet dependence be recognized as a legitimate impulse-control disorder worthy of its own classification in future revisions of the American Psychiatric Association's *Diagnostic and Statistical Manual of Mental Disorders*."[64]

If Google's primary intent was to incite anxiety and fearmongering, it would be the indisputable champion, hands-down. In fact, we might even argue that the fear of technology is doing more to manipulate and control our behaviour than technology itself. Jesus's admonition to be *"as shrewd as snakes and as innocent as doves"* (Matthew 10:16) seems particularly appropriate in this regard.

---

[64] Kimberly Young, *Caught in the Net: How to Recognize the Signs of Internet Addition—and a Winning Strategy for Recovery* (New York, NY: John Wiley & Sons, 1998), 235.

In the end, social media is just that—media, with the same concerns raised that were once raised over books, radio, and television. The internet is equally a gateway to addiction and credible research. The internet has revolutionized education, creating heretofore unimagined access to information in parts of the world where education has been censored and available only to the elite.

In 2002, UNESCO (United Nations Educational, Scientific, and Cultural Organization) began an initiative known as the International Day for Universal Access to Information (IDUAI), celebrated annually around the world on September 28. Their goal is that all countries should ensure public access to information and protect fundamental freedoms, in accordance with national legislation and international agreements.

During the international Open Talks global commemoration event held in Lima, Peru in 2019, Moez Chakchouk, Assistant-Director General for Communication and Information for UNESCO, said, "Public access to information can enhance the protection of human rights, bring about better governance, including by fighting corruption, and drive sustainable development."[65]

Arguably, these goals would be far less attainable without the world wide web.

Is there danger? Undoubtedly. Global corporations are as likely to practice the curious arts of manipulation as any individual. And while common sense and restraint are called for on our part, ultimately our safety lies not in avoiding the internet but in recognizing that there is equal danger in the recesses of our own minds. Are we being manipulated by the clever marketing present on social media? Of course. More to the point, as God's people, are we absorbing these techniques and then turning around and employing them in our churches?

MARKETING THE CHURCH

"What the heck are we doing? This feels so wrong!" Carlson flung down his pen and raked an agitated hand through already unruly hair.

It had been a difficult few months. The merger had not been seamless and the organization's new branding was radically at odds with what

---

[65] "International Day for Universal Access to Information," *UNESCO*. Date of access: May 2021 (https://www.unesco.org/en/days/universal-access-information).

they had been promoting for decades. There were obvious cultural clashes between the founding members of this Vancouver sporting goods company and the Quebecois who were now moving into senior leadership. The media and communications team was being told to lose some of the more identifiable aspects of their cultural identity in an effort to be more aligned with the new leadership.

"Are we ashamed of who we are?" Carlson asked. "People love that we are a small, grassroots, local startup. They love our story, and that's what draws them in. Why should we hide our roots?"

"We're not hiding them," one of the executive members said slowly, "just telling the story in a different way, a way that… more people will relate to."

"People?" Carlson raised his eyebrows sceptically. "What people? The new guys, the ones in charge? The ones with the most money to invest? Is that who we are serving now? Is that what we are about?"

There was a moment of embarrassed silence.

"Fine," he said, turning back to his computer screen with a defeated sigh. "Just tell me how you want to spin it."

***

As it turned out, Carlson and the other members of his team were right to be concerned. Over the course of the next couple of years, their new branding, although polished and professional, fell flat with their base of loyal customers and supporters. There was a general sense of disappointment that too much had been sacrificed, including traditional values and focus, and that the rich and complex story of their organization's history and culture had been exchanged for a shiny new trifold brochure advertising their products. The visionaries from Quebec, fortunately, realized that they had been imposing their own agenda, without consideration of context, and eventually sold their shares and left.

But the damage had been done. Within less than a decade, the company folded. "Spin" had not worked for them.

Is it working for the Church?

Professor Douglas D. Webster, in his book *Selling Jesus: What's Wrong with Marketing the Church*, critiques churches that strive to "create a market niche, focus on a target audience, meet a wide range of felt needs, pursue corporate excellence, select a dynamic and personable leader and create a positive, upbeat, exciting atmosphere."[66] He points out that such strategies, however sincere they may be in the motivation to spread the good news, may not be consistent with Spirit-led, Christ-centred spirituality.

Yet consumer Christianity is *de rigueur* globally. Why? Because it works. Marketing has the potential to combine psychology and technology with irresistible results. Companies pay excellent salaries to people who possess skills in persuasive communication, music, graphic art, data analysis, public relations, social media, etc.

A quick perusal through the employment section of ecclesial websites reveals that these skills are also highly valued by the Church. Pastors must not only have the educational prerequisites; they must also be able to work a crowd.

This is not what the early Church looked like.

Jesus appeared to fail utterly at self-promotion. Instead of majoring in the miraculous, he actually rebuked those who followed him for bread alone, or because of signs (John 6:26, Matthew 12:38–39). He criticized the religious elite whose support might have leant considerable credibility to his ministry. He dissuaded and dismissed the curious and insisted upon unadorned, uncomfortable proclamations that demanded a response from the listener.

Nothing kills a sale faster, Webster says, than demanding something from the audience that they are unprepared to give.[67]

Jesus insisted upon socializing with those who could do nothing to promote his popularity, including sinners, tax collectors, and women. He would gather a crowd, say outrageous and impossible things, then walk away and hide up in the mountain somewhere. He was renowned for being politically incorrect, and even unpalatable. "Eat my flesh and drink my blood" lost him a huge following.

Those who stayed squirmed. We can imagine how the conversation went.

"You ditching me, too?" Jesus in effect asked the twelve disciples in John 6:67.

---

[66] Douglas D. Webster, *Selling Jesus: What's Wrong with Marketing the Church* (Eugene, OR: Wipf and Stock, 2009), 21.

[67] Ibid., 103.

Simon Peter answered, "Lord, where the heck else are we gonna go?"

As far as effective marketing strategies are concerned, Jesus was a disaster. Worse still, his followers were just like him.

Early Christian preaching followed the example of Christ and involved attending services at a synagogue where the scriptures were simply read, then in a straightforward manner explained and discussed. There was no attempt at eloquence, embellishment, or flamboyance. Discussion took place during these meetings, but also during informal interactions preceding or following a meal.[68]

There also was no stage, no advertising, and no seeker-sensitive approach. This familiar kind of prosaic discourse came to be called a homily, from the Greek *homileó*, meaning friendly, companionable conversation. One did not take a course to do this, nor was there great emphasis on artful or persuasive speech. In fact, Paul later exclaimed that he disdained such techniques, writing that his message and preaching were not with *"wise and persuasive words, but with a demonstration of the Spirit's power, so that your faith might not rest on human wisdom, but on God's power"* (1 Corinthians 2:4–5).

In contrast, the surrounding Hellenistic culture of the day prized eloquence. Ancient Greece birthed the freelance educators known as the Sophists, who travelled around and charged money for their lectures, teaching the fine arts of public speaking and political politesse. The classic rhetoric of the day promoted by Plato, Aristotle, Cicero, and others began to give way to a more theatrical style of delivery designed to not only convince the mind but to sway the emotions.

This was in sharp contrast with the simple, earnest teaching of the early Church leaders. At least at first. Until Christianity became trendy. Success, after all, brings its own challenges.

Christianity had begun among the poor and uneducated classes. As more cultured, upper class Greeks began to show interest, the plain speech of the apostles and early Church leaders proved rather uninspiring. The dilemma arose as to how best to reach this latter group of potentially

---

[68] Valeriy A. Alikin, *The Earliest History of the Christian Gathering: Origin, Development, and Content of the Christian Gathering in the First to Third Centuries* (Leiden, Netherlands: Brill, 2010), 187, 198.

influential acolytes, without embarrassing or devaluing the founding congregations of working-class believers.

Indeed, keeping up with the times was in the Church's best interests.
In his book *A New History of Classical Rhetoric*, George Kennedy points out
that at this point the Church was beginning to see how affective rhetoric
could be employed to persuade "those in positions of power to take a more
sympathetic view of the Christians and especially to cease legal persecution
of them."[69]

The debate over employing persuasive rhetoric in sermons was docu-
mented by early Church fathers such as Tertullian, Jerome, Clement of Alex-
andria, and Origen. Tertullian foresaw the threat of worldly artifice invading
the Church: "What indeed has Athens to do with Jerusalem?" And Jerome
agreed heartily: "We ought not to drink the cup of Christ and the cup of
devils at the same time."[70] Both Cicero and Origen, however, conceded that
preaching must combine both instruction and persuasion, in a fusion of eloquence and godly wisdom. Augustine set the bar even higher in that regard,
for generations to come, insisting that preachers ought to strive to not only
teach but to delight and move the heart of the listener until he

> values what you promise, fears what
> you threaten, hates what you condemn,
> embraces what you commend, and rues
> the thing which you insist that he must
> regret, and if he rejoices at what you set
> forth in your preaching as something
> joyful, pities those whom by your words
> you present to his mind's eye as miser-
> able, and shuns those whom with terri-
> fying language you urge him to avoid.[71]

---

[69] George Kennedy, *A New History of Classical Rhetoric* (Princeton, NJ: Princeton University Press,
1994), 133.

[70] James J. Murphy, *Rhetoric in the Middle Ages: A History of Rhetorical Theory from Saint Augustine to the Renaissance* (Los Angeles, CA: University of California Press, 1974), 49, 53.

[71] Augustine of Hippo, *On Christian Teaching*, Book IV, xii.

Welcome to the fourth century.

During the Middle Ages, persuasive sermon delivery was known as the art of preaching. In the sixteenth and seventeenth centuries, it became known as ecclesiastical rhetoric and sacred eloquence. Since the end of the seventeenth century, it has been called homiletics.

Now, in the twenty-first century, we not only unquestionably accept the need to maintain cultural relevancy and fluency but we also have at our disposal previously unimagined resources of technology, psychology, media, and the arts, tools with which to teach, delight, and move our target audience.

Is this what Augustine had in mind when he set the trajectory for preachers? Unlikely. The early Church fathers didn't even have PowerPoint. We, on the other hand, have smoke machines, subharmonic bass, multimedia sensory input, essential oil diffusers, and mood lighting. Our sermons are topical, our pastors doctoral, our citations scholarly, our vernacular trendy, and our coffee fair trade and organic. The overall effect is impressive, effective, and exhausting.

Cutting-edge Christianity can only be maintained through ever-increasing efforts. Staying on top of current events, controversies, and cultural trajectories is a 24/7 commitment. Those pastors who do not burn out from the demands survive only if the church is successful enough to hire sufficient support staff to keep things afloat.

The pressure is unbelievable. Salaries must be sufficient to attract the best teachers, skillful worship leaders, and savvy tech support. The result is that a spirit of competition pervades the ecclesiastical scene today, with one church casting furtive glances to see what techniques other churches employ. We obsess over ambiance and vie for affection. Words are chosen to be carefully affirming, until it is nigh impossible to discern one's own level of sincerity.

Are we being manipulative? Or are we just being really, really nice? Is our motive to love God and draw others into his presence? Or are we trying to be popular? In today's churches, manipulation is not only fashionable; it is what the public *wants*.

Just as the early Church leaders looked out over hard-working, lower-class converts, then became flustered at seeing Greco-Roman lords and ladies among them, raising a finely tweezed and amused eyebrow, so our sincerest desire to see others come to know Christ gets thrown into a blender with our anxiety, ambition, and artifice. Ethical lines blur, stress levels spike, pastors fall into sin, children are neglected, marriages crumble, and churches split.

Mammon is worshipped.

Mammon then is not just about money. It is about success. This ancient idol demands that we worship it by polishing our own image. Money certainly makes it easier to influence others. But so do higher education, eloquence, and a sharp wit.

Today, many people are attracted to churches that have the trappings of success, whether it be a big building, impressive programs, or famous speakers. To some extent, this has fallen out of favour in the West. Millennials are not about flash; they are about depth and worthy causes. Many say that they are looking, as they say, for the real deal, for authenticity, and especially for an experience of genuine worship.

But Mammon, it seems, can also play the guitar.

WHEN MAMMON STRUMS

"I was feeling frustrated," my father-in-law admitted to me. "I longed to lead our church into whole-hearted worship. It isn't my primary role, I know—I am here to preach—but I wanted to challenge us into a deeper worship. We had been lulled into professionalism and performance with all the musical talent in our congregation, including members who are concert pianists or sing in the philharmonic choir. But something was missing.

"One day, I invited the elders and deacons to gather at my home and explained that we were going to worship—to express true things about God, to God. I told them simply, 'Let's all tell God, in turn, what he means to us. Let's acknowledge how great and how wonderful he is and thank him for all he has done.'

"Instead they prayed, 'Please, Lord, we're sorry. Forgive us and teach us how to worship…' They asked God's pardon for not having worshipped but made no attempt to actually worship!

"So I got on my knees and tried to model worship. It was an awful struggle. I chose words that reflected the truth about who God is and directed my proclamations to him. Then a sense of God's holiness came over me and I

was at the same time both terrified and deeply moved. I sobbed and my nose ran, but oh how I worshipped!

"The men remained with heads bowed and eyes closed. They never did understand. The next thing I remember was shaking hands with the elders and deacons at the door of our home. They all said, 'Very nice, John. Thank you.'"

***

What went wrong? These devout, mature Christians could not seem to understand what worship was all about. In fact, they were embarrassed by Dad's emotional display. They were more like the onlookers at Bethany, witnessing the jar of expensive perfume being poured out on Jesus by Mary.

Historian N.T. Wright, in his book *For All God's Worth*, writes, "Mary's uninhibited worship has shown up the onlooker's cold formality, has knocked at the door of deep emotion that they had carefully locked up."[72]

In the same way, my father-in-law's impassioned worship made the men uncomfortable because they did not share it. Having spent so many years, and so many Sunday services, focused intently on producing musical excellence in their worship activities, planning every excruciating detail of their program, they were now unable to be spontaneous. They had been in control for too long—in control of their emotions, attention span, and audience. To be genuinely moved in worship required a release of control which they could no longer experience. Worship had become, for them, about moving the hearts of others and gaining a reputation for excellence in the community. Their own hearts were immovable.

Worse still, they were not in the least bothered by this. They were quite comfortable using worship as a means to suit their particular ends. Their definition of success may have sounded more spiritual and altruistic, but they bowed to Mammon nonetheless.

Can manipulation and control enter into the holiest place, the place of our own hearts when we are in worship? The answer, lamentably, is yes. Both while we ourselves worship and when we operate in the role of leading others into worship, that line can be crossed. Most often it is because we

---

[72] N.T. Wright, *For All God's Worth: True Worship and the Calling of the Church* (Grand Rapids, MI: Wm. B. Eerdmans, 1997), 88.

lose sight of who God truly is and begin to see worship as a means to an end rather than as an end in and of itself.

The shorter catechism of the Westminster confession of faith asks, "What is the chief end [purpose] of man?" and then answers, "Man's chief end is to glorify God, and to enjoy him forever."[73] We were created to know God and to worship him. It is our primary raison d'etre. And although it is meant to be a source of indescribable joy to us for all eternity, worship is not for us; it is for God. It is his due.

We have been redeemed in order that we might enter into the worship of the one true God. That is the sole purpose of our salvation. Why then is it so hard to sustain? Why does it grow, for many of us, tedious, dutiful, and even boring?

N.T. Wright observes,

> How can you live with the terrifying thought that the hurricane has become human, that fire has become flesh, that life itself became life and walked in our midst? … Most of us [are] unable to cope…[74]

Or put another way, most of us find coping mechanisms that reduce the fiery pillar to something more manageable, something that does not cause our hearts to quake inconveniently.

And then our hearts lose the ability to quake at all.

Our beings and ways are meant to proclaim God's being and ways. What happens when we lose sight of who God truly is and begin to see worship as a means to an end rather than as an end in and of itself? When we cross over into using worship to increase church attendance, or to promote ourselves, we miss the mark. We may protest that this is not the case for us, that we are worshipping with passion, tears, and deep joy. But is this the goal?

---

[73] "Shorter Catechism," *The Orthodox Presbyterian Church*. Date of access: April 11, 2021 (https://www.opc.org/sc.html).

[74] Ibid., 1.

Emotional engagement in worship is certainly important. In fact, we could argue that it *must* be a part of our relational experience with God.

In what primary relationship would it be considered acceptable to feel nothing? A wife wants more than a steady source of income and someone to mow the lawn. She does not want to be married to an appliance. A child needs more than food and shelter from her parents. A psychiatrist might suspect a pathology of sociopathy in a mother whose heart remains unmoved by empathy, compassion, or grief over her child, and at the very least Social Services will have to get involved.

Emotion matters, to God and to us. Our hearts are meant to be warmed.

Unfortunately, this can too easily become our sole motive for worship. Worship, when it affects the heart, feels good. It gives us pleasure. And we can fall into a kind of addictive craving that draws us not closer to God but further and further away. We begin to worship for the rush, for the adrenaline-inducing, throbbing bassline, for the ecstatic high of a superb electric guitar riff, for the cathartic tears that fall in response to subjective, introspective lyrics.

None of these things are sinful. But if we are not vigilant we can go from being worshippers to being worship junkies.

In Deuteronomy 6:4–5, Israel was given the command to worship God with all their heart, soul, and strength. Woe betide us should we reduce this to worshipping with all our self-absorbed emotionalism, self-serving manipulation, and self-aggrandizing execution.

We can lose ourselves more easily than we might imagine, allowing our priceless psyches to become cheap trinkets for barter.

A HUNTER OF SOULS

The word *soul* occurs sixteen times in the New International Version's translation of the New Testament. Jesus once said, *"Do not be afraid of those who kill the body but cannot kill the <u>soul</u>. Rather, be afraid of the One who can destroy both soul and body in hell"* (Matthew 10:28, emphasis added).

Body, we understand. But what is soul?

Descartes seemed to draw a close correlation between the soul with the mind, saying that one resided in the other. He wrote about a "part of the body in which the soul exercises its function immediately… a very small gland so suspended above whereby the animal spirits in its [the brain's] anterior cavities have communication with those in the posterior."[75]

Neurosurgeons, obviously, have yet to discover any evidence of this. But perhaps Descartes's association is not that far off the mark. Our minds are what medical professionals reference in the "psych-" prefix of their disciplines of psychology and psychiatry. It is where we process emotion, access memories, find our sense of self, and resolve to act.

In the West, we often use this term interchangeably with the concept of *mind*, but in first-century biblical times the soul and mind were not the same thing.

Jesus uses the Greek word *psychē*, translated as "soul," when he references the all-encompassing biblical mandate of the Shema in Matthew 22:37. To the Deuteronomy 6:4–5 command to worship God with all our heart, soul, and strength, he substitutes the word "mind" for strength. That word used for "mind" comes from the Greek *dianoia*, from which we derive the word *dialectical*, connoting a kind of critical thinking that literally reaches "across to the other side" of a matter; it describes our capacity to analyze and reason. It would have been an appropriate addition for those of the first century, who were heavily influenced by the Hellenistic culture of logic and reason.

The word *dianoia* implies effort, the hard work of grappling with concepts in order to understand them, and was therefore a good substitute for the word *meod* used in Deuteronomy—a word that also conveys immense effort, and is therefore translated as "strength."

So when Jesus used the word *psyche* in his summary of the Shema, he was not talking about our ability to feel deeply or think hard, but about our ability to freely and fully be who God created us to be. The word literally means "breath" in Greek, an allusion to God breathing life, or personhood, into each human being. We might then say that his command is for our hearts to desire worship, our souls to *choose* worship, and our strength to *sustain* us in worship.

If the soul is that which gives us our God-breathed personhood—our freedom to choose what we will worship—what happens when it falls prey

---

[75] Robert Wilkinson, *Minds and Bodies: An Introduction with Readings* (New York, NY: Routledge, 2000), 178.

to manipulation? The Hebrew concept of personhood was not divided into body, mind, and spirit. Manipulation of feelings or thoughts was an assault on the totality of one's humanity, an ensnaring of the soul.

And it can happen at church. It is but a short step from the emotional to the volitional. In a worship service, various audio, visual, and even tactile stimuli (think of a pounding bass vibrating in your chest) can be used to flood our brains with the kind of neurochemicals that charge our emotions and extend our ability to sustain emotional engagement for as long as the stimulus continues. As heart and mind are both impacted, our soul can begin to lose its freedom to choose.

A friend of mine who was hired to be the senior sound technician at a large American church in Los Angeles was horrified to discover that they were using what is known as a sub-acoustic generator to produce a kind of white noise well below the range of human hearing. It is a demonstrated fact that such frequencies can induce a physical response in humans which may range anywhere from mild euphoria to incontinence, depending on the volume.

Sonic and ultrasonic weapons (USW) are currently in limited use or in research and development by military forces around the world. There are reports that China has developed handheld portable sonic weapons to subdue protestors.[76]

Do we ever consider our stage woofers and tweeters as potential weapons? They are. Those who already have sensory input challenges, such as those diagnosed with autism spectrum disorders, are especially vulnerable.

This is not to say we must now insist that all churches have "unplugged" worship, but we must be aware of and responsible with the use and misuse of media, music, and technology. For where heart, mind, and soul are no longer free agents, worship is a farce.

When the soul is manipulated, we lose the ability to make our own choices. We become passive automatons responding to whatever suggestions are made. Our souls are then dangerously pliant, at risk of anyone with selfish or malicious intent. Such a person can pluck our souls from wherever

---

[76] Stephen Chen, "Chinese Scientists Develop Handheld Sonic Weapon for Crowd Control," *South China Morning Post*. September 19, 2019 (https://www.scmp.com/news/china/science/article/3028071/chinese-scientists-develop-handheld-sonic-weapon-crowd-control).

they reside within us and collect them as trophies. They dangle like charms on the bracelets adorning the wrists of those who hunt for souls.

Such people do exist.

Ezekiel 13 talks about false prophetesses who capture people's souls with manipulative lies. The chapter is divided into two halves. In the first half (Ezekiel 13:1–16), he exposes false prophets who prophesy out of their own imagination (Ezekiel 13:2). They control the people to whom they prophesy, promising whatever those people want to hear. Then, in Ezekiel 13:17–23, we read of the Lord instructing Ezekiel to expose women who are hunting for souls. The New King James Version captures this vividly:

> Likewise, son of man, set your face against the daughters of your people, who prophesy out of their own heart; prophesy against them, and say, "Thus says the Lord God: 'Woe to the women who sew magic charms on their sleeves and make veils for the heads of people of every height to hunt souls! Will you hunt the souls of My people, and keep yourselves alive? And will you profane Me among My people for handfuls of barley and for pieces of bread, killing people who should not die, and keeping people alive who should not live, by your lying to My people who listen to lies?'
>
> "Therefore thus says the Lord God: 'Behold, I am against your magic charms by which you hunt souls there like birds. I will tear them from your arms, and let the souls go, the souls you hunt like birds. I will also tear off your veils and deliver My people out of your hand, and they shall no longer

> be as prey in your hand. Then you shall know that I am the Lord.
>
> "'Because with lies you have made the heart of the righteous sad, whom I have not made sad; and you have strengthened the hands of the wicked, so that he does not turn from his wicked way to save his life. Therefore you shall no longer envision futility nor practice divination; for I will deliver My people out of your hand, and you shall know that I am the Lord.'" (Ezekiel 13:17–23, NKJV)

If our working definition of *soul* is that part of ourselves, which defines our person and gives us freedom to choose, then what we have here is a picture of our ability to choose being stolen from us. False prophets and prophetesses sought to control the thoughts and wills of others, and apparently they succeeded. Charms and veils seem to be allusions to some form of divination, and some commentators feel these may have also been metaphorical symbols.

Either way, a veil suggests a concealment of dangerous power.

In the Old Testament, as in many conservative Muslim settings today, a veil was worn to protect the beholder from the dangers of lust. Women were veiled so the men who saw them might not be led into temptation by their beauty.

Moses was veiled because the radiance that suffused his face when he met with God was too intense to gaze upon, as well as to protect the people from the grief and dismay they would feel when they saw that reflected glory fade away.

A veil was also placed at the entrance to the holy of holies so no one would be destroyed by glimpsing the utter holiness of the Lord's presence.

Veils were for the sake of the beholder.

Ezekiel paints a picture of the prophetess as being a seductress deceptively veiling herself in order to give the impression of a threat—a wondrous, dangerous beauty, radiance, or power. It is highly suggestive, piquing one's curiosity, arousing the imagination, and luring the naïve into a trap. That is precisely why the false prophetess in Ezekiel wears one: to evoke mystery, desire, and fear in all who behold her veiled countenance. It is an affectation of power.

It is also, at least metaphorically, an essential accessory in the wardrobe of many in the Church.

There are times when we all want to look more intriguing than we actually are, more mysterious and powerful. Women might use makeup and men might namedrop. We hint at things we actually know very little about, wanting to give the impression that we are well-read. I am a writer; believe me, I know!

Even in the Church, there can be those who adopt certain mannerisms for the sake of impressing others. Religious vernacular, breathless sincerity alternating with thundering exhortation, physical manifestations that suggest spiritual anointing… these can all be assumed, or put on, like accessories. The more discerning—or cynical, as with postmoderns—see through these affectations in a flash.

More dangerous is one who is in fact rightfully "veiled" and uses that veil as a means of manipulating others. Genuine anointing can be corrupted for selfish gain. What does this look like?

Saul, remember, had a genuine and powerful encounter with God shortly after being anointed king by Samuel. While in Gibeah, he met a band of prophets, and *"the Spirit of God came powerfully upon him, and he joined in their prophesying"* (1 Samuel 10:10). This was noticed by others, who asked in amazement, *"What is this that has happened to the son of Kish? Is Saul also among the prophets?"* (1 Samuel 10:11)

The impact on Saul was profound. The Spirit of the Lord came upon him and he was in effect given another heart (1 Samuel 10:9) and *"changed into a different person"* (1 Samuel 10:6).

At first he seemed to respond with humility, not even telling his uncle of the reason he was late: that a prophet had just told him he had been chosen to be the first king of Israel.

Later, as Samuel cast lots to prove that God had been the one to appoint the first monarch, Saul was modestly seated among the baggage. He stood, almost reluctantly, to acknowledge his acceptance. Standing a good head and shoulders taller than anyone else, we can picture his flowing hair and rugged good looks which, combined with his humility, made the crowd go wild. They shouted, *"Long live the king!"* (1 Samuel 10:24)

Saul was beautiful, anointed, reverent, humble and… well, *hot*.

It took no time at all for all this to go to his head. Within a short span of days, a military crisis appealed to Saul's hero complex and in response he instituted a grotesque method of conscription to gather troops against the Ammonites. Bloody chunks of ox carcass were sent throughout Israel as a threat, as though to say, "Come and fight at my side or I will hack you into pieces."

Where was the beauty, the anointing, the Spirit of the Lord? It was all still there. Even the anger that burned within him was a righteous indignation that came, we are told, from the Lord (1 Samuel 11:6).

Nonetheless, Saul was already beginning to use the anointing to his own advantage, to exercise power and control over others. It was all downhill from there.

When those in the Church who manifest genuine qualities of godliness and spiritual anointing choose to use these qualities to gain personal advantage, they are no better than the false prophetess of Ezekiel 13, lowering dark eyes above a gossamer veil while beckoning others into thraldom.

For most of us, it starts small. We may be in the middle of a powerful ministry encounter or leading a tight worship set when, carried away by the rush of seeing others so deeply affected, we bask for just a moment in the glory. We are in the spotlight, with others gazing at us in adulation. Having brought them to tears, we think we can do no wrong. Over time, we begin to believe that we are as wonderful as others seem to think we are and use our stage presence to voice opinions, express criticism, give advice, win friends, and promote our favourite causes. Our motivation may be far from malicious—in fact, we may simply feel an obligation to use our influence for good.

But the temptation will come, inevitably, to cross the line into using this influence, this anointing, for our own good. We make our pitch to influence others at times when we feel we are in our "sweet spot," when others are most tender and receptive, moved by the presence of the Holy Spirit. Hearts are soft, minds are open, eyes are misty. We are able to see into the secret recesses of a person's heart and then tell them what they most want to hear, and in doing so we rob them of their soul, their *psyche*, their ability to be freely and fully themselves and to choose. That attractive person who may or may not be flirting with us becomes a coveted adornment, a thing to be collected and dangled from the charm bracelet of a witch.

Before we know it, another genuinely godly, anointed Church leader has fallen into sexual sin and the sullied, torn veil of seduction flutters down to litter the sanctuary floor.

There will always be a dangerous temptation for leaders, particularly skilled worship leaders, to play to the crowd more than they minister to God. When song and liturgy are based solely on what is most popular, or what evokes the most applause, souls are being hunted.

It is hard not to keep track of the events where we shine, the people we impact. We wear our accomplishments like charms on a bracelet. We finger them with fond pride, reminiscing of the time when we were given the mic at a conference, brought someone to tears with a prophetic word, had people clapping ecstatically at our worship leading…

Worship leaders in particular can be so overcome with the heady euphoria of ushering others into the presence of God that they may forget to go there themselves.

It's hard not to feed off the flock.

A DOORSTOP IN THE TEMPLE

The worship leader's priorities are to minister to God directly while at the same time serving God's people. They are meant to act like a kind of doorstop, both walking into the presence of God and yet making sure to lodge their foot firmly in the door so as to continually encourage and invite others to go in as well. The worship leader must do everything possible to keep that door ajar. Leaders who care nothing about discerning the hearts of the people in their own church might as well worship in front of a mirror. Yet leaders are not to care so much for the preferences of their congregants that they themselves neglect to enter into worship and instead only mirror whatever others want them to be. Both are false. Both are manipulative.

It is admittedly a very hard line to walk, between serving and leading. As a former worship leader, I was only too aware of how often I zigged or zagged on either side of that line.

The false prophetess in Ezekiel 13 turned a profit off the worship of others, and we must never make this our aim. To do so is to feed off the flock that is entrusted to our care.

Zechariah 11 describes the *"foolish shepherd"* who will not *"care for the lost, or seek the young, or heal the injured, or feed the healthy, but will eat the meat of the choice sheep, tearing off their hooves"* (Zechariah 11:15–16). This is the leader who cares only to profit from their own ministry and uses others to do so.

The means of feeding off the flock can be subtle, rationalized as being merely pragmatic. For example, when Jesus overturned the tables of the moneychangers in the temple, what was the reason for his anger? He said, *"My house will be called a house of prayer, but you are making it a den of robbers"* (Matthew 21:13).

The astounded merchants would have protested their innocence. They were providing, it would be argued, a valuable service. Those making the pilgrimage to Jerusalem to make an offering at the temple often travelled great distances. Not only would it have been inconvenient and logistically difficult to bring with them the livestock needed for the sacrifices, but there was also the question of having the right currency for the tithes and offerings. It only made sense that there should be a way to ease that burden, to make it a smoother and less complicated process. Setting up a booth in the temple itself was convenient and helpful.

"Away with such help!" Jesus might have cried out, indignant. "You are seeking to profit from their worship by making it easier for them!"

It was, it is, opportunistic in the extreme.

Worship can by turns be majestic, glorious, sad, exciting, and challenging. It can inspire sacrifice and a willingness to volunteer. In fact, it can inspire almost anything. When worship leaders discover their professional competence, and what that competence does to a congregation, they can slide into manipulation without realizing what they are doing. It can be a thrill to see people respond to a particularly rhythmic song, for instance, and know that one can evoke that response at will.

Leading worship is a noble calling, but it is a perilous one as well. It is to bring others to the holy of holies; not so cautiously that no one dares follow, and not so casually that we risk irreverence. True worship, from selfless motives, when expressed through Spirit-inspired artistic media, has tremendous power both to bless God and edify his people. The guitar must be strummed with humility. Mammon would have us wield it as a weapon.

In the worship arts, as in all high-profile church leadership roles, there is a temptation to worship this idol of success. Bowing before Mammon will also, inevitably, invite us to bow before other idols.

It is nearly impossible to worship Mammon, the idol of success, without at some point being drawn into an obsession with our own image. It is the most basic means by which we influence and control one another, yet it also has the shortest lifespan, biologically speaking. So it is that idols associated with our image exact a great price, for beauty is a moving target that is always just out of our reach.

We compulsively purchase every possible cosmetic enhancement to assure our continued desirability, jack up our line of credit to keep pace with the latest fashion trends, and pummel our flesh to fit seamlessly into skinny jeans.

Mammon welcomes our debt and suggests opening a line of credit with Molech, the idol who promises us eternal youth.

ETERNAL YOUTH: A CHILD FOR MOLECH

Jennifer Worth, in her book *In the Midst of Life*—one of a series that inspired the widely acclaimed *Call the Midwife* television series—wrote of her experience as a nurse. She began as a midwife and dealt almost exclusively with babies and new mothers, then later moved to the field of geriatrics and palliative care. She tells gruesome stories of elderly patients whose lives were prolonged through groundbreaking medical intervention and then went on to spend their last hours, days, months, or years in misery and pain. She shares vivid descriptions of incontinence, immobility, depression, decay, and the cold, efficient professionalism of those medical practitioners who insist upon prolonging life regardless of its quality.

While not openly advocating euthanasia, more recently called "medically assisted suicide," Worth grieves the lack of dignity and choice that comes with old age.

She tells this infinitely sad tale:

> [Mrs Ratski] lay immobile, hands restrained, in terrified silence. Soundless sobs racked her body, and tears streamed from her eyes. She could not swallow, because of the pain in her throat. Her mouth became completely dry and crusted, and had to be moistened and cleaned every hour, but even so her tongue was ulcerated and cracked. She did not pass any urine, so a nurse had to catheterise her, but she held her body completely rigid, to prevent anyone from parting her legs. Did she think she was being raped? I wondered. Maybe she had been, in a prison camp?
>
> …Mr Carter read through the notes. "I hear you have had trouble with her, Sister."
>
> "Yes, sir. She keeps trying to interfere with the dressings."
>
> "That is why you have tied her hands, I suppose?"
>
> "Yes, sir. It was the only way."[77]

Stories like this one horrify us. We cannot bear the thought that we, too, might one day face ugly decay and humiliation.

We are obsessed with youth and all that it represents: health, strength, and longevity. The prospect of aging is terrifying—and not just death; the

---

[77] Jennifer Worth, *In the Midst of Life: What Makes a Good Death?* (London, UK: Orion, 2011), 7–8.

process of dying represents the ultimate loss of control. We are willing to go to great lengths to forestall the inevitable.

While there is no doubt that the legalization of medically assisted suicide has brought peace of mind to many who suffer from painful, incurable, and fatal conditions, it also appeals to the young. The thought of controlling our own aging process and choosing our own time of death can be alluring. We can decide what last impression we will give, what last image will be left behind to memorialize our lives. We can die pretty.

In the meantime, obviously, everything possible is done to ensure that we stay pretty now. Christians worship at the altar of eternal youth no less than unbelievers. This is the altar of Molech.

Few perhaps realize that this god demands infant sacrifice.

Child sacrifice, expressly forbidden to the Israelites, was not uncommon amongst the pagan peoples of Canaan. In worship of Molech—also known as Milcom, or Malcham, an Ammonite deity—infants were routinely passed *"through the fire"* (Leviticus 18:21, NKJV) in a ritual sacrifice. Kings such as Ahaz (2 Kings 16:3) and Manasseh (2 Kings 21:6), having been influenced by the Assyrians, worshipped Moloch at the hilled site of Topheth, in the valley of Ben Hinnom, which by the first century was commonly known in the Aramaic language as *Gēhannā*. The site lay outside the walls of Jerusalem. There, infants were burned alive, at the hands of their own parents.

In Jeremiah 7:31, we glimpse the depth of God's revulsion at this practice: *"They have built the high places of Topheth in the Valley of Ben Hinnom to burn their sons and daughters in the fire—something I did not command, nor did it enter my mind."* What power could anyone possibly hope to gain from such atrocities?

In conventional, occult witchcraft, as in pagan folklore, there is the belief that a person will inherit the lifeforce of those creatures they kill. A pagan tribesman might kill a bear to inherit its strength, or slay a lion to inherit its courage. Would we be willing to murder a baby in the hopes of renewing or extending our own youth?

Some might say that we already do. Medical research is being done with living foetuses, either inside or outside the uterus—and, in many contexts, this also involves research on embryos. This human tissue is used most heavily for research regarding infectious diseases, especially HIV/AIDS; retinal function and disease; and normal and anomalous foetal development. In the past twenty-five years, these cells have been utilized to produce therapeutic treatments to fight cystic fibrosis, arthritis, and haemophilia, and stem cell research has led to dopaminergic neurons from aborted foetuses being experimentally transplanted into the brains of patients with Parkinson's disease.

None of this is new. Cells from aborted foetal tissue have been commonly used in research and medicine since the 1960s, when aborted foetuses were used to develop the WI-38 and MRC-5 cell lines, which led to the manufacture of vaccines against measles, rubella, rabies, chicken pox, shingles, and hepatitis A. Millions of people can be saved with one small clump of cells. It would be hard to make a case that this research has not been incredibly beneficial to humanity. Quite literally, we now live longer because of aborted foetuses.

And some of us look, and smell, way better.

While there is no definitive evidence of American-made cosmetics making use of cultured foetal cells, it is a promising new market in Europe, where such products are sold to promote healing for patients with severe wounds and burns.[78] Cosmetic companies promote similar products which they claim are effective in fighting psoriasis, eczema, and wrinkles.

To call this controversial would be a massive understatement. Recently in the United States, there was strong opposition to foetal tissue research by government scientists and academic researchers seeking grants from the National Institutes of Health (NIH) for studies involving foetal tissue.[79]

Then the COVID-19 pandemic hit and a life-and-death quandary arose—and at the time of this writing, it still exists. Organizations such as the Lozier Institute currently update their websites regularly to educate potential viral vaccine candidates as to which vaccines use foetal cell lines

---

[78] "Tissue Engineered Fetal Skin Constructs for Pediatric Burns," *The Lancet*, Volume 266, Issue 9488. September 2005, 840–842.

[79] Debra Goldschmidt and Susan Scutti, "Trump Administration Limits Research Using Fetal Tissue," *CNN*. June 5, 2019 (https://www.cnn.com/2019/06/05/health/hhs-fetal-tissue-research-bn).

like HEK 293, thought to be derived from the kidney tissue of a foetus aborted in 1972, in the development, production, or testing.[80]

There was some public outcry from pro-life (anti-abortion) advocates that certain vaccines are an ethical offence against humanity. The reality is that HEK 293 has been used for medical treatments and biological research for decades; it has become so ubiquitous that conducting research without relying on it in some form would be nearly impossible. In addition, the specific cell lines used continue to divide and reproduce themselves indefinitely and have not therefore created a need or market for new foetal tissue to be obtained for vaccine development.

Still, many so-called "antivaxxers," already opposing mandated vaccination against COVID-19 as a human rights infringement, cite the use of HEK 293 for vaccines as an additional ethical argument, along with a popular (though unproven) theory that vaccines can trigger an autism spectrum disorder in infants and children.

People are spitting mad on both sides of the debate.

Being the first global pandemic since the Spanish flu of 1918, COVID-19 has changed our world, our politics, and our priorities. Those most vulnerable—the elderly, the immunocompromised, and the global poor—clamoured for the vaccine and, in many cases, it was not available. Hospitals were at maximum capacity and didn't even have enough oxygen to treat the sick. Those in the developed West were divided, with the fear of a loss of liberty (being forced, for example, to wear a mask) clashing with the fear of loss of life. Libertarians insisted upon their right to self-determination, conservatives upon their right to financial independence; both extremes were grossly impacted by the pandemic. Conspiracy theorists abounded, national protectionism surged, walls were built, borders closed, and violent protests staged.

The majority of the world looked on in disgust, wondering how this controversy could even exist while the death toll in countries such as Brazil and India grew ever more appalling.

Ironically, Catholic leaders in the United States and Canada, along with other antiabortion groups, refrained from seeking to block government

---

[80] David Prentice, "Update: COVID-19 Vaccine Candidates and Abortion-Derived Cell Lines," *Lozier Institute*. September 30, 2020 (https://lozierinstitute.org/update-covid-19-vaccine-candidates-and-abortion-derived-cell-lines).

funding for the development of these vaccines, yet they continued to raise ethical objections to the use of cells derived from human foetuses electively aborted decades ago. On the one side were strident ethical and moral objectors; on the other, angry and dismissive pragmatists.

Most people simply wanted to survive. It has been a complex, polarizing issue where lives are at stake.

When it comes to medical research and treatment, it would be a cheap shot to accuse those who make use of aborted foetal tissue of sacrificing children to Molech. Cosmeceuticals that harvest foetal cells are easier to condemn, as they fuel the idolization of youth and beauty.

Again, though, none of this is new. Legalizing abortion did not lead to foetal stem cell research. The desire to be in control of one's life—admittedly, not always an illegitimate desire when considering the social injustices propagated on women historically—led to abortion.

Michael J. Gorman, in his book *Abortion and the Early Church*, tells us that abortion was commonplace in ancient Greco-Roman times. It was practiced most often in order to cover up illicit sexual activity among women of the upper class, so these wealthy women could retain their sex appeal. Prostitutes, likewise, depended on their beauty to secure their trade. A baby would not only be an economic inconvenience but could, afterward, make them physically less appealing. Plato and Aristotle recommended abortion to limit family size, for economic reasons.[81]

By the time of Christ's birth, abortion was so widespread that the early Christians were obligated to formulate a response regarding the practice, based largely on traditional Jewish theology, which valued the personhood of the unborn child.[82]

Abortion, at a time when other methods of preventing conception were unreliable, was practiced as a form of birth control. For the global poor, it still is. Perhaps the operative word here is, *control*.

Again, it cannot be disputed that issues of human rights and social justice are inextricably enmeshed with the ethical issue of abortion and

---

[81] Michael J. Gorman, *Abortion and the Early Church: Christian, Jewish, and Pagan Attitudes in the Greco-Roman World* (Eugene, OR: Wipf and Stock, 1998), 15.

[82] Ibid., 34–45. See also: Harold O.J. Brown, "What the Supreme Court Didn't Know: Ancient and Earthly Christian Views on Abortion," *Human Life Review 1*, Spring 1975, 5–21.

birth control. Allowing a human being to have undisputed stewardship of their own body is not being debated. The advancement and availability of effective birth control methods have given women a say in the direction of their lives, careers, marriages, and economic status. Not all control is bad, remember.

In my grandmother's day, the decision to marry was *de facto* a decision to have babies, whether one wanted them or not. In my mother's day, however, contraception was assumed to be normative. In my day, a Christian movement known as Quiverfull takes its name from this scripture: *"Children are a heritage from the Lord... Blessed is the man whose quiver is full of them"* (Psalm 127:3, 5). Adherents to this movement declared that birth control is a kind of rebellion; one ought to have as many children as God sees fit to send and allow him to be in control.[83]

This begs a question: are Christians who refuse to practice birth control surrendering control to God, or are they abdicating their own responsibility? Multiple births, especially for an aging mother, increase not only the economic burden on a family but also the risk of birth defects, natal and maternal death, and even neglect of other children. Are some children, in effect, being sacrificed for the sake of having even more children? Are the mothers who do this *trusting* God or avoiding decisions that are meant to be made in partnership *with* God?

These are difficult questions. Whatever one's view, it does not detract from the reality that twentieth-first-century access to contraception and abortion has played a significant role in the increase of sex outside traditional marriage. This in turn has had measurable consequences. Statistically, it has been observed that the more sexually active one is before marriage, the greater the likelihood of divorce after marriage.[84]

It could be said that the desire to be in complete control of our sexuality results in lesser, not greater, happiness.

Except for Molech, obviously. He is thrilled with our devotion.

---

[83] Kathryn Joyce, *Quiverfull: Inside the Christian Patriarchy Movement* (Boston, MA: Beacon Press, 2009).

[84] Joan R. Kahn and Kathryn A. London, "Premarital Sex and the Risk of Divorce," *Journal of Marriage and the Family 53*, 1991, 845–855. See also: Anthony Paik, "Adolescent Sexuality and Risk of Marital Dissolution," *Journal of Marriage and the Family 73*, 2011.

We are all idolators. It is in our sinful nature to chase after power and control, devoting ourselves to anyone or anything that promises to deliver that power into our hands. It would be a blatant lie to claim we do not want beauty or eternal youth. We hand over our money and our bodies, some would even say our children, in exchange for a dream that can never be fulfilled.

In the end, Molech makes a lousy beauty consultant and his products rot upon application. When we angrily demand our money back, he passes us off to his companions. We are introduced to Baal, Ashtoreth, Astarte, and their peers—fickle gods at best, and a poor substitute for the Lover of our soul.

But oh, it does feel good to worship them.

BAAL, ASHTORETH, AND THE LURE OF PLEASURE

Ernest Becker, in his book *Denial of Death*, describes modern man's obsession with romance and sexuality as a means of fulfilling our desire for cosmic heroism. Secular man, having turned his back on religion as a source of significance, still feels a primal need to "merge himself with some higher, self-absorbing meaning..."[85] Without God, the most appealing option is to search for one's true love, that perfect partner who "becomes the divine ideal within which to fulfill one's life."[86] The result is twofold: a trivialization of sex and a deification of love.

The apostle Paul perceived both of these dangers in the Corinthian church. Influenced by the Greek culture which made a point of distinguishing between the physical body and the spiritual self, the Corinthians were falling into two extreme views on sexuality. Some diminished its importance, reducing it to just one more appetite needing to be satiated: *"Food for the stomach and the stomach for food..."* (1 Corinthians 6:13). Others exaggerated its importance, so much that they saw sex as potentially competing with their higher values. They said, *"It is good for a man not to have sexual relations with a woman"* (1 Corinthians 7:1). Sex was so all-consuming and such a distraction, they felt, that the only way to be

---

[85] Ernest Becker, *Denial of Death* (New York, NY: Simon & Schuster, 1973), 160.

[86] Ibid.

spiritual was to be abstinent. To which, an astonished Paul replied, para-phrased, "What on earth makes you think you have that right? Your bodies belong not to yourselves, but to each other. Do not deprive each other!"

Paul's perspective on sex, romance, and marriage was revolutionary, promoting a radical surrender of independence and a whole-life commit-ment to vulnerability and oneness.

Tim Keller, in *The Meaning of Marriage,* describes this whole-life dona-tion of self:

> The Bible says don't unite with some-one physically unless you are also will-ing to unite with the person emotionally, personally, socially, economically, and legally. Don't become physically naked and vulnerable to the other person with-out becoming vulnerable in every other way, because you have given up your freedom…[87]

Sex and romance are God's gifts, created for a mutuality of yieldedness in marriage that mirrors the other-mindedness of Christ towards his Church, his Bride. It is about abdicating our rights, giving up our independence, as God did in the stark vulnerability of incarnation in order to be one with us.

Instead we have made it about our own personal fulfillment and a con-stant battle for control. And when sex and control cross paths, we enter the perilous domain of Baal, Astarte, Ashtoreth, and their ilk. In ancient times, these idols were worshiped for the sake of fertility; modernity worships them in search of sexual and romantic fulfillment.

These two extremes—undervaluing and overvaluing our sexuality—still exist today. Although modern Christians may not trivialize sex, the mod-ern Church has absorbed the secular, idealized notion of romance; whether intentionally or unintentionally, our church services are often designed to appeal to the restless heart in search of true love. While we cannot with

---

[87] Tim Keller, *The Meaning of Marriage: Facing the Complexities of Commitment with the Wisdom of God* (New York, NY: Penguin Books, 2016), 256.

integrity offer sex on Sundays, we can and do promote sensuality and romance. We may practice seduction—one of the curious arts, enticing others into following Jesus by promising the kind of intense delights associated with the sexual experience.

What does that look like?

We have already talked about how worship, particularly musical worship, can be used to manipulate our emotions and override our souls. The line between sensuality and spirituality has become so blurred as to be nearly unrecognizable.

For example, a Christian definition of modesty, which obviously differs according to the cultural context, seems to have become relative. By and large, what is acceptable in our social context is acceptable in our church, be that midriff tops and push-up bras, subjective self-centric lyrics, sensual gyrations while crooning into a mic, or the rush of oxytocin that comes with an octave vocal leap and grand crescendo.

The pervasive search for romantic and sexual fulfillment has shaped generations of Christians to look for love in all the wrong places, as the saying goes—and all the wrong ways.

In our pervasive search for romantic and sexual fulfillment, we may lose sight of the Lover of our soul and settle for seduction. When the Bride of Christ lowers her veil and gives a come-hither flutter of her eyelashes, the very adornments she has been given—the gifts of the Holy Spirit—become the means through which the curious arts are practiced.

SPIRITUAL GIFTS: PRINCESS OR PROSTITUTE?

Whenever we make the deliberate choice to pursue certain spiritual experiences for the sake of our own sensual pleasure or the seduction of others, we worship not God but idols of sexuality. When we align our church services to cater to our congregants' appetite for sensory pleasure, or even romantic, spiritual idealism, we collaborate with those idols and practice manipulation. Perhaps we think this sin most obvious in churches where the bank rocks out and the preacher is uber hip. That may simply be a result of youth being drawn in.

The worship of sensuality can actually be far less crass, and far more insidious. It can take what is precious and make it vile.

Tongues, prophecy, and healing are three of the ways in which the Holy Spirit may manifest his presence. They are God's gifts to the Church. They are also exciting to experience. Words of supernatural insight, when accurate, thrill and transform. To witness genuine healing, whether physiological, emotional, or relational, is moving and often overwhelming. Tongues and other ecstatic experiences can be profound and life-changing, inspiring us to renew our devotion to God, his word, and his people. Those who become competent and confident in allowing these gifts to be used in and through their lives will often be esteemed by others, and even given positions of power and influence in the Church.

None of this is bad, but it can distract us from both the origin and real purpose of the gifts.

The gifts of the Spirit are not for the individual alone, but primarily for the Body of Christ—in other words, for the edification of the entire Church. Although the Spirit's gift may be *for* me, it is not *about* me.

Paul's instructions regarding the gifts of the Spirit are corporate and given to the Church as a whole. The context of the description of gifts in 1 Corinthians 12 appears to be that of a gathering of believers where the gifts are bestowed upon the Church corporately, to be received and actively employed through individual members. This requires that we be sensitive to discern our situational context, to know what content and presentation is most helpful for which part of the Body. It means being under authority, submitted to those who are responsible for the well-being of others. It may also mean that we wait our turn in the queue.

We read in 1 Corinthians 12:7 that the gifts are distributed for the *"common good"* of those gathered. The body parts metaphor used in 1 Corinthians 12:4–7, when considered in the context of a gathering, is meant to ensure that everyone does not manifest the same gift at the same time, which would be both redundant and chaotic!

However, when we cease to see the gift as being for the sake of others, and instead pursue them for our own personal pleasure, or for the sake of the position of influence they offer us over others, we venture into enemy territory.

It is not wrong to feel pleasure when the Holy Spirit touches us. It is wrong to make that pleasure our goal. When we pursue the gift over the Giver, we are thrill-seekers, not God-seekers.

How can we know which category we fall into? We may judge ourselves by the reaction that we have when the thrill wears off. The God-seeker comes away from an experience of the Holy Spirit with his appetite for God increased. He will have a hunger for the word, fervour for evangelism, grief over sin, and craving for solitude in which to commune with God in prayer.

In contrast, the thrill-seeker leaves an experience of the Holy Spirit with that special glow of satisfaction that radiates most brilliantly when he describes his experience to others. There will be an insatiable need to talk about what he has experienced. Once the thrill has worn off, restlessness will set in. He may feel a sense of dissatisfaction, particularly if the gifts of the Spirit are not manifesting in his church to the degree he feels they ought. The thrill-seeker moves from church to church, from event to event, always seeking but never quite finding a peak experience that satisfies him. This kind of pursuit of sensual pleasure, even the wholesome and legitimate pleasure the Holy Spirit gives, is no different from the worship of sex.

The Church is destined to live in times of increasing spiritual anointing. Ephesians 5:25–27 tells us, *"Christ loved the church and gave himself up for her to make her holy, cleansing her by the washing with water through the word… to present her to himself as a radiant church."* And Revelation 21:2 describes us as *"a bride beautifully dressed for her husband."* We are going to ravish his heart with our beauty one day, and until then it is his good pleasure to adorn us with tokens of his love. These are the gifts of his Spirit, the manifestations of his person in and through his Bride.

What happens if instead of allowing him to beautify us for the wedding, we pawn the gifts off for our own selfish purposes? We easily forget that the preparation of his Bride involves not just anointing and adorning, but cleansing. With blessing comes judgment; they are two edges of the same sword. The outpouring of God's Holy Spirit on his Bride is likened to a refining fire: that which is gold will be made purer while that which is dross will be burned to ash. Our God is a jealous Bridegroom and consuming fire.

The Bride is still being made ready, but as her beauty increases she may feel tempted to cash in on that beauty.

Ezekiel 16:6–14 speaks vividly of the preparation which occurs as God readies his Bride for the wedding day. The passage refers to Israel, but the application of this prophetic metaphor to us as the Bride of Christ is deeply convicting.

In the first stage, we have our initial encounter with the future Bridegroom, as the Church is a squalling, unwanted newborn wallowing in our own blood and mucous. Abandoned infants do not live long in this state, and the Lord explains that he found us on the brink of death and rescued us.

> On the day you were born your cord was not cut, nor were you washed with water to make you clean, nor were you rubbed with salt or wrapped in cloths. No one looked on you with pity or had compassion enough to do any of these things for you. Rather, you were thrown out into the open field, for on the day you were born you were despised.
>
> Then I passed by and saw you kicking about in your blood, and as you lay there in your blood I said to you, "Live!" (Ezekiel 16:4–6)

The parallel here to the conversion experience is remarkable. We meet God in our uncleanness, our sin, and his word brings life. In the next stage, he passes by and sees us at a time when we are ready for love and claims us as his own.

> I made you grow like a plant of the field. You grew and developed and entered puberty. Your breasts had formed and your hair had grown, yet you were stark naked.
>
> Later I passed by, and when I looked at you and saw that you were old enough for love, I spread the corner of my garment over you and covered

> your naked body. I gave you my solemn
> oath and entered into a covenant with
> you, declares the Sovereign Lord, and
> you became mine. (Ezekiel 16:7–8)

"Mine!" God declares, dramatically sweeping his cloak over our nakedness. This is how, in ancient Israel, a man would pledge his troth and become engaged to a woman of his choosing. His fiancée, in turn, would gather the garment around herself and be clothed in his promise while pledging her own.

If there is a more breathtaking description of the baptism of the Holy Spirit, I have yet to find it.

Up until this point, the Bridegroom has interacted with his betrothed while she was still unclean. This is fascinating, from a theological perspective. Many of us have been taught that conversion to Christianity follows a strict sequence of actions which, in common vernacular, go something like this: "Sorry. Please. Thank you." The idea that God amorously claims and clothes us before we have even repented is staggering.

Although there is precedent. We read in Romans 5:8, *"While we were still sinners, Christ died for us."* And in Deuteronomy 7:6–8, Moses reminds Israel that God did not choose them and rescue them out of Egypt because of any merit, or apology, on their part. The Lord chose them simply because he loved them.

In the next section of Ezekiel 16, God moves into a stage of deeper intimacy with his betrothed, a time of greater refinement and purification. It is now that he begins the tender process of washing his beloved clean of the dried, caked-on blood, gently smoothing oil over her raw wounds and carefully dressing her nakedness:

> I bathed you with water and washed the
> blood from you and put ointments on
> you. I clothed you with an embroidered
> dress and put sandals of fine leather on
> you. I dressed you in fine linen and cov-
> ered you with costly garments. (Ezekiel
> 16:9–10)

There is a stark vulnerability here, as the Bride is again fully exposed, even examined. He could hardly wash us, after all, while fully clothed. This can be likened to that stage in our relationship with God where deeply buried issues are brought to light: past hurts, secret sins, buried shame. At this stage, we are most likely to coin the phrase "God is dealing with me, and I'm going through some stuff." Whether or not we ever really complete this stage, in this life, is another question. Sanctification is an ongoing process.

The Bride is entering a fourth stage now: the adornment. As we read the passage below, imagine the spiritual gifts—the wisdom, acclaim, resources, and God-breathed abilities with which the Lord bedecks his beloved:

> I adorned you with jewelry: I put bracelets on your arms and a necklace around your neck, and I put a ring on your nose, earrings on your ears and a beautiful crown on your head. So you were adorned with gold and silver; your clothes were of fine linen and costly fabric and embroidered cloth. Your food was honey, olive oil and the finest flour. You became very beautiful and rose to be a queen. And your fame spread among the nations on account of your beauty, because the splendor I had given you made your beauty perfect, declares the Sovereign Lord. (Ezekiel 16:11–14)

The Church is made beautiful, and will be made even more lovely than we can now imagine, through the adornment of the Holy Spirit.

This is the ultimate future of the Bride of Christ, but it also describes the unfolding of each and every Christian's present story. As we walk in grace and humility, we become beautiful to behold. The fame of our beauty goes out *"among the nations."* We are noticed, appreciated, affirmed, appointed, and admired. This is a time when the Church, and each one of us in it, may shine in genuine self-effacing glory, humbly ministering out of whatever gifts the Lord has seen fit to place in our hands.

It is also a time of deadly temptation, when the beautiful Bride can turn treacherous and unfaithful. Our beauty becomes a powerful tool for manipulation, and the adorning gifts of the Holy Spirit can become bribes to be offered for the increase of our own adulation.

The princess can so easily become a prostitute.

> But you trusted in your beauty and used your fame to become a prostitute. You lavished your favors on anyone who passed by and your beauty became his. You took some of your garments to make gaudy high places, where you carried on your prostitution. You went to him, and he possessed your beauty. You also took the fine jewelry I gave you, the jewelry made of my gold and silver, and you made for yourself male idols and engaged in prostitution with them. And you took your embroidered clothes to put on them, and you offered my oil and incense before them. Also the food I provided for you—the flour, olive oil and honey I gave you to eat—you offered as fragrant incense before them…
>
> In all your detestable practices and your prostitution you did not remember the days of your youth, when you were naked and bare, kicking about in your blood…
>
> I am filled with fury against you, declares the Sovereign Lord, when you do all these things, acting like a brazen prostitute! (Ezekiel 16:15–19, 22, 30)

When we are most beautiful, we are most in danger. That is the time for increased vigilance.

Jesus will return, remember. May he return to find us, his Bride, claimed, clean, anointed and resplendent, yet utterly heedless of the jewels that scatter on the ground as we rapturously throw ourselves into his arms. They are nothing. He is all.

NEBO, MARDUK, AND CBT

Where Molech, Baal, Ashtoreth, and Astarte would have us bow down before beauty, sex, and eternal youth, other idols have a more highbrow appeal. Nebo, described as the patron saint of scribes,[88] and his father Marduk were the ancient Babylonian gods of knowledge and learning. We bow down to them when we ardently pursue knowledge for financial security, fame, self-esteem, or positions of power.

Knowledge is a good thing and wisdom is to be coveted. Still, secular universities are full of students who pursue knowledge largely for the prestige and position it will give them in the world.

Bible colleges are no less full of those with similar motivations. To pursue even biblical knowledge for the wrong reasons is to worship an ancient idol.

Non-academic types may pursue knowledge in other ways, developing an unhealthy fascination with conspiracy theories, for example—as with the controversy surrounding election results while Trump ran for the presidency in the United States, or the supposed pharmaceutical scandals associated with the COVID-19 pandemic.

Those with religious inclinations might scour the internet for obscure prophetic voices and previously unpublished gospels. Others research UFO sightings, numerology, top-secret investment algorithms, and miracle weight-loss regimes.

We who covet power and control through knowledge may choose to pursue expertise in a subject matter that promises a path to secret, hidden wisdom and offers us keen insights that will give us an edge over others.

Consider, for example, the fields of psychology and counselling.

---

[88] Stephen Bertman, *Handbook to Life in Ancient Mesopotamia* (New York, NY: Oxford University Press, 2003), 121.

In 2017, there was a session at the American Counseling Association Conference & Expo in San Francisco entitled "Wounded Healers: How to support counselors-in-training who have experienced trauma." The session was taught by Allison Pow, a licensed professional counsellor in North Carolina and adjunct professor at both Wake Forest University and the University of North Carolina at Greensboro, alongside Amber Pope, a licensed mental health counsellor and program chair of the clinical mental health counselling program at Hodges University in Fort Myers, Florida.

Referencing their insights in the May 2018 issue of *Counseling Today*, Pow commented, "For a lot of people, past experience draws them into the counseling field, and trauma can play such a pivotal part in someone's life. It's a common thing that we see as supervisors and counselor educators."[89]

Trauma can shape resilient, empathetic, and skilled professionals. However, Pow warns that trauma survivors who pursue a career as therapists may also "unwittingly be using their role as a counselor to work through their own unprocessed material or to recapitulate an unhealthy power dynamic to feel that they're in control. Control is often something that people seek after going through trauma..."[90]

The association between having childhood adversity and choosing a vocation in the social work and mental health professions is a phenomenon first articulated by Jung's "wounded healer" archetype, to which Pow alluded.

Is this such a bad thing? It can be.

Psychology and counselling offer real possibilities for the practice of manipulation. Even inarguably helpful cognitive behavioural therapy (CBT) practices, which aim to alter behaviour by altering the thought patterns behind the behaviour, can be used opportunistically to influence those around us. For the self-serving, cognitive distortions in others can be intentionally induced. In modern parlance, this is called gaslighting—a form of psychological abuse that aims to exert control over another person by causing them to question their sanity, memories, or perception of reality.

---

[89] "Past Trauma in Counselors-in-Training: Help or Hindrance?" *Counseling Today*. Date of access: December 20, 2024 (https://ctarchive.counseling.org/2018/05/past-trauma-in-counselors-in-training-help-or-hindrance).

[90] Ibid.

Such mind games are more common than one might suppose. Recently, books have been written, both academic and popular, on the topic of what is known as *dark psychology*, the study of the psychological nature of those who prey on others by using manipulation and coercion to get what they want. Those practicing this craft may exhibit one or all of the traits encompassed within what is termed the *dark triad*: narcissism, machiavellianism, and psychopathy, all of which involve selfish, remorseless exploitation of others. The construct was articulated by researchers Delroy L. Paulhus and Kevin M. Williams in the *Journal of Research in Personality* in 2002 as a triad which presents complex, concurrent disorders that clinical psychologists seek to address in their clients.[91]

One would assume that therapists themselves would eschew the practice of dark psychology strategies on their clients, but the issue is not that black and white.

Leon Seltzer, in his book *Paradoxical Strategies in Psychotherapy,* identifies the strategies applicable to the four most common forms of therapy: psychoanalytic, behavioural, Gestalt, and systems approaches.[92] In some cases, it would seem that therapeutic manipulation is justifiable.

In a 2013 post to *Psychology Today*, Seltzer wrote that virtually every major school of therapy includes a

> surprising variety of indirect, noncom-
> monsensical techniques that might be
> designated paradoxical… some thera-
> pists hesitated to employ such unorth-
> odox methods for fear they might be
> misunderstood as manipulative. But I
> came to believe (as I continue to now)
> that if such devices can assist clients
> in achieving therapeutic goals, then, if
> anything, it would be almost unethical

---

[91] "Dark Triad," *Psychology Today*. Date of access: April 2021 (https://www.psychologytoday.com/ca/basics/dark-triad).

[92] Leon F. Seltzer, *Paradoxical Strategies in Psychotherapy: A Comprehensive Overview and Guidebook* (New York, NY: John Wiley & Sons, 1986).

> *not* to employ them—particularly when
> nothing else has succeeded in bringing
> about the desired change.[93]

Do altruistic motives suffice? Can mental health ends justify manipulative means? The therapeutic landscape is, it seems, coloured with shades of muted grey.

A therapist-patient relationship, just like an attorney-client relationship, is fiduciary in nature—that is, the therapist is ethically responsible for the mental well-being of his or her client and must prioritize that above all else. There are strict ethical codes set forth by, for example, the American Counseling Association, meant to protect clients from any harmful therapeutic methodologies.[94]

It is unlikely that a licence to practice would be granted to a therapist who exhibits clearly self-serving motivation, or who manifests intent to cause harm to a client.

However, therapists, albeit professional, are as broken and human as any of us. And their weighty profession can break them even further. Where those who have themselves been victimized seek to turn their painful experience into a means of social contribution by helping and healing others, great good is done. Where, however, trauma survivors are driven into careers as mental healthcare professionals because of a need to feel in control, great harm is done—not just to the client but to the therapist. The former is being used; the latter is feeding an escalating addiction for control. That addiction can be further compounded by the prerequisite need to be privy to the confidential details of another person's life, and counselling can then become a convenient way to get a "fix."

The misuse of counselling, including forms of pastoral or prayer counselling, is not new, nor is it necessarily birthed out of malicious sociopathy. Past hurts and traumas can leave scars that cause a person to feel unsafe,

---

[93] Leon F. Seltzer, "A New Take on Manipulation," *Psychology Today*. April 30, 2013 (https://www.psychologytoday.com/ca/blog/evolution-of-the-self/201304/a-new-take-on-manipulation).

[94] "2014 ACA Code of Ethics," *American Counseling Association*. Date of access: April 2021 (www.counseling.org/docs/default-source/default-document-library/ethics/2014-aca-code-of-ethics.pdf).

fearful, and unwilling to display their innermost emotions or disclose their deepest thoughts.

Trauma survivors search for a safe space in which to process their wounds. For some, that safe space may be created by always being the ones to lead others into vulnerable self-disclosure. As a close friend once told me, "I feel most comfortable when those around me are uncomfortable."

Added to this is the burden of establishing emotional boundaries that a professional counsellor is then expected to maintain, the need to offer neutral responses in the face of intense emotions, and the fact that therapists tend to demonstrate a heightened sensitivity to their environment. Such burdens are not insubstantial, exacerbating any pre-existing mental health issues of the counsellor.

Optimally, mental health professionals would seek counselling themselves when faced with personal crises, compassion fatigue, or burnout, and most do so. But those few for whom their profession, or ministry, is a way for them to maintain control cannot take the risk of making themselves vulnerable to anyone. Worshipping the gods of knowledge imprisons us in an ever-shrinking cell of isolation, pride, and loneliness.

All idols will ultimately disappoint and diminish us. Manipulation and control will only take us so far, until we lose the safety and significance we so desperately seek. The answer to our yearnings is not money, power, sex, or knowledge; it is a person, the living presence of God.

John Stott, in his commentary on the book of Acts, writes that

> idolatry is the attempt either to localize
> God, confining him within limits which
> we impose, whereas he is the Creator
> of the universe; or to domesticate God,
> making him dependent on us, taming
> and taping him, whereas he is the Sus-
> tainer of human life; or to alienate God,
> blaming him for his distance and silence,
> whereas he is the Ruler of Nations, and
> not far from any of us; or to dethrone
> God, demoting him to some image of

our own contrivance or craft, whereas
he is our Father from whom we derive
our being. In brief, all idolatry tries to
minimize the gulf between the Creator
and his creatures, in order to bring him
under our control.[95]

As we learn to feast on God, our palate changes. We *"taste and see that the Lord is good,"* increasing our appetite for communion with him (Psalm 34:8).

Ancient idols whisper, "He will not be enough. He will not meet your needs." The diabolical nature of this lie is twofold, both in content and focus. God will most assuredly provide for our needs, but more importantly he wills himself to be the provision of our deepest needs. Yet all too often our appetite for him is eclipsed by our craving for control.

We are like the Israelites in the desert, disgusted with manna and demanding steak.

GIVE ME MEAT!

The pattern has been set ever since Eden: we crave control, but we progressively lose our freedom as we pursue it. We give in to these cravings and end up sated, sick, and still hungry.

Numbers 11 recounts some of the drama in the desert as Israel grew dissatisfied with the miraculous, monotonous provision of manna. They complained bitterly, wailing,

> If only we had meat to eat! We remember the fish we ate in Egypt at no cost—also the cucumbers, melons, leeks, onions and garlic. But now we have lost our appetite; we never see anything but this manna! (Numbers 11:4–6)

---

[95] John R.W. Stott, *The Message of Acts: To the Ends of the Earth* (Leicester, Netherlands: Inter-Varsity, 1990), 270.

Was it wrong for the Israelites to crave meat in the time of manna? They could hardly pretend that their appetites were satisfied; God sees, and knows, our mortal frame and its weakness.

But rather than come to God in humble supplication for a change in the menu, their cravings led them to complain and fling slanderous accusations against their leader, Moses. They cried angrily, *"Was it because there were no graves in Egypt that you brought us to the desert to die?"* (Exodus 14:11) At issue was not that they had cravings, but that they chose to nurture them.

The Israelites consistently nurtured their own discontent. In the case of their demand for meat, the Lord's judgment upon them was a slaughter so extensive that the place where they camped became known as Graves of Craving, *"Kibroth Hattaavah, because there they buried the people who had yielded to their craving"* (Numbers 11:34, NKJV).

What lesson is here for us, as we are tempted to yield to our craving for control? God invites us to bring our desires to him, until he himself becomes the primary object of our desire.

Tim Keller, in his book on prayer, writes that our resolute pursuit of a relationship with God, through conversation and encounter, is

> the main way we experience deep change—the reordering of our loves. Prayer is how God gives us so many of the unimaginable things he has for us. Indeed, prayer makes it safe for God to give us many of the things we most desire.[96]

What God chooses to give us will always surpass anything we try to seize for ourselves.

Do we want health and strength? Daniel did, too, but he trusted the Lord and refused to be defiled by the rich fare of Babylon. The result was that he grew healthier and comelier than any of the other youths of the court.

---

[96] Tim Keller, *Prayer: Experiencing Awe and Intimacy with God* (New York, NY: Dutton, 2014), 18.

Do we seek fame? Daniel sabotaged his chances at a prestigious career by openly defying royal edicts and worshipping Yahweh where all could see him. Yet God granted him a position of influence second only to the king himself.

Do we dream of being wise and influential? Solomon received all of that and more, because he asked for none of it. Instead he asked God to grant him the skill to serve his people wisely. What Eve and Adam took for themselves, Solomon humbly waited to be given.

Do we look in the mirror and pine for beauty? Sarah was still desirable enough in her late sixties that Pharaoh lusted after her, much to Abram's dismay!

Whatever we grasp for ourselves will rot and decay, like hoarded manna. Whatever God gives will bear fruit forever.

Saul never managed to learn this truth, but the one who came after him, destined to be the next king, saw the tragic life of his predecessor. David was a simple shepherd and knew it. He resolved early on to keep his hands in his own pockets and trust God to give him the kingdom and keep him on the throne. This man, a man after God's own heart, knew the deadly risk of taking up the tools of the trade of the curious arts to forward his own agenda. He had seen with his own eyes what it did to Saul.

And so he resisted the temptation to take matters into his own hands—not always successfully, and at times escaping only by the skin of his teeth. But he did so with the kind of humility and integrity to which every leader should aspire.

David was far from perfect. Both before and after his coronation, he would give in to his indisputably strong cravings. While on the run from Saul, he would write poems full of outraged cries for violent vengeance. As an aging king in the grip of a midlife crisis, he would manipulate and murder in his lust for a bathing beauty on a rooftop.

These were times when he would falter, yet David's determination to trust God rather than take matters into his own hands would manifest throughout his tumultuous life.

What was his secret? He would not pretend to have no base desires but would deliberately, habitually cultivate a greater desire and a higher love:

One thing I ask from the Lord, this only do I seek: that I may dwell in the house of the Lord all the days of my life, to gaze on the beauty of the Lord and to seek him in his temple...

My heart says of you, "Seek his face!" Your face, Lord, I will seek. (Psalm 27:4, 8)

SIX
AFTER GOD'S OWN HEART

WE CANNOT KNOW David through historical narrative alone; he was a complex bundle of ambitions, impulses, and unrealistically noble ideals. In the historical accounts of his life, from 1 Samuel through to 2 Kings, his character can be cast as ambitious, brash, and politically cunning. We can attribute to him fear, weakness, or even artfully contrived innocence in those passages that depict him fleeing or refusing to assert himself before Saul. His ego was trigger-happy, for he was ready to kill Nabal for a slur. He lied to a priest and lived a lie among the Philistines. His remorse over the deaths of Saul, Jonathan, and Abner could have been sheer opportunism, seeking to secure the adulation of the people for his largesse.

How can we know the real David? Admittedly, the biblical narrative itself holds a degree of ambiguity regarding his motives. In his book on political power, Moshe Halbertal writes, "David's real motives are never nakedly revealed... One explanation could be that his intentions are hidden by political craft. Another could be that his motives are genuinely multiple and mixed."[97]

Who was David, really? As any musician will tell you, to know the artist you must look at the art. To see his heart, to know in what way he was a man after God's own heart, he must sing to us.

In the Psalms, we glimpse the true David, the one who is only hinted at in the historical books. We see beneath his actions to his heart, where there is no attempt at duplicity. David is raw, exposed, and embarrassingly needy. Reading Psalm 139 alone convinces us of his sincerity and shows us a man who was painfully aware of his faults and made little attempt to disguise them, because he knew that, with God, there was no point in doing so.

---

[97] Moshe Halbertal, *The Beginning of Politics: Power in the Biblical Book of Samuel* (Princeton, NJ: Princeton University Press, 2019), 59.

You have searched me, Lord, and you know me. You know when I sit and when I rise; you perceive my thoughts from afar. You discern my going out and my lying down; you are familiar with all my ways. Before a word is on my tongue you, Lord, know it completely...

Where can I go from your Spirit? Where can I flee from your presence?

...Search me, God, and know my heart; test me and know my anxious thoughts. See if there is any offensive way in me, and lead me in the way everlasting. (Psalm 139:1–4, 7, 23–24)

Reading the Psalms, we know that David was hardly given to emotional restraint or repression. The lyrics are full of heartfelt explosions of grief, anger, pain, and desperation, as well as love.

David's brand of guileless disclosure of strong emotion would have appealed to Saul; he, too, was a man of strong passions. Whereas Saul used those passions, however, to intimidate others and complain against the Lord, David directed his emotions, even the negative ones, upward.

This would be the pattern of David's life. He would one day sing out, *"Awake, Lord! Why do you sleep? Rouse yourself! Do not reject us forever. Why do you hide your face and forget our misery and oppression?"* (Psalm 44:23–24) And this would not be counted as a sin against God. What made it acceptable? How did it differ from the words of Job, the ones that warranted the Lord's rebuke? David was not pronouncing a bitter, critical accusation *against* God. Instead, in his anguish, he was crying out *to* God.

In the Psalms, David gives vent to the emotional turmoil in his heart and directs it to the only one who can comfort him. He would never hide his feelings from God, and neither should we. Indeed, it is quite impossible in the light of God's omniscience. God wants us to come to him in every emotional state and allow even our distress and pain to drive us into his arms.

Where Saul was a passive complainer and a bully, David was an active, decisive pursuer of intimacy with God. We can be sure then that David felt everything deeply, even as a boy. This would have been very attractive, even to a morose, despondent king with mental health challenges.

At least at first.

FIVE SMOOTH STONES

We have already described the David and Goliath story from the perspective of King Saul. The king was incensed at this uppity adolescent who smelled like sheep. He would always suspect David's motives, convinced that the boy was at least as ambitious and conniving as he was himself.

In reality, David was an oblivious teenager. He didn't pause to think of how ridiculous and offensive he sounded, demanding his older brothers, *"Who is this uncircumcised Philistine that he should defy the armies of the living God?"* (1 Samuel 17:26) Their eyes wide in disbelief, they might have responded, "And who the heck do you think *you* are?"

David barely seemed to be bothered by their resentment. He took no offence; as one who did not practice manipulation—like the intimidation of their mockery—he himself was tremendously difficult to manipulate, and therefore less likely to become defensive. He simply focused on the task at hand.

When David offered to take Goliath on, it was not with cheeky bravado. Saul would have been taken aback by how David spoke, neither boastfully nor with false humility, of his own courageous deeds while at the same time openly acknowledging his utter dependence upon God.

David told Saul, *"Your servant has killed both the lion and the bear; this uncircumcised Philistine will be like one of them, because he has defied the armies of the living God"* (1 Samuel 17:36). And then he revealed his heart, the source of his courage: *"The Lord who rescued me from the paw of the lion and the paw of the bear will rescue me from the hand of this Philistine"* (1 Samuel 17:37).

In other words, "I know I am brave, Your Majesty. But my bravery is not the point. It is God who will defeat this man, not me."

David guilelessly but politely declined Saul's armour, saying that he *"was not used to them"* (1 Samuel 17:39). To refuse such an honour would have offended Saul, but even the helmet—which would have fit, even if the rest did not—was taken off.

Then David walked out of the astonished king's presence to go down to a nearby stream in search of five smooth stones. The soldiers nearby would have watched, amused, at the ignorant youth whom they were sure was about to die.

Goliath was not amused. In fact, he was enraged. Sticks and stones? Where were the armed champions? This arrogant child was not even worth the effort of killing! But it was not with arrogant bravado that David now ran at him, but with faith in the one whose battle it truly was.

> You come against me with sword and spear and javelin, but I come against you *in the name of the Lord Almighty*, the God of the armies of Israel, whom you have defied. This day *the Lord* will deliver you into my hands, and I'll strike you down and cut off your head. This very day I will give the carcasses of the Philistine army to the birds and the wild animals, and the whole world will know that there is a God in Israel. All those gathered here will know that it is not by sword or spear that the Lord saves; *for the battle is the Lord's*, and he will give all of you into our hands. (1 Samuel 17:45–47; my emphasis)

Throughout David's life, he refused to be the hero of any story. He lived according to the songs he later wrote: *"Ascribe to the Lord, you heavenly beings, ascribe to the Lord glory and strength. Ascribe to the Lord the glory due his name..."* (Psalm 29:1–2).

"Not to me is the glory due," David consistently said. "It is God's alone. I am neither the hero nor the victim; in fact, the story is not even about me."

One would expect a more triumphal posture, considering what he was about to do. A confident shout was surely warranted, something like *"I can do all this through him who gives me strength"* (Philippians 4:13). This popular verse, however, is frequently misinterpreted. The central clause in the verse is not on us, the ones who are doing *all things*, but on Christ, the one who *strengthens*. A more literal translation of the Greek would read, "In him, in all, strengthening me, I am strong."

We are not the hero. God is. David understood this intuitively. His refusal to seek recognition as a hero would be a key strategy for resisting the pull of power, as in the years to come he would go on to surrender—not in meek defeat, but in firm faith—his rights, his position, his wife, his dreams, and eventually even his kingdom to the God he had come to know and love. Such surrender is the antithesis of manipulation and control, for it seeks not to be served but to serve.

David's heart, a reflection of God's own, continually prioritized the other, sacrificing himself for the sake of those under his care.

This is the kind of man David was. This was the kind of king he would become.

But it would take another fifteen years for the coronation to take place.

KEEPING MY ENEMY CLOSE

When Goliath fell, sheer chaos ensued. It was hard for Saul to even think straight; the Philistines, seeing their hero dead, turned and ran for the hills while the men of Israel and Judah pursued, shouting wildly in triumph. The Philistines were routed that day, their dead strewn along the Shaaraim road, their camp plundered. We can assume that David was part of the battle, and then Abner, the commander of Saul's troops, brought the boy back to Saul with the dripping head of his foe still hanging from his bloody hand.

Saul was stuck. Staring down in stupefied silence at the head of Goliath, he knew he had no choice but to join in the cheering. Moreover, he had publicly promised his daughter's hand in marriage to the man who defeated the Philistine giant.

Gnashing his teeth, Saul resolved to keep David close, as one would keep an enemy close in order to keep a careful watch.

David never went home again. Suddenly his whole world changed. For the next seven years, he would serve as both soldier and bard. He continued to be on call to soothe the king with music as needed, but he also undertook military missions. Each one was more successful than the last and Saul was forced to promote him, seeking as always the approval and support of his subjects. The troops and the officers were pleased with David. The women danced and wrote songs about David. Jonathan doted on David!

David, David, David… it was all too much for Saul. Such fame, such popularity, and the boy was still humble, content to come and play his lyre in the chamber of the king. It was infuriating.

Twice, listening to the gentle strumming, Saul lost control and in a jealous rage flung his spear at David, seeking to pin him to the wall. Twice, David escaped. Subject and king eyed one another from an entirely new perspective that day.

When seeing David every day became intolerable, Saul sent him away to take command of a thousand men. Out of sight, out of mind?

No such luck. News of David's unbroken chain of victories was sheer torment to the king. It was not only that David had military success, but that his character supported such success. In 1 Samuel 18:14, we read, *"In everything he did he had great success."* Another translation says that in everything David *"prospered"* (AMP). The Hebrew word used here is *maśkîl*, a cognate of a word which describes wisdom, prudence, and attentiveness. David's success did not go to his head. He remained humble, always learning. For Saul, this was maddeningly mature behaviour from someone so much younger than himself.

The day came when the king decided to keep his promise to give one of his daughters in marriage to the killer of Goliath. He first offered Merab, then perversely gave her to another man instead. When it was told to Saul that his daughter Michal was in love with David, he saw an opportunity to get rid of the young man. He set the bride price at one hundred Philistine foreskins and hoped David would die in the attempt.

Instead his future son-in-law came back with a double portion of these grisly trophies in a sack.

Feeling his power slip away was unbearable and Saul commanded his son Jonathan to murder David, but Jonathan managed to talk his father down. The king then glibly swore to his son that he would not harm David.

Although this was a blatant lie, David seemed almost eager to believe it and returned to his place at Saul's side, lyre in hand. Was it naiveté that brought David back, or was it that he refused to give up hope or stop longing for a restored relationship? He was, after all, a man after God's own heart.

A man whose heart was about to be broken.

UNDER THE NEW MOON

As Saul's violent outbursts became more severe, David's life was in constant danger. A night came when David's wife Michal decided that enough was enough. David must flee or die. He climbed stealthily out the bedroom window and ran to Samuel.

Three times Saul sent soldiers to kill David, but each time, upon encountering Samuel and his band of prophets, they fell under the Spirit of the Lord and themselves began to prophesy. And when Saul himself went, the same happened to him, but for him it brought only humiliation, as he stripped himself naked and lay on the ground in front of the prophet Samuel for twenty-four hours, mumbling incoherently.

Returning home in a foul mood, Saul encountered his son Jonathan, who refused to disclose the whereabouts of his fugitive friend. Saul was incensed and shouted,

> You son of a perverse and rebellious woman! Don't I know that you have sided with the son of Jesse to your own shame and to the shame of the mother who bore you? As long as the son of Jesse lives on this earth, neither you nor your kingdom will be established. (1 Samuel 20:30–31)

Of course, Saul was right, and perhaps some prophetic unction was in these wrathful words he barked out. Father and son glared at one another in mutual incomprehension.

How could you not care about being the next king? Saul might have asked his son.

As for Jonathan, he probably thought, *How could anyone not want David to be the next king?*

Despite the miserable role model Saul had been, Jonathan was not interested in the power and control his father had worked so hard to maintain.

Later that night, Jonathan and David met secretly in the shadow of a new moon. There was no hope and Jonathan finally admitted to David that the time had come to say goodbye. These two friends were in anguish at having to part. They swore an oath of friendship that would bind not just them but their offspring, and a heartbroken David disappeared into the dark.

THE WISDOM OF FOOLISHNESS

To the secular eye, David was a fool. He had every possible advantage and opportunity to take the throne, yet he adamantly refused to do so. He was wildly popular with the people, admired by the army, adored by the king's son, and fully endorsed by the prophet and judge responsible for anointing and appointing kings in Israel.

So why hesitate? Throughout the story, we see the stark contrast between the avarice and manipulative methods of Saul and the apparent naïve innocence of David.

But was he truly innocent? Being innocent is to be ignorant of evil and blind to its temptation, a condition no one can lay claim to since the fall. Once lost, we can never restore innocence. We can, however, seek purity. Purity is that which, though innocence be lost, refuses either to give in to evil or even pay much attention to it. It is a kind of single-mindedness which focuses upon *"whatever is true, whatever is noble, whatever is right, whatever is pure, whatever is lovely, whatever is admirable… excellent or praiseworthy"* (Philippians 4:8). Purity is that peculiar wisdom that allows some to walk blithely through great danger, following their hopes and dreams. It is the wisdom of starstruck lovers and fools.

It is the wisdom of the Magi.

In the beginning of the gospels we read of King Herod, a great and crafty manipulator not unlike Saul. When rumours of wise men seeking a newborn king reached him, he smelled danger and called for the chief priests. They told him that the ancient prophecies described Bethlehem as the place where the Messiah would be born, so Herod devised a plan to thwart this contender for his throne. Sending for the Magi, he asked them to reveal the exact time the star had appeared so he could estimate the age of the child he sought to kill. Then he slyly directed them to Bethlehem, saying, *"Go and search carefully for the child. As soon as you find him, report to me, so that I too may go and worship him"* (Matthew 2:7–8).

The picture is one of skilled diplomacy, veiling a malicious smirk.

The Magi didn't seem to suspect anything. How could they have been so easily taken in by Herod's duplicity? If they were so wise, where was their discernment? The Magi were indeed wise men chosen by God for a momentous and prophetic role in heralding the birth of Jesus, but their wisdom was not the wisdom of this world. They were not streetwise manipulators who could sense a con. Their wisdom, and their protection, lay in their single-minded purity; undistracted by evil, their gazes turned ever upwards to be guided by a star. Single-minded in their focus, Herod's scheme posed little threat.

True godly wisdom often comes with a trusting simplicity. Far from making us susceptible to victimization by those who would take advantage, such purity actually serves as protection. It shields us, as it did the Magi, because those who place a childlike trust in God are more likely to respond to his direction without hesitation, doubt, or cynicism. God uses the naïve because they are teachable, malleable, and sensitive to his guiding hand.

The Magi heeded dreams, visions, and guiding stars. Still following that star, they left Herod and found the Christ-child. They may have fully intended to report back the baby's exact whereabouts to Herod. Instead, warned by another divine dream, they returned to their country by another route (Matthew 2:1–12).

This is wisdom.

David instinctively sought to live by this kind of wisdom, and it pleased God that he chose to trust him rather than take the kingdom in his own strength.

The next seven years of David's life were spent on the run. He was urged by his men again and again to take the kingship by force, by violence, in vengeance and in meanness, and he had more than one opportunity to do so.

Instead he fixed his gaze upon some internal star, clinging to the God who was able to fulfill his promises and refusing to take matters into his own hands. Better to abide in a cave in the desert with integrity, he would insist, than to sit in a palace on a stolen throne.

His journey began as a hunted criminal would take him to the brink of disaster more than once, and even over the edge. Rather than scramble to save himself, he proved himself to be the king Samuel knew him to be. David's focus was to care for those around him, including those whose lives were endangered because of his own actions.

It did not always end well. There were times when he probably did not want to come out of the cave at all.

IN THE CAVE OF ADULLAM

David started his exile alone. He fled to the nearest priestly city, Nob, where he met with the priest Ahimelech, who was understandably alarmed.

"What are you doing here?" he asked.

David lied, explaining that he was on a secret mission for Saul and that his men were waiting to rendezvous with him elsewhere. It was not a proud moment, and one that David would bitterly regret,

Then he asked for food, for by now he was famished. Ahimelech offered him the only food on hand, the holy showbread, dedicated to the Lord and usually only available to priests for consumption (Leviticus 24:5–9). It was fresh, having just replaced the old (1 Samuel 21:6), implying that this was the Sabbath.

"Are there any weapons here?" David then asked.

Ahimelech gave him the sword of Goliath, which had been wrapped and reverently stored behind the ephod. Holding it aloft, David couldn't fail to be struck by the poetic irony. He, who had been commander of a thousand men under King Saul, had come full circle, holding in his hand the first sword he had ever owned, the weapon that had been won with a pebble in a sling.

He nodded slowly. "There is none like it…"

David left, not realizing that he had been recognized by Saul's chief shepherd, Doeg the Edomite. Saul's subsequent slaughter of the priests of Nob—along with their wives, children, and livestock—was the tragic consequence.

Unaware of what happened, David fled to the Philistines. Why not? Perhaps the enemy of his enemy would be his friend. But the king of Gath, Achish, was sceptical of him. David, realizing his danger, feigned madness—not difficult to do, having spent so much time with a mad king—and escaped by convincing Achish that he was no threat.

Later David would sing about this episode, recounting his escape: *"The Lord is close to the brokenhearted and saves those who are crushed in spirit. The righteous person may have many troubles, but the Lord delivers him from them all"* (Psalm 34:18–19).

This was when David decided to return to Judah and take refuge in a cave in the hills he knew so well from his years as a carefree shepherd boy.

In the cave of Adullam, David faced his fears head-on. All his bridges had been burned and both Saul and the Philistines wanted him dead. Saul had suffered under a delusion of paranoia, but David's persecution was real. Yet his response was radically different from that of the mad king. He did not rant, accuse, or take steps to avenge himself. He cried out to God and deliberately placed his trust in the hands of the only One who could save him, asking God to right this terrible wrong. One day David would write of this time and put it to music:

> Be merciful to me, my God, for my enemies are in hot pursuit; all day long they press their attack. My adversaries pursue me all day long; in their pride many are attacking me.
>
> When I am afraid, I put my trust in you. In God, whose word I praise—in God I trust and am not afraid. What can mere mortals do to me?
>
> All day long they twist my words; all their schemes are for my ruin. They

conspire, they lurk, they watch my steps, hoping to take my life. Because of their wickedness do not let them escape…

…in God I trust and am not afraid. What can man do to me? (Psalm 56:1–7, 11)

In another psalm that references this difficult time, David voiced a lament: *"Look and see, there is no one at my right hand; no one is concerned for me. I have no refuge; no one cares for my life"* (Psalm 142:4). This is exactly what Saul had once said to his men, but those words had been spoken to manipulate with guilt and intimidate his soldiers into obeying him. David's lament, in contrast, was expressed not to men but to God. He went on: *"'You are my refuge, my portion in the land of the living.' Listen to my cry, for I am in desperate need; rescue me from those who pursue me…"* (Psalm 142:5–6). Those seeking power use even their grief to manipulate others; those surrendered to God pour out their pain to him and ask for mercy.

David's next actions were also telling. Where Saul, in his need for power and control, moved from fear to blame, then rebellion and aggression, David's heart turned to the well-being of others. In surrendering himself to God, he became obsessed not with protecting himself but protecting others.

When David's father, mother, and other family members—their lives also at risk—joined him in the cave, he approached the king of Moab, a distant kinsman, to shelter them. By now, news of his situation had spread far and wide and he found himself joined by others, including the prophet Gad, an unlikely crew of those who were *"in distress or in debt or discontented"* (1 Samuel 22:2).

From their ranks would emerge those who one day became the *"mighty warriors"* of the future monarch (1 Chronicles 11:10). But at this moment they were just a ragtag company of misfits.

FOUR HUNDRED GRUMPY MEN

The group of malcontents would have looked far from promising, grumbling and unarmed, except perhaps for an assortment of spears, clubs, and farming tools.

Yet David saw what could be, what would be, so long as God was with him. This would be his army. Their loyalty and love were forged over bivouac fires at night, weary marches by day, fierce battles, and narrow escapes. David trained these men to be fighters, organizing them into undercover squadrons to guard the frontier of Judah against Amalekite and Philistine raiders intent on stealing sheep and burning crops. They formed a wall of defence in the south and stood guard *"night and day"* (1 Samuel 25:16) against the enemies of the very people from whom they were outcast—and they did so secretly, anonymously, faithfully, and thanklessly.

David may have been persecuted as a fugitive, but he was determined to care for his homeland, crown or no crown.

However, his confidence was about to receive a massive blow. News hadn't yet reached him of the murder of the priests at Nob.

At the mouth of the cave, a pale and dishevelled man appeared, shaking with exhaustion and trauma. He was Abiathar, son of Ahimelek and the sole survivor of Nob. He approached David, trembling. David's own heart faltered as he listened, stunned and mute, as the priest described the bloodbath the city suffered at the hands of Saul's men.

Afterward there would have been stone-cold silence among the men gathered there, save for a horrified gasp at the news that God's priests had been murdered by their own king.

The men looked to David, grim and ready for whatever command their renegade leader might issue. These men had been ruled by Saul, remember. They were used to an angry, vengeful leader who was quick to defend himself, blame others, and take swift, brutal action.

David's next words, however quietly spoken, would echo like thunder in the still expectancy of that moment.

"This is my fault."

David took full responsibility for the death of the priests and their families:

> That day, when Doeg the Edomite was
> there, I knew he would be sure to tell
> Saul. I am responsible for the death of
> your whole family. Stay with me; don't
> be afraid. The man who wants to kill you

is trying to kill me too. You will be safe
with me. (1 Samuel 22:22–23).

Were the men shocked by this public confession? Likely, yes. But that day David won the hearts of his mighty warriors and established a pattern that would last for the rest of his life.

He would not avoid facing the consequences of his actions, nor would he refuse to acknowledge his sins, although his resolve to be an honest and transparent leader would be sorely tested and David would have more than one occasion to repent and renew this inner vow.

It turned out that Abiathar had escaped Nob with the ephod, the linen pouch and two stones by which the will of God could be made known (1 Samuel 23:6). Perhaps David looked at those two small stones and thought back to the five small stones he had gathered for his battle against Goliath.

We know that David had already established a habit of inquiring of the Lord in this way and had done so through Ahimelek more than once (1 Samuel 22:15). He now continued that practice with Ahimelek's son, in every circumstance seeking God's direction, which Saul had failed to do. Saul's anxiety, remember, had led him to bark at a priest when he felt control of his troops slipping away (1 Samuel 14:19). David, in contrast, would not take a single step without consulting the priest and waiting on the Lord.

Not long after, he did just this. He then gave his fledgling army of motley recruits their first assignment. Having received direction using the ephod, David gave the command to attack a group of Philistines encamped around the Judean town of Keilah, where they had been looting.

David's men, green and untested, were taken aback. Was this a joke? The situation in Judah was bad enough for them. How much worse would it get if they came up against these Philistines?

David heard their concern. Rather than rebuke them for not instantly obeying, he had Abiathar consult the Ephod again, just to be sure. The answer from God was the same, as David had known it would be. It was his compassion for these untried soldiers that had led him to assuage their fears. He was confident the battle would be won, but he wanted them to have the same confidence. David was not interested in *controlling* his men but *encouraging* them.

The battle was won and the men exalted in their first victory.

Before there was time to celebrate, however, they learned that Saul was on his way. There was no time to panic and nowhere to run. This was it. Even now, David held them steady, again taking the time to call for the priest. The men must have been holding their breath as each question was put to the ephod.

"Will Saul come down?"

Yes.

"Will the people of Keilah surrender us to him?"

Yes.

"Right. Let's get out of here!"

It may be that David's men grumbled at the precious minutes wasted in consulting the Lord, but they would have to get used to the idea of serving a commander who had no intention of taking command until he received instructions from the Lord. God would be in charge.

F.B. Meyer, in his book, *David: Shepherd, Psalmist, King,* puts it eloquently:

> This was the holy practice of [David's] life; to wait on God, quelling the fever of his soul, and compelling the crowd of impetuous thoughts to be in abeyance until time had been given for the clear disclosure of the divine purpose and plan. Like a child that dares not take one step alone, like a traveller who is in a strange country who is utterly dependant upon his guide, so David lifted up his soul for the supreme direction which God only can give...[98]

David would have great need of this inner discipline, having the ability to pause, reflect, and own his thoughts before taking action. He learned not

---

[98] F.B. Meyer, *David: Shepherd, Psalmist, King* (Fort Washington, PA: CLC Publications, 2013), 12.

only to pause and inquire of the Lord through priests and prophets but to recognize the still, small voice of God directing him in critical moments.

The future king, determined not to seize the throne, would face many temptations to humiliate and usurp the man who stood in his way. Each time, he allowed Saul to escape—but really it was David who was escaping.

THE ROCK OF ESCAPE

Over the next eight years of roaming, David continued to amass friends and supporters from the countryside, including some of the elders of Judah (1 Samuel 30:26–31). Somewhere along the way, he picked up another two hundred men. He fled to the desert south of Hebron, where the wilderness of Ziph and Maon afforded more capacious strongholds and hiding places for a grassroots army of six hundred.

Here he had one last stealthy meeting with Jonathan, who assured his fugitive friend that Saul would never find him and that he, David, was destined to be king. The depth of selfless affection shown between these friends is remarkable, for Jonathan was forfeiting the kingship.

As a friend, Jonathan was peerless, with a love David would later declare to be *"wonderful, more wonderful than that of women"* (2 Samuel 1:26). Jonathan was more than a brother. Like David, Jonathan refused to claim his rights, refused to take even that which his own father was trying to thrust upon him. Instead he humbly surrendered himself to the future God had ordained. His highest hope was to serve one day at David's side: *"You will be king over Israel, and I will be second to you"* (1 Samuel 23:17)

Yet even in his commitment to David, Jonathan remained a good and loyal son to a harsh and unreasonable father. In fact, he would die in battle, fighting bravely for a mad king.

After this meeting in the lonely wilderness, David and Jonathan would never see each other again.

Saul, between skirmishes with the Philistines, continued to hunt for his elusive son-in-law, bringing with him a retinue of three thousand men. He scoured the desert, going from rock to rock, cave to cave, tireless in his hatred. There was murder in Saul's heart and David's men knew this. It is why they were so bewildered when David continued to spare the king's life.

At one point, Saul entered a dark cave to relieve himself, not realizing that David and his men were hidden in its recesses. We can imagine this moment of unbearable tension as David's men saw Saul squatting in the dark and turned to one another in elated incredulity. Surely this is the Lord's doing, putting Saul into David's hands!

Instead David sternly restrained them.

Goaded by the undeniable irony of the encounter, however, he crept forward in the dark and managed to cut off a piece of Saul's robe without the king noticing.

Afterward, we are told, David was conscience-stricken. He waited until Saul had left the cave and then followed him, making his presence known. He called out and Saul looked behind him. David bowed with his face to the ground, holding aloft the piece of fabric from Saul's robe, and cried out,

> Why do you listen when men say, "David is bent on harming you"? This day you have seen with your own eyes how the Lord delivered you into my hands in the cave. Some urged me to kill you, but I spared you; I said, "I will not lay my hand on my lord, because he is the Lord's anointed." See, my father, look at this piece of your robe in my hand! I cut off the corner of your robe but did not kill you. See that there is nothing in my hand to indicate that I am guilty of wrongdoing or rebellion. I have not wronged you, but you are hunting me down to take my life. May the Lord judge between you and me. And may the Lord avenge the wrongs you have done to me, but my hand will not touch you. As the old saying goes, "From evil-doers come evil deeds," so my hand will not touch you. (1 Samuel 24:9–13)

David was not seeking to humiliate his enemy, although there would have been ample justification to do so. Instead he generously offered Saul an out by implying that Saul had been deceived by listening to others. David even called him *"my father."*

These were not merely clever ploys on David's part. He was showing genuine respect, intentionally honouring a king whose own men struggled to respect him.

When David referred to himself as insignificant—*"A dead dog? A flea?"* (1 Samuel 24:14)—Saul began to weep. Acknowledging David's righteousness, Saul asked him to swear not to wipe out the royal family when he inherited the throne. David swore this oath and they parted ways.

But David stayed where he was, safe in the desert, with no thought of returning home to Gibeah. He and his men knew they could not count on King Saul; they were on their own.

During this time, David worked to keep his men, and even their families, housed and fed. He took upon himself the job of guarding Judah's southern borders from the Philistines. At one point, he sent ten men to travel to Carmel and meet with a wealthy man there named Nabal. Not only did Nabal withhold payment and food, but he actively insulted David and his men.

When David learned of this insult, he completely lost his temper and instructed his men to take up arms and march on Carmel.

Nabal's wife Abigail heard of the angry men en route and hurried out to meet them with provisions and profuse apologies. In doing so, without her wicked husband's knowledge or approval, she saved the lives of her entire household. She was forthright with David:

> When the Lord has fulfilled for my lord every good thing he promised concerning him and has appointed him ruler over Israel, my lord will not have on his conscience the staggering burden of needless bloodshed or of having avenged himself. (1 Samuel 25:30–31)

At hearing these words, David was brought to his senses. Was he no better than Saul? How could he have thought to avenge himself, after everything that God had taught him?

Chastened and grateful, David received the food and took his men back into the desert, displaying the humility that would be the trademark of his future rule.

The next day, Nabal found out what had transpired behind his back, but he was in a drunken stupor and died from what might have been a strike. Ever the noble knight, David heard of his death and grew concerned for the well-being of the man's widow.

Abigail became David's wife, alongside Ahinoam of Jezreel.

One wonders whether the news of this second marriage is what then impelled Saul to give his daughter Michal, David's first wife, to another man. It was a low blow, and one which David would one day set right.

Now, however, was not the time.

Saul was back on his trail, in hot pursuit of David, this time in the valley below Hachilah. David's scouts sent word and David ventured out with one of his mighty men, Abishai. They discovered Saul sleeping in a trench, his spear stuck in the ground beside his head and a jug of water by his side; his soldiers were snoring around him.

Abishai urged David to let him strike the dozy king. Refusing once again to take advantage of the situation, David deferred to the Lord:

> [T]he Lord himself will strike him, or his time will come and he will die, or he will go into battle and perish. But the Lord forbid that I should lay a hand on the Lord's anointed. (1 Samuel 26:10–11)

He did, however, take the spear and the jug.

Ascending the opposite hill, he called out loudly to the commander of Saul's troops, a man named Abner. Notably, his words were not designed to humiliate Saul. Instead he accused Abner of being negligent and faithless in failing to guard his king.

Saul recognized David's voice and saw his own spear in his young rival's hand. It was a moment heavy with symbolism, for this was the spear with which Saul, in jealous fits of rage, had hurled again and again in his attempts to kill David. Saul would no doubt have remembered the music, the soothing voice, and the shattered lyre against the stone wall.

We cannot assume, given the events that follow, that Saul came to his senses. But as one young soldier ran to take the spear from David and return it to the owner, Saul gathered what was left of his dignity and returned home. This time he offered no false assurances, nor did he implore David to come back with him. They remained enemies.

David knew he could not roam the desert forever, dodging from cave to cave with six hundred men to feed. He needed something more secure for them.

And so David became a double agent for the Philistines.

UNDERCOVER AT ZIKLAG

"This should have been unlocked an hour ago!" The man sounded irritated as he shifted his briefcase from one hand to the other.

Meanwhile, I searched for the right key. I had been awake for thirty-two hours, and brain fog was making it difficult to sort through the weighty mass of seventeen keys hanging from my security belt. These night shifts were brutal.

I finally found the right key and opened the dark classroom. The man stormed inside and flicked on the switch with an impatient gesture.

"About time," he muttered. "You people have no idea how important it is to be punctual."

I froze. For real? "You people"? As in, "you nameless, uneducated, insignificant, unappreciated, underslept, overworked and underpaid people"?

Well, you are most welcome, I wanted to say sarcastically.

I bit my tongue instead, since I needed this job.

Still, I could not resist a parting shot as I turned to walk away. "See you in class, professor!"

Startled, he spun around and narrowed his eyes. To his credit, he had the grace to look chagrined when he recognized me as one of his top graduate students. He gave a weak smile and an even weaker wave of his hand, but he could not quite bring himself to say anything. There was no "Thank you," no "Sorry."

That's okay, *I thought to myself.* I'm not doing this for you anyway.

***

I never imagined myself working night shifts, much less as a security guard, but during the economic crash of 2008 my husband lost his job and my part-time work as a worship director wasn't enough to live on. At the same time, our daughter was eager to launch into university and we had already agreed to help with tuition. Unable to bear the thought of her being disappointed, I sought the Lord earnestly about our financial situation.

One morning, as I was praying and doing my Bible reading in the book of Ruth, I was struck by Naomi's love for her daughter-in-law, which resonated with my own heart. I read—and wrote down—Naomi's reassuring words in Ruth 3:1*: "My daughter, shall I not seek security for you, that it may be well with you?"* (NKJV)

Shortly after that, my phone rang. It was my sister-in-law, who worked for the university my daughter hoped to attend. She knew I had been looking for some way to secure an education there for my daughter, and this university gave full tuition benefits for full-time employees and their dependents.

"Hey," she said. "Would you be willing to do *anything* for your daughter?"

"Uh, well, sure, of course," I stammered. Then I paused and asked cautiously, "What exactly do you mean by *anything*?"

When she explained that the security department was the only one currently hiring, I burst out laughing, thinking about Naomi and Ruth.

Here's hoping, I thought wryly, *that it will indeed "be well" with me!*

The next year was a blur. I got used to long hours, endless walking, a dorky uniform, and the death of my ego. I was an artist, a musician, and gifted in ministry. No one cared. "Just get my door unlocked on time please."

My daughter was overwhelmed with gratitude, and then with crushing guilt as she saw my bleary eyes each morning when I arrived home to collapse into bed, hobbling painfully on swollen feet.

By year two, she couldn't stand it any longer and begged me to quit. I refused.

"Well then, why don't you use the benefits too?" she burst out in frustration. "You always wanted to finish your graduate degree!"

I balked. Twelve-hour night shifts, plus essays? Who was she kidding?

"If you won't do it for your own sake, then do it for mine," she argued. "I can't handle this guilt!"

It made a weird kind of sense, and I enrolled. Once I got over sitting in class in full uniform among a bunch of hip postmodern Gen Xers in skinny jeans and flipflops, I was fine. In fact, more than fine. I loved it. Scholarships and grants added motivation, and my best research was done in the guard hut at 3:00 a.m.

The hardest part, sleep deprivation notwithstanding, was the sense of having a dual identity. As a student, I excelled and was respected. As a guard, I was invisible and dismissed. Switching hats was hard, especially since classes often took place while I was on duty. In the middle of parsing a passage of New Testament Koine Greek or debating the ontological argument for the existence of God, my radio might go off; I would need to grab my keys, tighten the laces on my clunky steel-toe boots, and head out. I felt like a middle-aged, nerdy version of Batman—scholar by day, security guard by night.

Who was I, really? I was whoever my loved ones, especially my daughter, needed me to be.

Just like David.

David would have done almost anything for his men, been whoever they needed him to be. He felt responsible to provide for them, even if it meant becoming a double agent.

Travelling westward with his six hundred followers, David presented himself before Achish, king of Gath. This time the monarch received him kindly, convinced beyond doubt that David was genuinely defecting. Not only did he allow David and his men to live in Gath, but he also gifted them the town of Ziklag for a possession.

Breathing a sigh of retrained relief, David helped his men to settle down, even bringing their wives and children to live with them. Once assured that they were safe and provided for, and that their cover was intact, he began to live a double life.

From Ziklag, he carried on an active campaign of warfare against the enemies of Israel under the pretence of raiding against his own countrymen.

Then he gave the plunder to Achish. By day he was the king's mercenary; by night, Israel's unsung hero.

Over the course of the next year, Achish's friendship with David steadily strengthened. So complete was the Philistine king's trust that he appointed David his chief bodyguard.

A day finally came when the multitude of Philistines united their varied forces into one vast army and the troops prepared to march into battle against Israel, with David and his six hundred followers marching in the rear. The air was thick with tension. Were they actually going to be forced to fight against their own people?

It is significant to note that while this was going on, Saul reached the frayed ends of his mental and moral rope. Samuel had passed away by now and was no longer there to hear his appeals. God no longer spoke to Saul, either by prophet or by dream. David and his men had joined forces with the enemy. King Saul was alone in his madness.

This is when he sought out the witch at Endor. The consultation ended badly and Saul came to understand that he and his son were about to die.

Bath in Gath, David and his men were about to be forced to betray Israel, but disaster was averted at the last moment. When the Philistine leaders saw David and his men in the war parade, they balked. Could these Israelites really be trusted to fight against their own kinsmen? Reluctantly, Achish was forced to dismiss David and his band. They headed home to Ziklag in relief… only to discover that their town had been sacked by the Amalekites. Their flocks, herds, property, wives, and children were all gone.

A loud wail of despair burst forth from the men. Their nerves had already been stretched to the breaking point and they railed at David, blaming him for the loss. They were ready to stone him, so intense was their anguish at losing their sons and daughters.

If ever there was a time for David to act quickly, this was it.

We are prompted now to remember the many times when Saul, in similar straits, was willing to do anything to maintain the loyalty of his troops, whether it be threats, bribes, or even taking the priestly knife into his unsanctified hand and killing the sacrifice on the altar rather than wait for Samuel and inquire of the Lord.

Was David tempted to do the same? Would it have been wrong to quickly take charge and rally the men to pursue the Amalekites?

For David, yes.

Despite the urgency of the moment, he steadied his breathing and raised his hand for silence. As the grim-faced men looked on, ready to kill their leader, David called for the ephod. Perhaps even the priest Abiathar was somewhat disconcerted. Was there any need, really, to doubt the will of God in this matter? Wasn't it obvious?

This was still the pattern of David's life: to assume nothing, to consistently allow God to be the one in control, even when the need for action seemed critical.

Perhaps with forced calm, David asked the Lord,

> "Shall I pursue this raiding party? Will I overtake them?"
> "Pursue them," he answered. "You will certainly overtake them and succeed in the rescue." (1 Samuel 30:8)

His features hardened with resolve as he turned to face his men and ordered them to march out and save their families.

Despite the fact that the men had just returned from a three-day march, they lost no time. An hour later, they had reached the Brook Besor, and David realized the men were exhausted and dehydrated. In fact, some were unfit to go on.

Two hundred stayed at the brook while the rest forged ahead.

Along the way, they encountered an Egyptian slave who had been part of the raid on Ziklag. He led them to the Amalekites' encampment—and twenty-four hours later the Amalekites were all dead. David and his men had not only recovered their livestock, possessions, and family, but they took new booty as well.

Returning to the Brook Besor, some of the men griped that the loot should not be distributed among those who had stayed behind. David rebuked this selfish attitude; those who remained behind would not be punished for their weariness.

Once again, David's concern for his men stands in stark contrast with Saul, a leader who felt it necessary to dismember an ox and send out the body parts to bully fighting men into resentful obedience. Not only did David defend and reward the weary soldiers who stayed behind, he made generosity among the ranks *"a statute and ordinance"* (1 Samuel 30:25) for Israel. Paul Abramson remarks, in *David's Politics: Servant, Rebel, King*, that "David is not yet a king, but he has become a law giver."[99] In this, he was acting like the monarch he would one day become, passing laws meant to protect the weak and reflect not only God's justice but his mercy.

Where does such confidence come from? It comes from a heart of compassion.

Years later, when David attained the throne, the people of Israel acknowledged that his authority had not begun with his coronation but had been active in his selfless service to the people even while he was still an outcast. Saul may have been king, they would say, but David was the one really leading them (2 Samuel 5:2).

After joining the two hundred men left by the brook, David sent a portion of the spoils to his key supporters throughout Judah. Taking into account the whole of David's story thus far, we can be sure that these gifts were not intended as manipulative bribes but tokens of gratitude. His men happily embraced their families and David gladly spread the joy with a generous hand.

In the back of his mind, however, he didn't stop wondering how the battle was going between Saul's army and the combined forces of the Philistines. Though tired of the injustice of Saul's persecution, David remained concerned for the well-being of his fellow Israelites, who were vastly outnumbered. Had he been allowed to fight for Israel, his six hundred men might have been invaluable.

Now it was too late.

THE SONG OF THE BOW

Saul's army was wholly routed by the Philistines on Mount Gilboa. Jonathan, faithful to his abusive father, died fighting, as did two of his brothers.

---

[99] Paul R. Abramson, *David's Politics: Servant, Rebel, King* (Lanham, MD: Lexington Books, 2016), 40.

Saul, desperate to be in control right up to the end, chose to die by his own hand, falling on his sword rather than allowing himself to be humiliated by the enemy.

This was a bitter day for Israel. The Philistines moved in to occupy town after town without any resistance as the inhabitants fled.

The next day, the Philistines returned to the battlefield to strip the slain. They shouted exultantly upon recognizing the bodies of Saul and his three sons. Their heads were cut off and their bodies hung from a wall.

Later, brave citizens of Jabesh Gilead snuck in by night to retrieve the bodies and bury them.

When David later learned the news of the battle from a runner who had escaped Saul's camp, his heart lurched. He wept, knowing that his friend Jonathan was dead. All that loss had been so preventable, so unnecessary.

In the throes of grief, the not-quite king passed his second law. The first, at the Brook Besor, had been one of generous love. The second was a command to lament the fall of an evil king whom few would even miss. David was resolved not to take any pleasure in Saul's defeat, but to order that all Israel learn to sing the Song of the Bow, memorializing the best of his dead father-in-law. The heart of God, which refuses to stop loving even those who hate him, poured out of David's mouth: *"Daughters of Israel, weep for Saul…"* (2 Samuel 1:24) Repeating the mournful refrain, he led all of Israel in a royal lament: *"How the mighty are fallen!"* (2 Samuel 1:27)

"The king is dead; long live the king."

SHALL I GO UP?

The entire nation of Israel held their collective breath, waiting to see what David would do next. Would he assume command aggressively, wiping out anyone suspected of lingering loyalty to the now-deceased Saul? Saul's one surviving son, Ishbosheth, was a contender for the throne. Would David storm the capital and seize control?

Anticipating this, a nursemaid left in charge of Jonathan's five-year-old son, Mephibosheth, tried to flee with the young boy, but in her fright she fell and the boy was rendered lame for life.

In the meantime, everyone was on tenterhooks, expecting an invasion of six hundred loyal warriors to secure the throne for David.

Instead, true to form, David asked for the ephod to be brought to him. Having come this far by surrendering control over to God, he had no intention of changing his habit now.

"Shall I go up?" he asked, and the Lord responded in the affirmative.

In a solemn exodus from Ziklag, David and his men, together with their families, possessions, and livestock—all only recently recovered—made the trek to Hebron, where the citizens went out to crown him king of Judah. This humble shepherd finally received that which he had refused to take in his own strength.

Psalm 18, possibly written to commemorate the occasion, is full of hyperbolic allusion that seems to encompass, in one song, the whole scope of the last seven years of David's life. The majority of these verses attribute his victory to God alone, who David thanks: *"He rescued me from my powerful enemy, from my foes, who were too strong for me"* (Psalm 18:17). We hear his sense of wonder: *"you have made me the head of nations; people I did not know now serve me"* (Psalm 18:43).

As Judah's monarch, David used his new authority not to intimidate, threaten, or bribe the masses, as Saul had repeatedly done. Instead his first royal act was to send a message to the brave, loyal men who had risked their lives to rescue the bodies of Saul and his sons. David commended them:

> The Lord bless you for showing this kindness to Saul your master by burying him. May the Lord now show you kindness and faithfulness, and I too will show you the same favor because you have done this. (2 Samuel 2:5–6)

No doubt they were a little stunned.

Unimpressed, Abner, the commander of Saul's army, proclaimed Ishbosheth king of Israel.

Over the course of the next seven years, David may well have had cause to miss his days as a free-roaming renegade. Despite the fact that his rule grew *"stronger and stronger, while the house of Saul grew weaker and weaker"* (2 Samuel 3:1), the divided kingdom weighed heavily on David's shoulders. It was disheartening to be surrounded by constant treachery and ambition.

Abner and Ishbosheth eventually clashed, and Abner defected to David, only to be ambushed and killed by David's commander-in-chief, Joab.

Such ruthlessness was to be the trademark of Joab's career.

Grieved by the senseless murder of Abner. David gave him an honourable funeral and song of lament. Of Joab, David said grimly that he and the other sons of Zeruiah were too harsh for him (2 Samuel 3:39).

Ishbosheth, hearing of his commander's death, panicked. Two of his servants, thinking to ingratiate themselves with David, then stabbed Ishbosheth in the stomach while he slept in the heat of the day. They brought his head to David, confident of praise… but David was furious. His promise to Jonathan to spare the royal family, and his oath to Saul not to wipe out the entire line, was getting harder and harder to fulfill.

David had the men executed and buried Ishbosheth's head beside Abner.

It is a bloody awful job, being king.

The trickiest time of his life was just beginning.

SEVEN
THE CHASTENED KING

THE DAY FINALLY came when Judah and Israel at last united to declare David their king. He was thirty years old.

Strategically, David decided to move his residence to Jerusalem, which straddled the border between the lands of Judah and Benjamin, hoping no doubt to further cement the new allegiance between these two segments of the kingdom.

When he later decided to relocate the Ark of the Covenant to Jerusalem, the people were thrilled, for the Ark had languished in Kiriath-jearim for twenty years (1 Samuel 7:1, 2 Samuel 6:3). The united kingdom was about to have not just a new capital but a centralized location for worship. David was, as they say, on a roll. He could do no wrong in the eyes of the people.

In the eyes of God, however, he was about to receive a severe chastening.

When David first set out to bring the ark to Jerusalem, he was either uninformed or perhaps dismissive of the directions Moses had given regarding the reverent handling of this holy relic. It was not to come into contact with human hands but be carried by Levites who touched only the poles inserted through rings attached to the sides (Numbers 4). He did not follow these stipulations.

As David led a military escort of thirty thousand men, he felt ecstatic. The religious and emotional fervour mounted as the king, *"wearing a linen ephod… [danced] before the Lord with all his might"* (2 Samuel 6:14). Sincerity and joy, however, would not atone for irreverence.

When the oxen pulling the cart stumbled, Uzzah, one of the priests charged with transferring the Ark, put out his hand to prevent it from falling. God struck him dead.

One can only imagine the sudden, deafening silence that befell the people.

David was not just a little upset at Uzzah's death; the Hebrew word used in this passage means to burn with anger (חָרָה *charah*). This event, for David, had been meant to be the pinnacle achievement of his life. The God whose faithful mercies he had long sung was to have been honoured this day, with all Israel pouring out their praises and renewing their vows of faithfulness and worship. He was livid.

But the killing of Uzzah, which put an abrupt stop to the festivities and left everyone confused, placed David in a difficult situation. What were his options? Pretend that it had been an accident? Blame Uzzah? Blame God? Be like Saul? Instead David assumed full responsibility.

The procession immediately halted. David, acknowledging his unworthiness, said, *"How can the ark of the Lord come to me?"* (2 Samuel 6:9)—for if a sanctified Levite could be struck dead for a careless act, how much more danger would there be for him?

There is a depth of humility in this self-awareness.

Either David dismissed the crowd or they dispersed on their own. The Ark was hastily taken to the home of Obed-Edom, a Levite who lived nearby. Over the next three months of sober reflection, David saw nothing but blessing and prosperity poured out upon the house of Obed-Edom.

Only then did he dare to dance again. Perhaps it was essential that he do so, knowing now the importance of having not only passion but reverence in worship. In dancing again, he would model for his people both contrition as well as the joy of the forgiven. David knew he had done wrong. His open, honest acknowledgement gave him the courage to approach the God he loved, which he now did with all his heart, mind, strength, and soul. The rule of his life was to hold together in healthy tension this balance of humility and confidence, acknowledging his own insignificance and yet daring to make bold requests:

> Lord, what is man, that You take knowledge of him? Or the son of man, that You are mindful of him?
>
> …Bow down Your heavens, O Lord, and come down; touch the mountains, and they shall smoke…

> Stretch out Your hand from above;
> rescue me and deliver me out of great
> waters, from the hand of foreigners...
> (Psalm 144:3, 5, 7)

Structure and reverence are crucial elements that anchor the wild abandon of love; the Ark needed to be steadied in the way God had ordained so that everyone could dance fearlessly, glorifying him without danger. Such attentiveness did not diminish passion. Rather, it enriched it.

This time David was far more careful about heeding the regulations regarding the transportation of the holy Ark: the priests and Levites consecrated themselves in order to bring up the Ark with the poles on their shoulders, as Moses had commanded.

We might expect David's approach to be more cautious, a sober reflection on his failure to show proper reverence previously. Yet he took centre stage with even greater freedom, clad only in the priestly garment of an ephod, whirling like a gleeful child who had been disciplined, forgiven, and embraced.

After setting the Ark in a tent that had been pitched for this purpose in Jerusalem, David offered sacrifices to the Lord. In contrast to Saul, who took up the sacrificial knife to keep his men from deserting him, David was simply thankful. Later he would appoint singers and musicians to minister to the Lord before the Ark (1 Chronicles 15:1–3), establishing a new worship order led by those for whom worship would be a full-time vocation (1 Chronicles 15–16).

When the sacrifices were over, David sent the people home, giving each a loaf of bread, a cake of dates, and a cake of raisins. The ceremony had been a rousing success and his spirits were high as he returned to his home.

There, he was met by a surly, offended wife. Michal was appalled at his earlier lack of decorum. She scoffed, *"How the king of Israel has distinguished himself today, going around half-naked in full view of the slave girls of his servants as any vulgar fellow would!"* (2 Samuel 6:20) Michal was her father's daughter, it seems.

For David, this would have been like getting splashed in the face with cold water. Did she honestly think he cared about his image? That he had been trying to seduce or manipulate onlookers? Was she confusing him with Saul?

Before his angry wife, David stiffened, and replied, *"I will celebrate before the Lord. I will become even more undignified than this, and I will be humiliated in my own eyes"* (2 Samuel 6:21–22). The marriage, such as it was, ended that day.

For the first time in more than fifteen years, David was able to rest. His enemies were subdued, his people united, and his rulership unchallenged. Where a lesser man might have grown slack and self-indulgent, David used the time to consider his priorities. His first concern was, as usual, not for himself.

While there was justifiable cause to devote his time and energy to building his own palace, he realized that the Ark of God still resided in a tent. He proposed to build a magnificent temple in which to house the Ark. To this, Nathan the prophet responded that God did not need a house, nor would David be the one to build it, being a man who had shed much blood (1 Chronicles 28:3).

Instead the prophet relayed a message, paraphrased: "It is I, the Lord, who will establish a house for *you* — a house that will endure forever" (2 Samuel 7:11). God went on to say that David's line, household, and kingdom, would endure forever.

Rocked by this, David sat before the Lord feeling overwhelmed and asked, *"Who am I, Sovereign Lord, and what is my family, that you have brought me this far?"* (2 Samuel 7:18)

For the next few years, David continued to have both political and military success. His exploits ended in victory and, unlike Saul, he did not feel the need to bully or threaten his troops. He was surrounded by a loyal company of brave warriors whose exploits he celebrated and whose fame he himself promoted (2 Samuel 23:8–39, 1 Chronicles 11:10–47). He searched out survivors in the lineage of Saul and found and cared for the crippled son of Jonathan, Mephibosheth. The loose tribal confederacy of Israel came together as a united nation under a monarch they adored. These were glorious years, as *"the Lord gave David victory wherever he went"* (2 Samuel 8:14). David was a rock star. He could do no wrong.

Until he did.

YOU ARE THAT MAN!

"Brad told me that he loved me—a love so strong, so pure, that it had to be of God. I was pretty lonely by then, and I believed him." Dianne grimaced, remembering. "What a little fool I was! But once we started, I couldn't say no. Our affair went on for years."

Brad was her pastor.

"My husband had been neglecting me for almost a decade," Dianne went on to explain. "I was so desperate to feel loved, to feel that I had worth. Brad not only affirmed me sexually, but spiritually. We prayed together and I felt close to God. It was crazy!"

She described to me how they had studied Bible passages in the Old Testament that seemed to support polyamory. The pastor had assured her that it was possible, even healthy, for a man to have many wives, but that the law did not allow for that. So they would have to settle for being lovers, keeping it a secret from their spouses.

"I bought it all," Dianne said. "After all, he was my pastor. He must know more than me, right? How could I refuse him? I trusted in his authority." Then her face grew dark. "It wasn't real authority. I know that now… it was just power."

***

Dianne eventually discovered that she was just the latest in a long line of married women with whom the pastor had been having sexual relations. Furious and humiliated, she confessed the entirety of her sordid affair to her own husband.

The marriage did not survive. Dianne's husband could not understand the powerful hold Brad had exercised over her.

A pastoral role had given him the right to persuade and govern, but Brad had used it to coerce and seduce. More than half a dozen women had felt powerless to resist him.

Eventually his sins were exposed and he was forced to find another career. And Dianne was forced to find another husband.

The story of David's affair with a married woman is infamous. It happened in the springtime, a time when kings headed off to war. David, who was about fifty, stayed home ont his occasion. Why? There is speculation that the decision may have partially been due to his age. He was not a young man and his army did not want to risk losing him (2 Samuel 18:3, 21:15–17).

By age seventy, David was feeble enough to be bedridden, but at fifty his men may have already been feeling protective of him.

Whatever the reason, we read of him pacing back and forth on the palace rooftop one evening, perhaps bored, perhaps fretful. He then saw a beautiful young woman washing herself on a nearby roof.

He later asked one of his servants to discover her name and the answer soon came: *"Bathsheba, the daughter of Eliam and the wife of Uriah the Hittite"* (2 Samuel 11:3).

What David did next was not only a heinous abuse of power, but the kind of betrayal he had sought to avoid his entire life, for Bathsheba was not only the wife of one of his top soldiers (2 Samuel 23:39); she was also the daughter of one of his mighty men (2 Samuel 23:34) and the granddaughter of Ahithophel, one of David's chief counsellors (2 Samuel 15:12).

The Bible offers no excuses for his temptation. We merely read that David sent for her, had sex with her, and sent her away pregnant.

It gets worse. The shame of what he did, perhaps magnified by the contrast of his publicly acclaimed morality to that point, impelled him to attempt a coverup.

David recalled Bathsheba's husband from the siege of Rabbah, hoping he would sleep with Bathsheba while on leave. Uriah had too much integrity to do so, however, declaring,

> The ark and Israel and Judah are staying in tents, and my commander Joab and my lord's men are camped in the open country. How could I go to my house to eat and drink and make love to my wife? As surely as you live, I will not do such a thing! (2 Samuel 11:11)

The man's uprightness failed to deter David. Having given into self-serving idolatry—lust, intimidation to fulfill that lust, and now deception to avoid the consequences—he lost his moral ground quickly. David's foray into the curious arts was eroding his will, just as it had done with Saul.

The next night, he set about getting Uriah drunk and urging him to visit his wife. Again, Uriah stubbornly refused to go home.

David then wrote a letter to Joab, instructing him to abandon Uriah in the heat of battle. And that is, in fact, what happened. Luring him into a vulnerable position while fighting, Joab suddenly removed the supporting men and left Uriah exposed and alone. He died, betrayed by king and commander both, and David acquired Bathsheba as his seventh wife, to his own shame. The national hero, the songster of Israel, had shown a despicable side to his character.

What was David feeling throughout this time? It couldn't have been easy to keep this awful secret. Possibly we glimpse some of the internalized stress David wrestled with in these verses: *"When I kept silent, my bones wasted away through my groaning all day long. For day and night your hand was heavy on me; my strength was sapped as in the heat of summer"* (Psalm 32:3–4).

Whatever the context of the writing of this psalm—and it may well have been a reflection of David's state of mind during the Bathsheba incident—it tells us that this shepherd-king-minstrel was in torment while his sin remained a secret. It was almost a relief when it finally came to light.

Nathan the prophet felt convicted to confront the king. He invented a story, spinning the tale of a rich man who took a cherished ewe from a poor man's flock in order to prepare a meal for a traveller. This provoked David's keen sense of justice. Incensed, he agreed that such a man should be put to death.

The rhetorical trap snapped shut. "You are that man!"

David crumbled, knowing all too well that he had stolen another man's wife when the traveller—lust—came calling.

The story contains echoes of Saul's shallow admissions of guilt. But unlike Saul, David humbly faced the consequences—and they were severe, for the baby died and God assured him that even worse developments were coming: *"Out of your own household I am going to bring calamity on you"* (2 Samuel 12:11).

How did David's response differ from Saul's? When Saul was told that his kingship was being taken from him, he became ever more self-serving, mentally unhinged, and pursuing every means to stay in a position of power and control, even to the point of consulting a witch.

We see David's heart response in the song he wrote after the event: *"For I know my transgressions, and my sin is always before me. Against you, you only, have I sinned... Do not cast me from your presence or take your Holy Spirit from me"* (Psalm 51:3–4, 11). This last was spoken, no doubt, because David remembered all too well how the Spirit had departed from Saul, and he knew that he deserved no better.

Then, having turned both inward and upward, he resolutely turned outward. What now? How could this experience be used for good? How could he help others to be better than he had been? There was contrition in his heart, but also the other-mindedness that so typified his life and reign: *"Then I will teach transgressors your ways, so that sinners will turn back to you"* (Psalm 51:13). What exactly would David teach them? The answer comes shortly after: God cannot be bribed or otherwise manipulated through the curious arts. He isn't interested in the blood sacrifices of bulls and rams from a cold, calculating, or transactional heart: *"My sacrifice, O God, is a broken spirit; a broken and contrite heart you, God, will not despise"* (Psalm 51:17).

This theme runs throughout David's psalms.

> My guilt has overwhelmed me like a burden too heavy to bear... I am feeble and utterly crushed; I groan in anguish of heart. All my longings lie open before you, Lord; my sighing is not hidden from you. (Psalm 38:4, 8–9)

> Out of the depths I cry to you, Lord; Lord, hear my voice. Let your ears be attentive to my cry for mercy. If you, Lord, kept a record of sins, Lord, who could stand? But with you there is forgiveness, so that we can, with reverence, serve you. (Psalm 130:1–4)

You, God, know my folly; my guilt is not
hidden from you. (Psalm 69:6)

Search me, God, and know my heart;
test me and know my anxious thoughts.
See if there is any offensive way in me,
and lead me in the way everlasting.
(Psalm 139:23–24)

Humility, contrition, and yearning—not sinlessness—are the hallmarks
of the true worshipper. David would not again return to the shadows where
sin could master him. He boldly allowed it to be exposed and, more boldly
still, resumed his throne in the full, glaring light of God's judgment.

Michal had once accused him of not guarding his personal dignity, and
he had retorted that he would become even more undignified than that.
The public exposure of his fervour for God, twirling and jumping from sheer
happiness, was now matched by the public exposure of his lust, lies, and
murderous sin. He would avoid neither one.

SIN: NOT A PRIVATE MATTER

David may have sought to hide his sin at first, but once convicted he made
no attempt at keeping them private. Now risen from the dust and detritus,
he washed his face and sat down to a meal. His servants were dumbstruck;
after days of mourning and fasting and pleading with God, only for Bathsheba's baby to die, they had expected him to go mad with grief.

Those who embrace the open disclosure of their sin before God grow
not weaker but stronger. Shame, once brought into the open, loses its power
over us. In the face of the accuser, we can say, "You don't know the half of
it! But God knows the whole, and he has forgiven me."

David continued to live an open and exposed life before his subjects
and before God. We might imagine him singing Psalm 51 for the first time,
perhaps in some public act of temple worship. There would have been no
showmanship, no arrogance, no basking in the spotlight of infamy. He simply announced to the whole world that his highest offering to God was his
own brokenness.

The confession of sin was never intended to be a private matter. This notion causes those of us in the West to squirm uncomfortably. Our culture in North America has been pioneered and settled by strongly individualistic people, many of whom were immigrants fleeing oppression, desperate for personal freedom. They came to a vast land where there were no rules, no regulations, or standards to conform to. They could believe and live as they pleased.

At its best, such individualism can breed a strong motivation to defend the oppressed, oppose injustice, and cherish freedom. At its worst, it can nurture pride, relativism (the lack of any absolute right or wrong), and the privatization of sin. Religion becomes a very personal and private matter. Sin, if we believe in it at all, is between us and God alone. We in the Western Church are careful to avoid invading the privacy of our brothers and sisters, and we often shy away from personal enquiries regarding our own walk with the Lord.

Moses would have found us a bewildering lot.

Such attitudes did not characterize the Jewish culture. From the beginning of their history, it was clear that God viewed them not just as individuals but as a group. He dealt with them as families, ancestral lines, tribes, and nations. Singular pronouns were often used to address groups of people. For example, the name *Edom* referred to all the descendants of Esau and *Israel* meant all the descendants of Jacob (Numbers 20:14–18). Singular pronouns were even used to address the whole of God's people, such as when he spoke of them as his bride, or wife (Ezekiel 16).

Because God dealt with them in this way, we can see that they were not independent of one another but interdependent. We see this interdependence play out clearly in scripture, with both blessing and judgment falling on the many because of the righteousness or sin of a few, or even one.

We read in 1 Chronicles 21 how David's sin in taking a census resulted in a devastating plague. Joshua 7 tells us that Achan's possession of unholy gold led to a major military defeat in Israel. In 2 Samuel 21, Saul's murderous acts caused a three-year famine some thirty years after his death! Numbers 16 relates the rebellion of Korah, Dathan, and Abiram, which ended in the death of hundreds at God's hand, including their own wives and children.

Is it unjust for God to punish so many because of the sin of certain individuals? Or was he intent on teaching them that sin is far from a personal, private matter between the individual and God? While it may be at least those things, it must also be seen to be far more. Individual sin, even hidden, can lead to corporate judgment.

One begins to understand why the people of Israel were told to take the Law so seriously, even to the point of stoning those who disobeyed it. They had to keep very short accounts when it came to sin. Too many lives depended on it.

The Mosaic Law made no allowance for a private, silent confession to God in the privacy of one's own room. Sin was not a private matter. It was a community event! It involved the purchase or procurement of specific animals (or produce), a sometimes-lengthy trip to the temple, and a rather tedious interaction with at least one Levitical priest. The very sacrifices chosen might clue in the neighbours as to what the particular sin was that was being confessed. "Aha! No oil or frankincense on the barley this time. Must be adultery!"

Confession of sin was complex, costly, and inconvenient. But it was *not* private.

Sacrifice was the means through which confession, atonement, and reconciliation were accomplished, and a public act.

Perhaps we think that all changed when Jesus came onto the scene. Did it?

The first thing Jesus challenged was the Pharisee's understanding of the Law, revealing deeper truths. Lusting after a woman was the same as the sin of adultery. Venting our anger on another person was as serious as the sin of murder. What came out of our mouths was far more defiling than what we put into our mouths. Jesus taught us that it was not the letter of the Law (rules and regulations) that mattered so much as the spirit of the Law (attitudes and motives of the heart). A dead pigeon on the altar was not as important as a repentant heart.

From this, one might surmise that we no longer need the public sacrifice or the priest anymore. Yet we are told that Jesus did not come to abolish the Law, but to fulfill it (Matthew 5:17). What does this mean? Certainly, we can see that by his death the ultimate sacrifice has already been made, once and for all, and no other is needed. In this, the Law was fulfilled. Also, Jesus himself now takes the place of the high priest, interceding for us before the throne of God (Hebrews 8:1). Do we then need a priest at all?

Yes and no.

Jesus, in coming not to abolish but fulfil the Law, did not do away with the priestly office; he extended it to us. We are now called a holy priesthood (1 Peter 2:5–9, Revelation 1:6), allowed into the holy of holies (Hebrews 6:19, 20) and given the authority to steward creation (Genesis 1:28) and rule with him over the inaugurated new creation (Revelation 5:10, 1 Corinthians 6:2–6).

The Hebrew word *radah*, sometimes translated as our dominion over the earth, is defined in Psalm 72 as a mandate to save, serve, and protect. As King, Jesus used his authority against sin, death, evil, and injustice. He then imparted that authority to us (Mathew 28:16-20), an authority that isn't meant to be exercised *over* others but *for the sake* of others. This is the mandate of our royal priesthood. It isn't that priests are no longer necessary but that Jesus has admitted us all into the priesthood so we might function corporately as his chosen people rather than as separate, saved individuals who only relate to God privately about our sins and to each other barely at all.

The corporate identity of the Jews in the Old Testament has not been dissolved with the coming of the Messiah. It has been established with even greater depth and clarity. Jesus sees us as his own body. Romans 12:5 quotes Paul as saying, *"so in Christ we, though many, form one body, and each member belongs to all the others."* We read also, *"Because there is one loaf, we, who are many, are one body, for we all share the one loaf"* (1 Corinthians 10:17) and *"Even so the body is not made up of one part but of many"* (1 Corinthians 12:14). Toes cannot hop off the ecclesial foot and confess their sins privately.

If sin was not a private matter under the old covenant, it is even less so now. Private sin has corporate consequences, just as wounding the foot makes the whole body lame. As we read in 1 Corinthians 12:26, *"If one part suffers, every part suffers with it; if one part is honored, every part rejoices with it."* This is not a plea for empathy; it is a statement of body dynamics.

Just as confession of sin in the Old Testament involved walking in the midst of the camp, openly going to the priest with a sacrifice everyone can see, so we are called to openly minister to one another in a priestly capacity. Confession is meant to be spoken aloud and witnessed.

The words used in the New Testament for "confession" are *exomologeomai* and *homologio*. Both words mean to speak out publicly, to agree with one another, and to profess aloud. Jesus emphasized that the confession of our faith is to happen *"before others"*—that is, out loud and witnessed (Matthew 10:32–33). Romans 10:9 says that confession *"with your mouth"* is essential for salvation. It is not enough that we offer up silent acknowledgment; confession is to be spoken aloud.

OUT FROM UNDER THE COVERS

We are meant to be an exposed people. In God's kingdom, exposure is our shield, contradictory as this might sound. Jesus warns that *"there is nothing that is covered that will not be disclosed, or hidden that will not be made known"* (Matthew 10:26) and adds that those things which are *"whispered in the ear in the inner rooms will be proclaimed from the roofs"* (Luke 12:3). Even the gift of prophecy serves to expose, or lay bare the secrets of the heart (1 Corinthians 14:25). Paul reminds us, in 1 Corinthians 3:12–15, that on the day of judgment we will face the test of fire, and even we who survive will watch in dismay as those things in us that are burned up before our eyes—eyes that should have been plucked out, hands that should have been cut off while there was still time. Our sins will indeed one day find us out (Numbers 32:23).

Paul exhorts us to expose *"fruitless deeds of darkness"* (Ephesians 5:11), because sin has no power over us once it is exposed to the light. The sin we conceal is the sin that controls us. Satan knows this and capitalizes on it, amplifying our shame with accusations and encouraging it to the point where we refuse to openly confess our sin and find freedom. The enemy loses his grip on us when we bring our sins to the light and speak plainly about them to our brethren. His accusations crumble in the face of our bold-faced confession.

The dark is utterly defeated in the light. Jesus came to expose the darkness and expose himself as the source of all light (John 1:5). Like him, we are meant to bring light to the world, yet many of us prefer to cower under the covers when it comes to our sin. It would be better, perhaps, to voluntarily come out from under the covers now, rather than wait until the day when all coverings will be swept away by the Lord.

Otherwise, we may end up like Ananias and Sapphira, a couple who were anxious to establish a reputation among the first-century believers for their noble generosity. Ananias laid a considerable sum of money at the feet of the apostles in a manipulative bid for power, the goal of which was to impress. We know this retrospectively, because the author of Acts tells us they sold a property and pretended to be generous but secretly agreed to keep back some of the proceeds for themselves. This hidden sin was exposed through Peter's prophetic insight. It is a painful story to read.

> Then Peter said, "Ananias, how is it that Satan has so filled your heart that you have lied to the Holy Spirit and have kept for yourself some of the money you received for the land? Didn't it belong to you before it was sold? And after it was sold, wasn't the money at your disposal? What made you think of doing such a thing? You have not lied just to human beings but to God."
>
> When Ananias heard this, he fell down and died. (Acts 5:3–5)

Shortly after, the dead man's wife appeared, having no inkling that the apostle Peter had just spoken her husband to death, as it were. Peter asked Sapphira about the money and gave her a chance to come clean and disclose their deception.

But she lied as well—and within moments, she dropped dead.

When news got out, we are told that *"great fear seized all who heard what had happened"* (Acts 5:10).

God, not Peter, took the lives of this couple. Right at the church's inception, God was using death to awaken his people to the seriousness of hidden, private sin.

Eugene Peterson offers us an interesting translation of 2 Corinthians 4:2:

> We refuse to wear masks and play games. We don't maneuver and manipulate behind the scenes. And we don't twist God's Word to suit ourselves. Rather, we keep everything we do and say out in the open… (MSG)

In the Old Testament, confession of sin was an involved, time-consuming, costly, and inconvenient process. It still is. We no longer need the sacrifice—Christ has himself supplied it—but there is still a cost and effort involved. The cost is to our pride, personal space, privacy, and individualism as we humble ourselves to confess our sins to one another.

Is the cost too dear?

David said, *"I will not sacrifice to the Lord my God burnt offerings that cost me nothing"* (2 Samuel 24:24). James 5:16 encourages us, saying, *"Therefore confess your sins to each other and pray for each other so that you may be healed. The prayer of a righteous person is powerful and effective."* We need each other's prayers whether we like it or not. We have no right to private sin, and no justification for turning a blind eye to the sins of our brothers and sisters. Their sin is our own, we are accountable to God as a people, and he calls us to be accountable to one another. The defiant individualism that has infused us in North America is to yield to the Spirit which calls us to be one body.

This is easier said than done. Open confession of sin is not always met with empathy in the Church. The slightest hesitation, a raised eyebrow, an intake of breath can all bring shame crashing down around our ears. Also, some sins are far more painful to admit than others, especially when they have led us to harm those who are weak, disempowered, or dependent on us in some way. We feel deep shame when we abandon our responsibilities and neglect or damage those in our care.

Ask David. Ask *any* parent.

THE SAGA OF A LOST SON

Over the next number of years, an axe hung over David's head. He knew that his sins would have consequences, regardless of his repentance. Nathan had prophesied calamity coming from David's own household, and we might picture him vigilant and anxious as he hovered over his children.

A fateful day came when David's firstborn son Amnon committed the same crime as his father, but in an even more reprehensible fashion; he raped his own sister Tamar. David's subsequent inaction is perplexing. Perhaps by not bringing Amnon to justice for his terrible crime, David thought to model the mercy he himself had once so desperately needed.

If this is so, David's compassion was grossly misunderstood by another of his children, Absalom. Seething in rage, Absalom nurtured a vengeful plan against Amnon for two years. In full view of his brothers, he murdered Amnon, heir to the throne. Then the brothers all bolted and Absalom fled to his grandfather's house for refuge.

Three more years passed while David wept bitterly, not only for the death of Amnon but for the loss of Absalom.

Meanwhile, Absolom's bitterness festered. His father would neither condemn him to death nor restore him to the palace, so he lived in a kind of relational limbo, growing more and more angry.

Absalom's grandfather, it turned out, was only too happy to throw fuel on that fire.

Absalom's mother Makah was the daughter of a king, Talmai of Geshur. The Bible describes Geshur as having been allotted to the half-tribe of Manasseh during the occupation of the Promised Land, but its inhabitants, the Geshurites, could not be expelled (Joshua 13:13). It was against the Geshurites that David undertook his clandestine raids while he lived in Ziklag (1 Samuel 27:8). It seems that Talmai quickly switched allegiance from Saul to David when David became king, even going so far as to secure peace by offering his daughter Makah in marriage. Absalom was the son of that union.

When Absalom fled to his grandfather Talmai, he felt sure that he would find an ally in this man who had once been his father's bitter enemy. During these years in Geshur, Absalom likely began to dream about usurping his father. Reliving his resentment again and again only fed it and made it grow stronger. His accusations and self-justifications multiplied to the point of pushing out all other coherent thought, until eventually Absalom hatched a plot to become king.

Absalom was not wrong to be critical of his father. However, he wasn't looking to convict David of the injustice or to right the wrong done; he simply wanted to inflict pain. A critical spirit and sharp tongue are a deadly combination.

Those skilled in rhetoric can find criticism a potent weapon in gaining control over others. Well-spoken, articulate critics can persuade others that they are in the right. Criticism, especially when combined with sarcastic humour, projects a convincing illusion of intelligence—it is illusory because it actually takes very little intelligence to find fault. The critic weaves a spell, exposing the flaws and misdeeds of others in order to draw a crowd, who then watch with fascination as the victim's character is destroyed with a few pithy phrases. It is not unlike the fascination of watching an animal stalk and kill its prey. In the end, though, the stalker is himself stalked.

In the Church, we confuse criticism with discernment. Discernment is motivated by love, its aim being the reconciliation of brethren who have been estranged. Criticism does not seek reconciliation; it simply seeks to be right.

The word criticize, in the Greek, is *krino*. It is also at times translated as judge. That is why the critic is doomed to suffer the same fate he hopes to impose on those he criticizes.

> Do not judge, or you too will be judged. For in the same way you judge others, you will be judged, and with the measure you use, it will be measured to you.
>
> Why do you look at the speck of sawdust in your brother's eye and pay no attention to the plank in your own eye? (Matthew 7:1–3)

We hear this verse often. We conscientiously try to put it into practice. No one wants to be accused of being judgmental. But notice what happens when we translate *krino* another way: "Do not criticize, or you too will be criticized. For in the same way you criticize others, you will be criticized, and with the measure you use, it will be measured to you."

Do we realize how profoundly true this is? It is true psychologically, spiritually, socially, and eternally.

Psychologically it is true because when we harbour criticism about other people, we grow convinced that they, in turn, are equally critical of us.

Spiritually it is true because, as with the practice of all forms of manipulation, we sow control and reap bondage. By using others for our own selfish gain, we are ourselves used by the enemy.

Socially it is true because even as we seek to draw others to form an admiring circle around us, we in fact alienate them, as they fear becoming the next object of our criticism. In this way, we isolate ourselves, preventing any genuine relationship. Over time, we cannot see people clearly at all, except through the lens of a critical spirit.

This erects a wall, just as it did between David and Absalom. Behind that wall, mistrust grows. We add more bricks all the time, projecting our critical attitudes onto ours. We indulge in gossip as a means of self-consolation, which allows us to mitigate any sense of guilt by manipulating others into siding with us. We become self-righteous.

It is a vicious spiral. Those who listen to our gossip grow to fear us and pull away. As they do, we become paranoid that they are now gossiping about us. We lose our grip on reality, as Saul did at Endor.

This is what was happening with Absalom.

Meanwhile, back in Jerusalem, David's commander-in-chief, Joab, was clearly frustrated with his sovereign. Between the injustice of the rape, the unpunished murder of Amnon, and David's inconsolable mourning over Absalom, the kingdom was fraying. Something needed to be done.

Thinking back on the success of the prophet Nathan in breaking through to David in the matter of Bathsheba and Uriah, Joab decided to try the same approach.

Joab sent for an old woman with a reputation for wisdom and instructed her to present a sob story about her son to David, to awaken his sympathies. Joab knew David longed for some legitimate excuse to bring Absalom back (2 Samuel 14:1), so he intended to provide him with that excuse.

As the woman proceeded with her charade, David's suspicions were awakened. He asked whether Joab had put her up to this, and she admitted the truth.

There may be some grudging respect in David's question; it had been an elaborate and time-consuming endeavour on Joab's part.

David turned to his commander and said, *"Go, bring back the young man Absalom… [but he] must go to his own house; he must not see my face"* (2 Samuel 14:21, 24). It was yet another bad decision, contributing to the cascade of disastrous consequences that now seemed unstoppable.

Absalom did return to Jerusalem, and two more years passed without him seeing his father. When the limbo of his situation became unbearable, Absalom forced a meeting with David by burning Joab's fields. This at last resulted in him being brought to the palace.

After years of holding a grudge and indulging in gossip and criticism, the relational chasm between father and son was wide. David longed to cross it, but for Absolom this was impossible; once you have talked about someone behind their back for that long, you can never really look them in the eye. Reconciliation was the last thing on Absalom's mind.

A MINISTRY OF RECONCILIATION

Emotionally, David was caught between a rock and a hard place. Having failed to execute justice in the matter of Amnon and Tamar, he hardly felt himself to be in a position to confront his son over Amnon's murder. The haunting spectre of Uriah would not have been far from David's mind, either. Who was he, David, to point the finger at another murderer?

Yet in avoiding the issue of sin and consequence, David propagated yet another injustice, and in the end he burned whatever was left of the bridge between himself and his estranged son. Without open confrontation and repentance, there could never be any reconciliation.

There in the palace, they were together at last. We can imagine father and son standing stiffly apart, each eying the other and thinking of what had never been said, what would even now remain unsaid. Absalom had yet to openly accuse his father of neglecting to execute justice for his sister. David had yet to deal with Absalom's murder of Amnon. It was a mess.

Scripture tells us that David had been longing for his son, but once in his presence he seemed to falter. How could he help Absalom drop his defences, confess his sin, and allow the Spirit of a merciful God to heal his mind and melt his heart? As a father, he yearned; as a king, he wrestled; as a man, he respected his son's silence and hoped for a crack in the armour.

There was none. The prince was a stone.

They approached one another cautiously and then exchanged an awkward, meaningless kiss. With that, David sent his son away.

In order for reconciliation to take place, sin must be brought out into the open. This sometimes requires confrontation.

Confrontation requires a level of courage that neither seemed to possess.

Scripture leaves no room for indirect confrontation through gossip and slander; when we are compelled to confront sin, it is meant to be in a straightforward and direct fashion. Absalom, like any good Jew, would have known this from the Torah. Leviticus 19:17 reads, *"Do not hate a fellow Israelite in your heart. Rebuke your neighbor frankly so you will not share in their guilt."*

This parallels our understanding of New Testament teachings about confrontation being for the sake of reconciliation. In Matthew 18:15 we read, *"If your brother or sister sins, go and point out their fault, just between the two of you. If they listen to you, you have won them over."* Here is a procedure to follow that few dare implement. Yet without this kind of straightforward approach, relational rifts remain unaddressed, which affects our own relationship with God.

Further, scripture tells us that it does not matter who started the argument or who is in the wrong. If we are the ones who have committed the wrong, we are also responsible for initiating reconciliation. Matthew 5:23–24 tells us,

> Therefore, if you are offering your gift at the altar and there remember that your brother or sister has something against you, leave your gift there in front of the altar. First go and be reconciled to them; then come and offer your gift.

In God's kingdom, there is zero wriggle room for leaving an offence unaddressed.

The Matthew 18 passage goes on to lay out an actual procedure to follow in pursuit of reconciliation. We begin face to face, one on one. If nothing is resolved, we ask others to become involved; these are people who are equally invested in bringing about a reconciliation or in rescuing a brother or sister from the bondage of sin. If that falls flat, church leadership is invited to step into the process, again with reconciliation in mind. The final step, should all else fail, is that the unrepentant person should be treated as *"a pagan or a tax collector"* (Matthew 18:17).

Yet even in this extreme circumstance, Jesus is not saying that such a one should be shunned or expelled from the community. How did Jesus treat pagans and tax collectors? He sought them out, called them to follow him, and discipled them. The worst that can happen in a failed conflict resolution, biblically, is that we end up evangelizing the one who refuses to repent, loving them back into fellowship.

How often are we willing to follow this tedious procedure? It is more common that we begin by discussing our brother's sins with others, perhaps asking their advice or soliciting their prayers. From there we take our accusations and gossip straight to a person in authority, even the pastor himself.

This is not the kind of confrontation to which Jesus calls us. We must be direct, discreet, and determined not to convict or condemn but to bring our brother back into a restored relationship. If reconciliation is not our goal, we have no grounds for confrontation.

This may rankle. Is it not our responsibility to proclaim the truth? Yes, of course. But are we sure we are able to perceive the truth? Indulging in criticism erodes our discernment faster than any other sin because it hampers love. Ephesians 4:15 reminds us that we must speak the truth in love. Why is this so important? Unless real love motivates us, we have no ability to perceive truth. Criticism and discernment cannot operate at the same time. Truth without love is not truth, as God perceives truth.

N.T. Wright proposes love as a mode of "knowing." In an article which expounds upon this idea, he writes that paying attention to Jesus as a real figure of first-century history can point some ways forward for the Church and, through the Church, for our misguided and muddled world. And for all this—and for the multiple resultant tasks in theology and mission—we need to understand, and put into practice, new ways of knowing: specifically, an epistemology of love.[100]

What does this look like? Consider Paul's mockery of the Corinthians' pretensions to any kind of special knowledge, *gnosis*:

We know that "We all possess knowledge." But knowledge puffs up while love builds up. Those who think they know something do not yet know as they ought to know. But whoever loves God is known by God. (1 Corinthians 8:1–3)

Commentators point out that there is a footnote ascribed to the last verse in this passage, noting that an early manuscript and another ancient witness translate the latter phrase as "But whoever loves truly *knows*."

Wright ends by saying that

love is the mode of knowing that provides continuity between the present age and the age to come. Love is the constant between our present incomplete knowledge and the full knowledge yet to come…[101]

---

[100] N.T. Wright, "Love to Know," *First Things*. February 2020 (https://www.firstthings.com/article/2020/02/loving-to-know).

[101] Ibid.

When we see our brother—or son, or father, or king—with compassion and empathy and even grief, we will know not just how to confront sin but *why*. Our hearts will yearn for restoration of relationship, for forgiveness, for oneness. Priorities will shift, trivialities be shrugged off, past hurts forgotten, and hopeful futures envisioned. We will not demand sackcloth and ashes but, like the overjoyed father of the returning prodigal, sweep the lost brother up in a bear hug before they can even finish their apology—or better still, whether they apologize or not.

Christ, while we were yet sinners, died for our sins. His was the "knowing" of love and saw right into our dark crevices and through to the other side, offering open arms of forgiveness and reconciliation to generations yet to be born, yet to repent.

Without love, we are blind. Criticism distorts our emotions and clouds our minds. True spiritual discernment requires that we see things as God sees them. We must share his perception of reality. When we entertain critical thoughts, our hearts grow hard, we analyze, we critique, and our perception of reality becomes twisted. Only love opens our eyes. And the way in which we experience that unconditional, heart-melting, paradigm-shifting love is by living openly ourselves, allowing God—and our brothers and sisters—to confront us with our own sin. We cannot remove the speck from our brother's eye until we have dealt with our own sin. We must begin, and continue always, in a posture of humble self-examination and confession of sin.

No, it will not always end in tearful reconciliation, healed relationship, or restored marriage. The story of David and his angry son was destined to end tragically, with the conflict drawing in more of the royal family, nobles, army, and citizens, until the entire nation was engulfed in civil war. Through it all, David never backed away from the pain or ceased longing to embrace his son.

Absalom, on the other hand, gave his kisses away to others as campaign promises.

KISSES AT THE GATE

The subtlety of Absalom's next manipulative moves makes one shudder. His plan to kill his father and replace him as king was precise, detailed, strategic, and demonic. The insanity of unforgiveness had warped him such that he felt completely justified in plotting patricide. He had conveniently forgotten any religious checks and balances, such as the passage in the Torah which puts the presumption of criticizing one's leaders on the same plane as reviling God: *"Do not blaspheme God or curse the ruler of your people"* (Exodus 22:28). No such warning even crossed his mind as he deviously stole the hearts of the people.

> In the course of time, Absalom provided himself with a chariot and horses and with fifty men to run ahead of him. He would get up early and stand by the side of the road leading to the city gate. Whenever anyone came with a complaint to be placed before the king for a decision, Absalom would call out to him, "What town are you from?" He would answer, "Your servant is from one of the tribes of Israel." Then Absalom would say to him, "Look, your claims are valid and proper, but there is no representative of the king to hear you." And Absalom would add, "If only I were appointed judge in the land! Then everyone who has a complaint or case could come to me and I would see that they receive justice."
>
> Also, whenever anyone approached him to bow down before him, Absalom would reach out his hand, take hold of him and kiss him. Absalom behaved in this way toward all the Israelites who came to the king asking for justice, and so he stole the hearts of the people of Israel. (2 Samuel 15:1–6)

This was slick political manipulation of the highest order. The chariots, horsemen, and runners were intended to impress, even intimidate, others by creating an aura of false authority. The city gate was where judicial issues were heard and ruled upon; Absalom took a position which would intercept people before they ever arrived. In an affectation of respect, he reached out to take the hand of those who bowed down before him, lifting them up and kissing them as if implying that they were peers. They were unaware of the seduction being used to bewitch them.

Absalom then inquired with carefully feigned concern, hearing their various issues, and then, through faint praise and mild slander, stirred up dissatisfaction with David's government. We might imagine his lowered voice and the sense of camaraderie he created through crafty gossip, expressing both sympathy and regret that he was not in a position to enact the justice they deserved. These subtle allusions to injustice would have brought to their minds the matters of Bathsheba, her murdered husband, and the raped daughter for whom justice had been denied until he, Absalom, rose up in righteous vengeance.

David's words in Psalm 55 may or may not have been written during this time of treason, but the words are apt: *"His talk is smooth as butter, yet war is in his heart; his words are more soothing than oil, yet they are drawn swords"* (Psalm 55:21). Seven years of harboured bitterness had allowed Absalom to hone his skills at the curious arts to deadly perfection.

Saul would have been proud to have a man like Absalom as his son.

It is unlikely that David was ignorant of this political manoeuvring on the part of his son. Why then did he avoid dealing with it outright? This king who had humbled himself before God and his people, openly proclaiming his utter dependence on the Lord's mercy, seemed to be clinging to the hope that his son would soften his heart and come back to him.

Having come this far by refusing to take control of others for his own benefit, David maintained his stance. Either God was for him or not. If not, then *"human help is worthless"* (Psalm 60:11; 108:12).

Psalm 3, which was written on the occasion of this treason, reflects David's conviction that vindication could only come from, and be of, the Lord. He wrote, *"But you, Lord, are a shield around me, my glory, the One who lifts my head high"* (Psalm 3:3).

Undeterred by filial sentiment, Absalom mounted a growing conspiracy with two hundred men—including Bathsheba's grandfather, Ahithophel, who had been serving as David's counsellor—and sounded a trumpet to proclaim himself king. The entire nation was about to be engulfed in civil war. David had lost his throne.

DEATH OF A DREAM

It is said that one does not truly know a person through the greatness of their achievements, but by how they respond to failure. Martin Luther King Jr. said, "The ultimate measure of a man is not where he stands in moments of comfort and convenience, but where he stands at times of challenge and controversy."[102] In a crisis, a real leader doesn't hide behind others, blame his enemies, assume a posture of self-righteous protectionism, or make a futile and selfish last stand that is sure to cost the lives of his followers.

David was a real leader. He acted immediately and decisively to protect his people. Rather than fight, he ordered his household and the six hundred men of his personal guard to flee, lest Absalom *"put the city to the sword"* (2 Samuel 15:14). As always, his thoughts were first and foremost on the safety and well-being of others, not himself. He left Jerusalem not in fear or disgrace but in surrender to the One who held his fate in his hands.

Among his retinue, he spotted Ittai the Gittite, a man who had only just arrived in Jerusalem the day before, seeking refuge. He told the man to go back, along with his men, rather than be forced to find himself on the run. The man refused and the sad exodus continued as people lined the streets, weeping to see David leave the city.

Crossing the Kidron Valley, David encountered Zadok the priest, along with other Levites, and realized they had brought the Ark of the Covenant with them in support of David. The temptation to hold on to this vestige of power and prestige would have been strong, yet again David intentionally surrendered his rights to self-protection. He told Zadok,

> Take the ark of God back into the city.
> If I find favor in the Lord's eyes, he will

---

[102] Martin Luther King Jr., *Strength in Love* (Boston, MA: Beacon Press, 1963), 26.

> bring me back and let me see it and his
> dwelling place again. But if he says, "I
> am not pleased with you," then I am
> ready; let him do to me whatever seems
> good to him. (2 Samuel 15:25–26)

This was not weakness or despair or David's part. It was a solemn pledge to trust in God's sovereignty and justice.

Before the priests left, David arranged for Hushai the Arkite to be his man on the inside, sending him information through the sons of the priests. David was not giving up but standing back, vigilant and alert to discern what God may be doing, and ever ready to respond.

Continuing his flight, David's next encounter was perhaps the most offensive of all. A relative of the deceased King Saul came out from the city of Bahurim, cursing and spitting mad. Pelting David and his men with rocks and dirt, the man yelled,

> Get out, get out, you murderer, you
> scoundrel! The Lord has repaid you for
> all the blood you shed in the house-
> hold of Saul, in whose place you have
> reigned. The Lord has given the king-
> dom into the hands of your son Absa-
> lom. You have come to ruin because
> you are a murderer! (2 Samuel 16:7–8)

Incensed, David's men were ready to cut off the man's head, but David stopped them. His next words made it clear to all that he had no intention of taking back the throne unless God, and God alone, gave it to him. David told them,

> Leave him alone; let him curse, for the
> Lord has told him to. It may be that
> the Lord will look upon my misery and
> restore to me his covenant blessing

instead of his curse today. (2 Samuel
16:11–12)

Any power which might have infused the man's curses was cancelled
by the power of David's words of humility, faith, and surrender. David had, in
effect, offered *blessing* in the face of *cursing*, allowing God to be the one to
decide which words to empower.

For make no mistake: words do have power.

THE POWER OF WORDS

Just as we are created in the image of God, so our power of speech is meant
to reflect his divinity. By the power of his spoken word, all things are made
or unmade. By the power of our spoken words, we also can build up or tear
down. To purposely communicate love, wishing someone well, is to bless.
Likewise, the deliberate communication of hate is the essence of cursing.

God himself does not curse us, in the malevolent sense of the word. In
Eden, he blessed the fruitfulness of his creation (Genesis 1:22). We implicitly
understand that for Eve and Adam to walk outside his blessing, through willful and self-serving acts of idolatry, would be to leave that circle of blessing
and enter a state of un-blessedness, or cursedness.

This is both a judicial proclamation and a warning. Fire will burn. Sin
will kill. In this sense, all divine curses have already been pronounced; they
are eternal because of the eternal nature of God's law. The eating of the forbidden fruit took all mankind out from under God's blessing, bringing both
biological and ecological consequences upon humanity.

Moses referred to this when the Israelites were about to enter the Promised Land: *"However, if you do not obey the Lord your God and do not carefully follow all his commands and decrees I am giving you today, all these
curses will come on you and overtake you"* (Deuteronomy 28:15). This was
not a threat but a reality which the people had already been experiencing
in the desert. God was not hovering over them with a big stick, waiting for
them to mess up; they already had. He was pointing them back to the realm
of blessedness, making a way for them to dwell in that realm amidst temptation. Even referencing the curses of disobedience was, in fact, a blessing for
them; how else were they to know how to guard their steps?

To say that God does not actively curse us is not to say that God does not have the power and right to do so. But he does not need to. Jesus's cursing of the fig tree in Matthew 21:18–22 was a symbolic act, not one directed toward a person. And the famous sevenfold declarations of woe in Matthew 23, directed toward the hypocritical Pharisees and scribes, were not imprecatory curses being hurled by an angry God; they were rebukes full of furious grief from a God who is *"crushed by [our] adulterous hearts"* (Ezekiel 6:9, NKJV).

God does not need to actively curse us; he points to the blessing-free zone and shows us how not to cross the border.

There is a realm of cursedness that exists outside God's blessing. When we forsake fellowship with him, we come under the Law, and being in sin we come under the cursedness of its consequence (Galatians 3:10). The astounding thing is that grace and blessing continue to pursue us even as we reject them, and they are always available to us when we turn in penitence and gratitude to Jesus. Galatians 3:13 assures us, *"Christ redeemed us from the curse of the law by becoming a curse for us, for it is written: 'Cursed is everyone who is hung on a pole.'"* The curse of the Law fell on Christ on our behalf so the righteousness of God can now fall upon us (2 Corinthians 5:21). Jesus paid a hefty price to rescue us from a divine curse. Ironically, we are quite casual about pronouncing curses of our own.

Do our intentional words of cursing and blessing have relevance in the modern world? Can curses do real harm? As well one might ask whether blessings can do real good. The question may boil down to whether we can so communicate our love and hate as to work on the one hand healing and on the other sickness and death.

The answer is yes.

Communication is far more than the mere impartation of information. Consider poetry, dance, music, and art. All are potentially powerful and effective means of communication meant not just to inform but to affect one's emotions. When intentional communications are used to bring harm, they are a curse. Think of the last mean-spirited text or email that literally ruined your day. If you, like me, have had occasion to be on stage and look out over an audience only to notice the angry glare of someone who clearly is not a fan, you understand the power of nonverbal communication.

But by far the most potent form of communication, and therefore the most powerful and potentially destructive, comes through the spoken word.

Ancient peoples believed in the power of curses. Leviticus 20:9 warns, *"Anyone who curses their father or mother is to be put to death. Because they have cursed their father or mother, their blood will be on their own head."* This infers that the people were in fact prone to cursing their parents at that time.

The Bible contains many examples of what we could call legitimate curses, divine consequences merited by individual action. For example, Jeremiah cursed the false prophet Hananiah, saying, *"Therefore this is what the Lord says: 'I am about to remove you from the face of the earth. This very year you are going to die, because you have preached rebellion against the Lord'"* (Jeremiah 28:16). False prophecy was condemned by God and Jeremiah declared this with power and conviction. In the seventh month of that same year, Hananiah the prophet died.

In 2 Kings 2:23–24, Elisha cursed a mocking crowd of youth in the name of the Lord. The curse brought bears out of the woods, and they mauled thirty-two people, presumably to their deaths. The rightness or wrongness of this curse has been debated, but there is a strong case to be made that Elisha may have been invoking the divine consequence of their choice to challenge his authority as a prophet, invoking the legitimate judgment due by them breaking God's command: *"Do not blaspheme God or curse the ruler of your people"* (Exodus 22:28).

Noah cursed Ham's son, Canaan, saying that Canaan would become the slave of Shem. Ham, having gazed upon his father's nakedness—possibly with sexual connotations—would see the consequences of his sinfulness affect his own children.

Jacob cursed Simeon and Levi on his deathbed for their *"anger, so fierce, and their fury, so cruel!"* (Genesis 49:7)

None of these curses were in any way casual, nor were they spoken in a petty, momentary fit of pique. The same cannot be said for the kind of cursing we are prone to, including those of us in postmodern cultures of cynicism who do not believe in such things.

We pronounce curses over one another all the time. "You'll never amount to anything." "You're just like your loser father." "Wait till you're a mother; then you'll understand what real suffering is." "Enjoy your health while you can. It won't last long." We pronounce curses when we roll our eyes in annoyance, grimace, sniff disdainfully, mock, and speak cuttingly. It is the form of manipulation requiring the least skill. Anyone can do it.

We shrug these things off, perhaps apologizing for our tempers from time to time. We do not realize that we have flung deadly missiles with demonic precision. We have become so desensitized in the practice of casual cursing that we are ignorant of the severity of sin involved.

It does not take a calamity of extreme proportions to provoke most of us to curse. Minor annoyances are usually quite sufficient: unreasonable employers, a nagging spouse, financial strain, frustrated ambitions, car problems, or a bad head cold. Feeling unloved and abandoned by a God who seems cold, remote, and indifferent to our pleas, we may even curse God. Self-pity, anger, and despair provoke us to blame God for his injustice and callous disregard. Slander is in fact a form of cursing. It is the name-calling of Matthew 5:22, where a man is called an empty-headed idiot and Jesus warns that the slanderer is in danger of hellfire.

Negative communications of this sort hurt us emotionally, psychologically, and even physically. The hateful gestures and expletives from the driver you just inadvertently cut off can cause your blood pressure to spike and your limbs to tremble as adrenaline rushes through you. You might subsequently have your judgment impaired and your safety compromised. An accident could easily ensue.

This is not a divine curse but a natural consequence of someone's ill-wishing, yet God has created us with the ability to affect each other this way with our words.

What about the stories brought to us by missionaries and people from cultures which practice cursing through voodoo and magic? Can such unwarranted curses have an impact? If the curse is not legitimate—that is, it is neither divine in origin nor lawful in invocation—it can and should be brushed aside.

Proverbs 26:2 tells us, *"Like a fluttering sparrow or a darting swallow, an undeserved curse does not come to rest."* Undeserved curses cannot alight. In other words, they cannot remain upon us as a permanent pronouncement of judgment, unless we allow them to do so. They are like birds, only pausing on a branch before flying off. They do not roost. An undeserved curse cannot build its proverbial nest in us. It has no home in our lives if we have done nothing to incur divine judgment.

But it can still make a mess when it stops to perch. The bird must be shooed and the curse rejected.

Words have power—to wound or heal, to curse or bless. When we encounter hateful communication and inexplicable adversity, the enemy's aim is quite clear: Satan wants us to sin, in word and deed. He wants us to hit back against our enemies and God for having allowed the hurt.

Satan wanted Job to *"curse God and die"* (Job 2:9). The enemy's intent was to incite Job to sin with his lips. This is important, because words both reflect what is in the heart and also actively defile the heart (Matthew 15:11). James 3:6 reminds us that the tongue defiles the whole body. On virtually any page in the book of Proverbs, you will find warnings to the same effect. Words both precede and provoke action, particularly sinful action. They can destroy relationships, defame character, poison hearts, pervert minds, and cause us to curse God and die.

David was a word-crafter. As a psalmist, he knew the power of verse, metaphor, rhythm, and cadence. He was ever careful to choose his words in ways which did not usurp God's authority or insult Saul, that he might not sin. He prayed, *"Set a guard over my mouth, Lord; keep watch over the door of my lips"* (Psalm 141:3).

This was not the duplicity of insincerity. David was not repressing or denying his feelings. On the contrary, he was explosive in his anger and despair, just as he was open regarding his passion and sorrow.

Yet his expression of these emotions was not directed to would or win the hearts of men. David's deepest feelings were expressed to his God, in prayer and song. These psalms were then preserved for others to hear, since it's unlikely that he paused while on the run from Absalom, for example, to sing. Those who knew him best would have known what he was feeling, what it cost him to hold back from venting those feelings, and would have loved him all the more for this self-restraint. They knew David didn't want civil war, but war came nonetheless.

EVERY MAN TO HIS TENT!

The ousted king was on the run, no doubt feeling too old to again be a fugitive. Meanwhile, Absalom's first act as king was to sleep with his father's concubines, fulfilling the woeful prophecy of Nathan: *"Before your very eyes I will take your wives and give them to one who is close to you, and he will sleep with your wives in broad daylight"* (2 Samuel 12:11). It was humiliating for David, yet even now took no action, waiting to see what God would do.

He did not have to wait long. Absalom mustered all his forces to pursue his father and wipe out his troops. In response, David readied his men for battle. There was no eagerness in this; he was weary with grief, knowing that the fight was inevitable but still adjuring his men, *"Be gentle with the young man Absalom for my sake"* (2 Samuel 18:5).

Joab, the bloodthirsty commander of David's army, ignored this request and killed the king's son while he hung helpless with his long hair caught in the branches of a tree.

With Absalom dead, the insurrection dissolved and the war was over.

A runner hurried to bring the news to David, but the king only asked after the safety of his son. Hearing that Absalom was dead left him shaken and in tears. He cried out that it should have been his life that was forfeit, not his son's. This was not shallow melodrama but a deep sense of shame, knowing that his own sin had brought the nation to this place and caused the death of his son.

Victory was overshadowed with grief. The cheering troops faltered and then fell silent. Joab became angry. Determined to shake David out of his despondency, he told the king that the very men who had risked their lives to defend him now felt unappreciated. David, mindful of his soldiers, roused himself; he needed to bring order and unity to this fractured kingdom. It was too late.

Israel was divided in her loyalties and its people debated whether or not to welcome David back to Jerusalem at all. The dispute was moot, since David had a right to return. But he would not force his reign upon Israel.

Sending his priests into the city to negotiate, David waited to be invited. When a short time later they asked for their king to return, thousands rushed down to the Jordan River to meet him. Those from Judah and those from Israel eyed one another, vying for the privilege to escort the king back to his palace. The northern tribes felt excluded, eclipsed by Judah in this cere-monial welcome. Their discord sowed the seed of yet another civil conflict.

Before long, a trumpet sounded and the men of Israel deserted David to rally to a troublemaker named Sheba, from the same Benjaminite tribe as Saul. They stormed off, shouting, *"Every man to his tent, Israel!"* (2 Samuel 20:1)

Under Joab, this latest rebellion was quashed and Sheba killed. The years that followed were more settled, barring a few battles and a three-year famine.

An uneasy truce was struck between the northern and southern king-doms, one that would last until the death of David's son Solomon.

We can assume that both David and Joab wanted to do all in their power to strengthen this alliance, Joab through a show of ruthless force and David through humility, integrity, and genuine sacrificial love for his people.

The contrast between these two men may provide a key to understand-ing the perplexing event that follows.

In 2 Samuel 24, David called for a census. We read in 1 Chronicles 21 that the motive for his act was misguided, provoked by Satan and allowed by God.[103] Joab was against it from the start. It was not forbidden to take a census, but there was something wrong in this, something that angered God to the point of killing seventy thousand people through a punitive plague that raced through the land afterward.

What happened? Most commentators suggest that this census was an offence because it was not initiated at God's request, seemed to include the Levites (which was forbidden for military conscription), and was motivated by David's self-reliance and pride.[104]

There is no doubt that a census would have been useful to David in terms of assessing his manpower and resources. He had much on his mind as he aged and was giving greater consideration to the son who would suc-ceed him.

However, self-reliant ego-tripping hardly fit with his rule of life thus far. In fact, David was far more likely to put himself at personal risk or remain

---

[103] Tony W. Cartledge, *1 and 2 Samuel* (Macon, GA: Smyth & Helwys, 2001), 699–700.

[104] Ibid.

stubbornly impassive rather than trust in his own strength. On more than one occasion, David consistently acknowledged his weakness and dependence upon the Lord, saying, *"You are my Lord, my goodness is nothing apart from You"* (Psalm 16:2, NJKV).

Further, had his census been meant to bolster military morale and showcase David's pride and strength, it seems unlikely that Joab would have objected. Joab loved power and was cunning. His modus operandi had always been to intimidate, dominate, and betray. Reckless, hot-headed Joab had often been impatient with David, a monarch who never ruled with an iron fist.

A census, if done to assess military might, might have been seen by Joab as being strategically advantageous. He would never have exempted the Benjamites, for example, and he would have welcomed a chance to insult the tribe of Saul by rubbing their noses in the fact that they were now servants of David.

It is hard to imagine Joab objecting to a census. Why was it repulsive to him?

In Old Testament times, a census was preliminary to a draft of soldiers and a levying of taxes for the service of the Tabernacle (Exodus 30:11–16). But this passage in 2 Samuel makes no mention of the head tax being collected, so the census appears to have been for enumeration purposes only.[105]

While we can imagine that Joab might actually have been in favour of assessing the numbers of fighting men, it is possible that David proposed to do so in a way that refrained from burdening the people. This would definitely fit with his personality up to this point. Did he, for example, intentionally not collect the taxes for the service of the Tabernacle? If we consider that David may have allowed his desire for unity and peace to override the mandate for tax collection, not only does the ensuing plague make sense but we can appreciate why Joab would have been so angry. Joab was a man who measured things in terms of military might and power, dominating through fear; to exempt the men from the head tax would have presented a weakness men could exploit. If David were being in any

---

[105] John D. Rayner, *An Understanding of Judaism* (Oxford, UK: Berghahn Press, 1997), 59–60.

way conciliatory, such as by refusing to collect the census tax, Joab would have strongly objected. There was no place for leniency in his army.

If the tax exemption was in fact a component of this ill-fated census, then God would have been right to condemn David for allowing concern for his people to take priority over love for God, in that any census was meant to result in *"an offering to the Lord"* (Exodus 30:14), a provision for the worship of God in the Tabernacle. Failing to collect this so-called ransom price of one half-shekel per man would have incurred a plague, according to Exodus 30:11–16. It is possible that this is one of the reasons for the ensuing disaster.[106]

The plague that swept over the nation was brutal, with seventy thousand people losing their lives in just one day. True to his nature, David cried out to God on behalf of others:

> Was it not I who ordered the fighting men to be counted? I, the shepherd, have sinned and done wrong. These are but sheep. What have they done? Lord my God, let your hand fall on me and my family, but do not let this plague remain on your people. (1 Chronicles 21:17)

The Angel of the Lord, sword poised to strike, paused.

ON THE THRESHING FLOOR

Knowing where the plague had been stopped, the prophet Gad sent David to the threshing floor of Araunah the Jebusite, intending to right a great wrong. Araunah and his sons, we are told, saw the Angel and knew that the sword of death hovered threateningly over their farm. They would not have known that the plague had been halted there, or why. As David and his escorts approached, they would have been alarmed. Why was the king coming to their farm?

---

[106] Song-Mi Suzie Park, "Census and Censure: Sacred Threshing Floors and Counting Taboos in 2 Samuel 24," *Horizons in Biblical Theology,* Volume 35, Issue 1. January 1, 2013.

Araunah bowed low and David explained that God had sent him to build an altar and offer sacrifices. David offered to pay the full price for the land, but Araunah shook his head emphatically. Immediately, and wisely, he offered up his property, including wood for the fire and oxen for the sacrifice, for the king's pleasure.

David, perhaps reflecting upon the taxes he had failed to collect for the service of the Tabernacle, knew that he could not accept the gift. The ransom money he may have deliberately failed to collect was to have supported the Tabernacle and temple services as a memory of the Lord's atonement.

> Receive the atonement money from the Israelites and use it for the service of the tent of meeting. It will be a memorial for the Israelites before the Lord, making atonement for your lives (Exodus 30:16)

His debt was weighing on him as he faced the Jebusite. He shook his head and said, *"No, I insist on paying you for it. I will not sacrifice to the Lord my God burnt offerings that cost me nothing"* (2 Samuel 24:24).

This is nothing, David might have thought to himself, *compared to what I owe.*

If the account in 1 Chronicles account is correct, this threshing floor marked the site of the future temple (1 Chronicles 21:28–22:1). This is where David seemed to realize that preparing his people for the formalized worship of the Lord was the last and highest priority of his life. He knew he would have to do everything in his power to ensure Israel never forgot that they had been redeemed by the Lord, and never again neglect to render unto him the worship due his name.

The threshing floor of Araunah became a permanent monument to the humility of this king, and we might imagine that a scythe lies buried somewhere deep beneath the foundation of the site upon which today sits the Dome of the Rock, left behind where the farmer let it fall, reminding us that the person who follows after God's own heart will turn every occasion of sin into an opportunity for surrender and worship. On this literal and proverbial threshing floor, the wheat was trampled, beaten, and tossed into the wind so that the chaff might be blown away and the kernel fall to the ground. David's heart, like wheat, yielded to the threshing.

As David's last days drew near, his thoughts turned to succession.

There is a gentle, poetic justice in God's choosing of Bathsheba's son, Solomon, as the next king. Ever reticent to evoke conflict, David waited far too long to acknowledge him as heir to the throne, and Joab, impatient as always, backed David's son Adonijah (1 Kings 1:5–11) while David remained in denial about the whole affair (1 Kings 1:6).

After putting down the ensuing insurrection, David arranged for Solomon to be anointed, transferring the symbols of monarchy to him and presenting him publicly as the new king while David himself still lived (1 Kings 1:32–35, 39–40). The king then made a few suggestions to his son, advising him to eliminate certain potential threats upon David's death, including both Joab and a man who had cursed him.

We must not think David vengeful. The king was mindful of his vows and never eager to shed more blood. Rather, he was protective of his son and, more to the point, protective of his people. David wanted to eliminate the possibility of further civil unrest, which would result in needless deaths.

Because David had already shed so much blood as king, God appointed Solomon the task of building the temple (1 Chronicles 22:7–10). David, having secured the threshing floor, began to train Solomon for the kingship and the establishing of formal temple worship. He surrounded his son with a capable team of builders and artisans and provided vast stores of materials for the construction of the temple. God's house, David insisted, must be *"of great magnificence"* (1 Chronicles 22:5).

David also took on the task, so well suited to his heart, of organizing the worship that would take place in the temple, even though he would never live to see it. He assured himself that this ministry would not just survive but thrive under his successor.

In making preparations, David was in essence writing his will, bequeathing to all who would follow afterward in the worship of the one true God the priceless inheritance of humility, surrender, and sacrificial love.

NOT SO WITH MY HOUSE

David had built his own house to be within view of the Tabernacle so he would see the smoke rise with each sacrifice, hear the orchestrated music of 24/7 worship, and perhaps even distinguish the words of his own psalms being sung. He did all he could to equip Solomon to reign, in the process ensuring that the Levites were financially provided for, that they might be free from other duties and employed in the work of day and night worship (1 Chronicles 9:33, 16:37, 2 Chronicles 8:14).

Now more than seventy years old and frail, David had done his utmost to leave behind a legacy worthy of God's favour. We attribute to him the words of Psalm 71:

> Do not cast me away when I am old;
> do not forsake me when my strength is
> gone... Since my youth, God, you have
> taught me, and to this day I declare your
> marvelous deeds. Even when I am old
> and gray, do not forsake me, my God,
> till I declare your power to the next gen-
> eration, your mighty acts to all who are
> to come. (Psalm 71:9, 17–18)

David was ready, at last, to die. There was none of the frantic clinging to life we saw in Saul, no desperate last-minute bid for power, no bargains struck with prophet or seer. David had never been about power and control but about humility and surrender. His prayer at the inauguration of his son Solomon reflected this: *"Everything comes from you, and we have given you only what comes from your hand"* (1 Chronicles 29:14).

Throughout his life, David had fought the temptation to seize and grasp that which he ought instead to have received from the hand of God alone. He had known commendable victories and spectacular failures.

At the end, as elsewhere throughout his history, he ascribed all success to the mercy of God. In his final oracle, attributed to the Spirit of God speaking through David, humility exists in dynamic tension with the acknowledgement of God's favour. In his last words, David is lauded as the chosen one of the Almighty, calling himself *"the man exalted by the Most High, the man anointed by the God of Jacob, the hero of Israel's songs"* (2 Samuel 23:1) through whom the spirit of the Lord spoke. The passage goes on to describe the glory of righteous rule as being like *"the light of morning at sunrise on a cloudless morning, like the brightness after rain that brings grass from the earth"* (2 Samuel 23:4).

Some translations contain a familiar note of contrition, with David adding, *"Although my house is not so with God, yet He has made with me an everlasting covenant, ordered in all things and secure"* (2 Samuel 23:5, NKJV). In this, we can hear an echo of David's awestruck question, spoken when God first spoke that promise to him through the prophet Nathan: *"Who am I, Sovereign Lord, and what is my family, that you have brought me this far?"* (2 Samuel 7:18).

And in the stillness of his final breaths, perhaps God whispered in reply, "You are a man after my own heart."

CONCLUSION
DANCING DUST

DAVID DIED FIRMLY convinced of his own unworthiness, yet confident in the faithful mercies of the God who had chosen him. His legacy of humble surrender, vulnerability, and other-mindedness would not be passed on unchallenged in the DNA of his descendants, but his exemplary life would shine for a thousand years, until the birth of one who would call himself *"the Root and the Offspring of David, and the bright Morning Star"* (Revelation 22:16). Jesus, son of David, would rise up and claim the throne of the kingdom of God on earth, defeating sin and shame and death for the sake of those whom his Father loved.

Jesus Christ's victory would be won not through intimidation, seduction, or deception but rather through the same means that David won God's heart: surrendering his destiny into the hands of a trustworthy Father. Jesus scorned the curious arts of manipulation and rebuffed Satan's temptations of power, prestige, and pleasure, finding his sustenance in his Father's words alone for forty long, hungry days in the desert.

Like David with Saul in the desert cave, Jesus would not take control by force but instead wait for God to bestow on him the mantle of a king. He would refuse to defend himself before Pontius, choosing to hang mute on the cross while mockers demanded he summon his angelic hosts and wrench himself free. Like the dethroned David leaving Jerusalem to walk through the Kidron Valley—also known as the Valley of the Shadow of Death—he was scorned and spat upon and humiliated. Trusting in divine vindication alone, Jesus surrendered his divinity, his rights, his freedom, his life, and in so doing conquered all.

Jesus would also challenge us to revive the temple worship of his ancestor David by daring to redefine that temple as being *himself*, his own body, the place where God meets with man, where sacrifice is offered, where forgiveness is found, and where the fiery cloud of God's presence bursts into flame and heaven and earth slam together and become One.

Then, at Pentecost, the body of Jesus became us—the Church, a temple of living stones which cannot help but cry out in praise. The Church is the means by which the fiery cloud of God's presence is destined to invade, rescue, redeem, and fill the whole earth.

Did David glimpse any of this near the end of his life? Did he realize the prophetic nature of his own songwriting, and that of the musicians and poets he had raised up? We can imagine him listening, bedridden, as faint music carried through the window to capture his fading mind with the majestic mystery yet to be realized in the coming Messiah.

> You are my son; today I have become your father. Ask me, and I will make the nations your inheritance, the ends of the earth your possession. (Psalm 2:7–8)

> The Lord says to my lord: "Sit at my right hand until I make your enemies a footstool for your feet." (Psalm 110:1)

Would he wonder at the significance of a lament that would one day slip from the parched lips of a dying Messiah—*"My God, my God, why have you forsaken me?"* (Psalm 22:1)—or groan at the image of such a one surrounded by enemies who would pierce his hands and feet?

Did David, drawing his final breath, imagine the resurrection? Perhaps not. Yet he had, in his lifetime, experienced the undeserved and unstoppable mercies of his God; he would have known, deep down, that such love cannot die. He had learned to cling to that love, to hold out empty, sin-stained hands and dare to ask for more.

David knew the redemptive power of divine love, a power that lies not in what is taken by force but only in what is humbly received. The sweet psalmist of Israel walked through the valley of the shadow of death and feared no evil. His final words would one day be on the lips of another king, the King of

Kings, who would greet death, saying, *"Into your hands I commit my spirit"* (Psalm 31:5, Luke 23:46).

Tim Keller, renowned author and speaker, is at the time of this writing recently deceased from pancreatic cancer. Knowing of his imminent death, he wrote perhaps his most poignant, albeit short book, entitled *On Death*. He writes of the reason for our confidence, a reason King David knew well:

> It's in death that God says, "If I'm not your security, then you've got no security, because I'm the only thing that can't be taken away from you. I will hold you in my everlasting arms. Every other set of arms will fail you, but I will never fail you."[107]

Facing death, David was not afraid. There were arms waiting. Somewhere, on the other side, this man after God's own heart knew that he would encounter the heart of God and dance as he had never danced before.

Perhaps in this moment he brought to mind the words he had penned in Psalm 103, reminding himself that God

> knows how we are formed, he remembers that we are dust. The life of mortals is like grass, they flourish like a flower of the field; the wind blows over it and it is gone, and its place remembers it no more. (Psalm 103:14–16)

For this shepherd-king who had learned the hard lessons of surrender, these words would have evoked no anxiety or regret, only quiet confidence in the kindness of the God who forms our fragility. We are dust, but we are dancing dust—and the dance goes on after death.

---

[107] Tim Keller, *On Death* (New York, NY: Penguin Books, 2020), 27–28.

This depth of confidence and peace can feel elusive, never more so than when we face death. Mortality chafes and the fading flower of youth, beauty, and strength can cause us to rage, like Saul, at such helpless impermanency. We demand more choices, more time.

More control.

We thrash about, clutching at straws of beauty, money, knowledge, and fame. The power they promise remains ever tantalizingly out of reach and we desperately clutch at the false hope that by controlling others—controlling, if possible, God himself—we will somehow control our own destinies.

And so we learn the art, or craft, of manipulation: intimidation, seduction, and deception—the tools of the trade of the curious arts. With those tools we build an idol in our own image, as King Saul did, and then it rules over us. In the end it will crush us, toppled by a holy, jealous God. Our one free choice—the choice of masters—will have been spent in vain.

It doesn't have to be this way.

God invites us onto another path—the way of King David, the way of Jesus, a way of humble surrender, raw vulnerability, and other-minded sacrificial love. It is the way of an upside-down kingdom in which weakness is our greatest strength, intimacy is not attained through seduction but as a gift offered to the brokenhearted, and bullies are confounded as cheeks are turned, cloaks shared, feet washed, and enemies blessed. It is the way of the servant-hearted who find, even while embracing a lifestyle of seemingly inconsequential service, they have somehow risen to become God's royal priesthood, his treasured possession.

We conquer through clinging, as Jacob did. To bare our souls is to be shielded by the armour of God. To die to Self is to overcome death. To renounce our rights is to inherit eternal riches. Trusting our destinies to him, we can exchange the powerlessness of asking "Why?" for the purposefulness of asking "What?" We can marvel as he weaves together the threads of our suffering and confessed sin into a living tapestry that glorifies him and takes our breath away. We, the Church, will be the Bride whose beauty ravishes God's heart.

Can you see it? Perhaps not yet. When we look at ourselves, we see idolatry baked into our bones by the blazing furnace of our own ambition, jealousy, greed, and lust.

But that is not who we are. Our truest self is seen reflected in the eyes of the lover of our souls. That is the image we must learn to seek in others as we see them through the Father's eyes of compassion, with love as our mode of knowing. The image of God in each individual will then dazzle us with its beauty and we will cringe at the thought of ever seeking to manipulate or abuse the sacredness of another's personhood for our own benefit. God will teach us to cup the fragility of each other's hearts with reverence and infinite care. Then and only then will we speak truth in kindness. Then and only then will we joyfully embrace each opportunity to expose our secret fears and battered egos. Then and only then will we know what it is to love and be loved.

We will yield, we will serve, and we will be free.

ABOUT THE AUTHOR

NIKKI T. WHITE is an award-winning author (*Identity in Exodus*), speaker, and prolific writer with Multiply, the global mission agency of the North American Mennonite Brethren conference. Following undergraduate studies in fine arts in Mexico, White returned to Canada to spend twelve years serving in worship ministries in the Vineyard church movement, as well as completing graduate seminary studies at Trinity Western University.

White's prayer training resources have helped churches of all denominations equip their ministry teams with a helpful, biblically balanced perspective on the charismatic. Her role with Multiply has taken her to remote locations around the globe to gather stories of transformation—from victims of terrorism in Colombia, persecuted believers in Myanmar villages, and Indigenous church planters in the Amazon jungle. White has a passion for facilitating life-changing, culture-bridging encounters with Jesus wherever she goes.

Prayer training resources are hosted at www.multiply.net/prayer-ministry and her personal website can be viewed at www.whitestoneid.ca

BIBLIOGRAPHY

"2014 ACA Code of Ethics," *American Counseling Association*. Date of access: April 2021 (www.counseling.org/docs/default-source/default-document-library/ethics/2014-aca-code-of-ethics.pdf).

Abramson, Paul R., *David's Politics: Servant, Rebel, King* (Lanham, MD: Lexington Books, 2016).

Adler, Margaret, *Drawing Down the Moon: Witches, Druids, Goddess-Worshippers, and Other Pagans in America Today* (New York, NY: Penguin Books, 2006).

Alikin, Valeriy A., *The Earliest History of the Christian Gathering: Origin, Development, and Content of the Christian Gathering in the First to Third Centuries* (Leiden, Netherlands: Brill, 2010).

Alter, Robert, *The Art of Biblical Narrative* (New York, NY: Basic Books, 1981).

Augustine of Hippo, *On Christian Teaching*, Book IV, xii.

Becker, Ernest, *Denial of Death* (New York, NY: Simon & Schuster, 1973).

Bernays, Edward, *Propaganda* (New York, NY: IG Publishing, 2005).

Bertman, Stephen, *Handbook to Life in Ancient Mesopotamia* (New York, NY: Oxford University Press, 2003).

Brown, Harold O.J., "What the Supreme Court Didn't Know: Ancient and Earthly Christian Views on Abortion," *Human Life Review 1*, Spring 1975, 5–21.

Bunyan, John, *The Pilgrim's Progress* (London, UK: Hurst, Robinson, and Co., 1820).

Calvin, John, *Institutes of the Christian Religion*, Chapter 17:12. Date of access: October 21, 2024 (https://www.ccel.org/ccel/calvin/institutes.v.xviii.html).

Cammaerts, Emile, "The Laughing Prophet: The Seven Virtues and G.K. Chesterton," *Chesteron.org*. Date of access: January 9, 2025 (https://www.chesterton.org/wp-content/uploads/2020/04/The-Laughing-Prophet_ACS-Books.pdf).

Cartledge, Tony W., *1 and 2 Samuel* (Macon, GA: Smyth & Helwys, 2001).

Chen, Stephen, "Chinese Scientists Develop Handheld Sonic Weapon for Crowd Control," *South China Morning Post.* September 19, 2019 (https://www.scmp.com/news/china/science/article/3028071/chinese-scientists-develop-handheld-sonic-weapon-crowd-control).

"Church of England 'Office of Visitation,'" *Book of Common Prayer* (Gainesville, FL: Shanti Publications, 2020).

"Dark Triad," *Psychology Today.* Date of access: April 2021 (https://www.psychologytoday.com/ca/basics/dark-triad).

Dawson, John, *Take Our Cities for God: How to Break Spiritual Strongholds* (Lake Mary, FL: Charisma House, 2002).

Dell, Katharine M., "Job," *Eerdmans Bible Commentary*, eds. James D.G. Dunn and John William Rogerson (Grand Rapids, MI: Eerdmans Publisher, 2003).

Edwards, James, *Romans: Understanding the Bible Commentary Series* (Grand Rapids, MI: Baker Books, 2011).

Erickson. Millard J., *Introducing Christian Doctrine* (Grand Rapids, MI: Baker Books, 2001).

Ferguson, Sinclair B., and David F. Wright, eds., *New Dictionary of Theology* (Lisle, IL: InterVarsity Press, 1988).

Frankl, Viktor E., *Man's Search for Meaning* (Boston, MA: Beacon Press, 2006).

Goldschmidt, Debra, and Susan Scutti, "Trump Administration Limits Research Using Fetal Tissue," *CNN.* June 5, 2019 (https://www.cnn.com/2019/06/05/health/hhs-fetal-tissue-research-bn).

Gorman, Michael J., *Abortion and the Early Church: Christian, Jewish, and Pagan Attitudes in the Greco-Roman World* (Eugene, OR: Wipf and Stock, 1998).

Guinness, Os, *A Free People's Suicide: Sustainable Freedom and the American Future* (Lisle, IL: IVP Books, 2012).

Guinness, Os, *Last Call for Liberty: How America's Genius for Freedom Has Become Its Greatest Threat* (Lisle, IL: InterVarsity Press, 2018).

Guinness, Os, and John Steel, *No God but God: Breaking with the Idols of Our Age* (Chicago, IL: Moody Press, 1992).

Halbertal, Moshe, *The Beginning of Politics: Power in the Biblical Book of Samuel* (Princeton, NJ: Princeton University Press, 2019).

Hearn, Daniel Allen, *Legal Execution in New England: A Comprehensive Reference, 1623–1960* (Jefferson, NC: McFarland Publishing 2008).

"Integrity," *Merriam-Webster*. Date of access: October 21, 2024 (https://www.merriam-webster.com/dictionary/integrity).

"International Day for Universal Access to Information," *UNESCO*. Date of access: May 2021 (https://www.unesco.org/en/days/universal-access-information).

Joyce, Kathryn, *Quiverfull: Inside the Christian Patriarchy Movement* (Boston, MA: Beacon Press, 2009).

Kahn, Joan R., and Kathryn A. London, "Premarital Sex and the Risk of Divorce," *Journal of Marriage and the Family 53*, 1991, 845–855.

Kartzow, Mariane Bjelland, *Gossip and Gender: Othering of Speech in the Pastoral Epistles* (Berlin, DE: Walter de Gruyter, 2009).

Keller, Tim, *The Reason for God: Belief in an Age of Skepticism* (New York, NY: Penguin Random House, 2008).

Keller, Tim, *Counterfeit Gods: When the Empty Promises of Love, Money, and Power Let You Down* (London, UK: Hodder and Stoughton, 2010).

Keller, Tim, *Prayer: Experiencing Awe and Intimacy with God* (New York, NY: Dutton, 2014).

Keller, Tim, *The Meaning of Marriage: Facing the Complexities of Commitment with the Wisdom of God* (New York, NY: Penguin Books, 2016).

Keller, Tim, *On Death* (New York, NY: Penguin Books, 2020).

Kennedy, George, *A New History of Classical Rhetoric* (Princeton, NJ: Princeton University Press, 1994).

Kidner, Derek, *Genesis* (Lisle, IL: InterVarsity Press, 1967).

King, Martin Luther, Jr., *Strength in Love* (Boston, MA: Beacon Press, 1963).

Lewis, C.S., *The Problem of Pain* (New York, NY: Harper Collins, 1944).

Luhrmann, Tanya, *Persuasions of the Witch's Craft* (Oxford, UK: Blackwell, 1989).

Mather, Cotton, *Wonders of the Invisible World* (Charleston, SC: Bibliolife, 2009).

Mather, Cotton, *Memorable Providences Relating to Witchcrafts and Possessions* (Ann Arbor, MI: ProQuest, 2010).

"Matthew 6," *Bible Hub*. Date of access: April 9, 2021 (https://biblehub.com/commentaries/barnes/matthew/6.htm).

Meyer, F.B., *David: Shepherd, Psalmist, King* (Fort Washington, PA: CLC Publications, 2013).

"Miroslav Volf: Loving for No Reason," *SparkBible*. Date of access: March 19, 2021 (https://sparkbible.com/r/biola-university/miroslav-volf-loving-for-no-reason-biola-university-chapel).

Morris, Thomas V., "The Hidden God," *Philosophical Topics* 16(2), 1988.

Murphy, James J., *Rhetoric in the Middle Ages: A History of Rhetorical Theory from Saint Augustine to the Renaissance* (Los Angeles, CA: University of California Press, 1974).

Murray, Douglas, *The Madness of Crowds: Gender, Race, and Identity* (London, UK: Bloomsbury, 2019).

Owen, John, *The Works of John Owen, Volume VII*, Rev. William H. Goold, ed. (New York, NY: Robert Carter & Brothers, 1853).

Paik, Anthony, "Adolescent Sexuality and Risk of Marital Dissolution," *Journal of Marriage and the Family 73*, 2011.

Park, Song-Mi Suzie, "Census and Censure: Sacred Threshing Floors and Counting Taboos in 2 Samuel 24," *Horizons in Biblical Theology,* Volume 35, Issue 1. January 1, 2013.

"Past Trauma in Counselors-in-Training: Help or Hindrance?" *Counseling Today*. Date of access: December 20, 2024 (https://ctarchive.counseling.org/2018/05/past-trauma-in-counselors-in-training-help-or-hindrance).

Pereboom, Derk, "Free Will, Evil, and Divine Providence," *God and the Ethics of Belief: New Essays in Philosophy of Religion*, eds. Andrew Dole and Andrew Chignell (Cambridge, UK: Cambridge University Press, 2005).

Peretti, Frank, *This Present Darkness* (Nashville, TN: Thomas Nelson, 1993).

Peretti, Frank, *Piercing the Darkness* (St. Charles, IL: Crossway, 2003).

Prentice, David, "Update: COVID-19 Vaccine Candidates and Abortion-Derived Cell Lines," *Lozier Institute*. September 30, 2020 (https://lozierinstitute.org/update-covid-19-vaccine-candidates-and-abortion-derived-cell-lines).

Rayner, John D., *An Understanding of Judaism* (Oxford, UK: Berghahn Press, 1997).

Richardson, Don, *Peace Child* (Bloomington, MN: Bethany House, 2005).

Ryle, J.C., "The Hand of the Lord!" *Being Thoughts on Cholera* (London, UK: William Hunt, 1865).

Ryle, J.C., "This Is the Finger of God," *Being Thoughts on the "Cattle Plague"* (London, UK: William Hunt, 1865).

Scott, James, *Domination and the Arts of Resistance: Hidden Transcripts* (London, UK: Yale University Press, 1990).

Stott, John R.W., *The Message of Acts: To the Ends of the Earth* (Leicester, Netherlands: InterVarsity, 1990).

Seltzer, Leon F., *Paradoxical Strategies in Psychotherapy: A Comprehensive Overview and Guidebook* (New York, NY: John Wiley & Sons, 1986).

Seltzer, Leon F., "A New Take on Manipulation," *Psychology Today*, April 30, 2013 (https://www.psychologytoday.com/ca/blog/evolution-of-the-self/201304/a-new-take-on-manipulation).

Serafim, Bishop of Ostroh, *The Soothsayer Balaam: Or The Transformation Of A Sorcerer Into A Prophet, Numbers 22-25* (London, UK: Rivingtons, 1900).

Seuss, Dr., *The Cat in the Hat* (New York, NY: Random House, 1958).

"Shorter Catechism," *The Orthodox Presbyterian Church*. Date of access: April 11, 2021 (https://www.opc.org/sc.html).

Smith, Christian, *Soul Searching: The Religious and Spiritual Lives of American Teenagers* (New York, NY: Oxford University Press, 2005).

Spurgeon, C.H., "God's Providence," *The Spurgeon Center*. Date of access: December 17, 2024 (www.spurgeon.org/resource-library/sermons/gods-providence/#flipbook).

Stewart, Pamela J., and Andrew Strathern, *Witchcraft, Sorcery, Rumors, and Gossip: Departure in Anthropology* (Cambridge, MA: Cambridge University Press, 2004).

Tertullian, *Apologeticum*, 50.13.

"Tissue Engineered Fetal Skin Constructs for Pediatric Burns," *The Lancet*, Volume 266, Issue 9488. September 2005, 840–842.

Volf, Miroslav, and Judith M. Gundry-Volf, *A Spacious Heart: Essays on Identity and Belonging* (Harrisburg, PA: Trinity Press International, 1997).

Volf, Miroslav, "Good, Evil, Suffering, and Silence," *The Table Video*. February 7, 2018 (https://cct.biola.edu/good-evil-suffering-silence-miroslav-volf-full-interview).

Von Rad, Gerhard, *Wisdom in Israel* (London, UK: SCM, 1972).

Wagner, C. Peter, *Engaging the Enemy: How to Fight and Defeat Territorial Spirits* (Grand Rapids, MI: Baker Group, 1995).

Webster, Douglas D., *Selling Jesus: What's Wrong with Marketing the Church* (Eugene, OR: Wipf and Stock, 2009).

White, Lynn, "The Historical Roots of Our Ecological Crisis," *Science* 155, 1967.

Wilkinson, Robert, *Minds and Bodies: An Introduction with Readings* (New York, NY: Routledge, 2000).

Worth, Jennifer, *In the Midst of Life: What Makes a Good Death?* (London, UK: Orion, 2011).

Wright, N.T., *For All God's Worth: True Worship and the Calling of the Church* (Grand Rapids, MI: Wm. B. Eerdmans, 1997).

Wright, N.T., "Love to Know," *First Things*. February 2020 (https://www.firstthings.com/article/2020/02/loving-to-know).

Wright, N.T., *Into the Heart of Romans* (Grand Rapids, MI: Zondervan, 2023).

Young, Kimberly, *Caught in the Net: How to Recognize the Signs of Internet Addiction—and a Winning Strategy for Recovery* (New York, NY: John Wiley & Sons, 1998).

Also by Nikki T. White

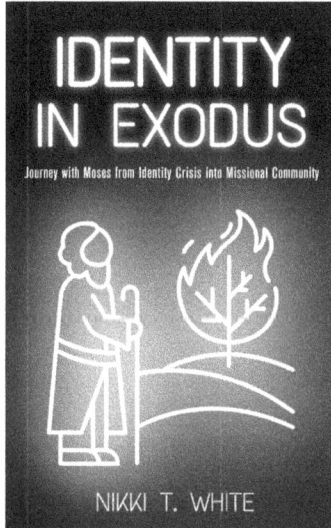

IDENTITY IN EXODUS

MOSES WAS A misfit. Are you?

Those of us whose sense of self has been buffeted by trauma, mental illness, culture shock, post-modern ideologies and the like—we are kindred spirits to this biblical patriarch. Journeying through the book of Exodus, Nikki White explores the topic of identity crisis in the life of Moses, inviting us to discover—through the ordinary, extraordinary, and unthinkable events of our lives—a new identity of purposed and purposeful mission.

In the ancient story of Moses, White finds many modern parallels to the stories of this current generation. She examines the different forms of identity crisis faced by millennials, missionaries, migrants, the marginalized, and the grievously misunderstood. Interspersing their stories throughout the book, White offers well-researched insights into some of the sources of identity crisis in North America. Relating the ways in which God has woven her own personal brokenness into his overarching story of redemption, she leads readers to see how God can impart profound meaning to the seemingly random chapters of life.

This book helps us to find our identity and calling within the bigger scope of God's divine narrative. For we, like Moses, are being *sent*.

.